D1246803

THE STATE OF PAKISTAN

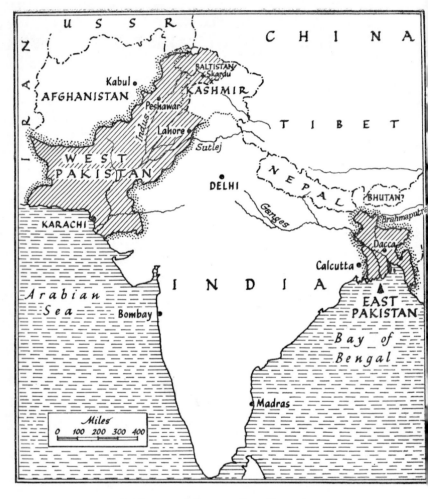

Pakistan and Surrounding Countries

THE STATE OF
PAKISTAN

L. F. Rushbrook Williams

Quondam Fellow of All Souls College, Oxford
and University Professor of Modern Indian History
in the University of Allahabad;
formerly Director of Public Information
with the Government of India:
sometime Foreign Minister of the State of Patiala:
later Eastern Services Director with
the British Broadcasting Corporation and
a member of the Editorial Staff of *The Times*

with maps by N. S. Hyslop

FABER AND FABER
24 Russell Square
London

First published in mcmlxii
by Faber and Faber Limited
24 Russell Square London W.C.1
Printed in Great Britain by
Latimer Trend & Co Ltd Plymouth

TO MY WIFE

by the same author

★

THE STATE OF ISRAEL

ACKNOWLEDGEMENTS

I am grateful to many Officers of the Central Government of Pakistan and of the Governments of East and West Pakistan for facilitating my visits to the localities—some of them very remote—which I was anxious to see, as well as for giving me much of their time. When so many of them have helped me in numerous ways, it would be invidious to mention individuals, but I am particularly grateful for the assistance I have received from the Press Information Department in arranging my tours of the places which I selected to visit, including the details of travel, reception, and accommodation; in permitting me to reproduce photographs: and in allowing me to make use of official maps as the basis of the maps in this book.

I must make it clear, however, that the opinions which I have recorded are my own, and do not express the views of these Governments or of their Officers.

I am also grateful to the Editors of *The Times* and of *The Round Table* for permission to reproduce sketch maps of the Cease-Fire Line and of the Indus Basin respectively.

L. F. R. W.

CONTENTS

ILLUSTRATIONS

MAPS

FOREWORD

Perhaps I should explain the rather personal angle from which this book is written. It is nearly fifty years since I first came to British India, fresh from All Souls, a specialist in the history of the Mughal Empire. My work gave me a certain insight into the Indian aspects of the Islamic tradition, upon which I founded a School of Mughal Studies at Allahabad which won some reputation. I was soon taken from academic life and immersed in administration. I worked with Lionel Curtis and Edwin Montagu. I came into contact with the men and women who were leading the nationalist movement which later bifurcated between India and Pakistan. My successive periods of deputation to several of the former Princely States, where I worked under Indian superiors, helped me to meet these men and women on equal terms, and to form friendships of which I shall always be glad.

The number of Englishmen who remember personally the Founding Fathers (and Mothers) of the Indian Republic naturally diminishes as time passes; but so much has been written about the Indian nationalist movement and its leaders that there is no need of another book.

The case of Pakistan is different. Iqbal and Jinnah never enjoyed the international reputation of Gandhi, Tagore, Jawaharlal Nehru and his great Father. The Pakistani nationalist movement, even at the moment of its triumph, was condemned by those who did not understand it as a mere petulant fragmentation of the seamless fabric of the British Raj. Thus, the western world's view of Pakistan lacks the background of informed sympathy which India has found so helpful; and there is still a disposition to wonder why Pakistan exists, and, indeed, to think of her as a piece of India which has seceded politically, with slender justification.

This nation of 94 million people, inhabiting 365,000 square miles, the greatest Islamic State in the world, has not received enough attention, and has been accorded too little understanding. Since the Revolution of 1958, President Ayub Khan's frank and lucid policy statements, like his visits to other countries have helped to put

Pakistan on the map; but even in 1961, few except Pakistanis even
raised their eyebrows when a film of the Queen's visits to India and
Pakistan was exhibited under the title of the Royal Tour of *India*.
This general ignorance about Pakistan and what she stands for is
partly the fault of the Pakistanis themselves, who seem often too busy
doing things for their country to spend time telling other people why
they are doing them. They will say, quite frankly, that if you are
interested in Pakistan, and want to know 'what makes her tick', you
will be most welcome to come and see things for yourself.

Not everyone can do this; and as I have been fortunate enough to
see for myself how Pakistan grew, and to know the men and women
who strove to bring her to birth and who later guided her destinies as
a free nation, I have tried to give the kind of picture of Pakistan which
might interest people who want to know more about her without
specializing in her constitutional, political and economic problems.
This picture has no claims to completeness; just because it is a personal one, it is based on what my wife and I saw and heard for ourselves in the course of many visits to a country and to a people whom
we have come to love.

It is our fervent hope that Pakistan and India, who share between
them the land where the best years of our life have been spent, may
yet come to feel for each other the deep affection in which we hold
them both.

West Pakistan
East Pakistan
Hampshire
1961–2

Chapter 1

WHY PAKISTAN EMERGED

Pakistan and India have reacted upon each other so intimately that some reference to Hindu-Muslim relations in the former British Raj, which gave birth to both, is unavoidable if the outlook of present-day Pakistan is to be understood. Anyone who visits the new India today will discover that the controversy out of which Pakistan originally emerged has never really died down: it is still alive. Some of my Indian friends insist that the creation of Pakistan is the culminating example of British machiavellian intrigue. 'When you British found your position impossible', they say, 'you backed the Muslim League against the Congress, in accordance with your traditional policy of "divide and rule", and proceeded to prejudice our future by partitioning the sub-continent with Mr. Jinnah as your willing tool.'

Against this theory I would cite two arguments. Anyone who knew Mr. Jinnah will bear me out in maintaining that he was never, at any time in his life, the 'tool' of anyone—least of all, of the British. And no one who followed as closely as I did, first as an official in turn of the Indian and British Governments and of the BBC, and next as Asian leader-writer on *The Times*, the agonized efforts of the British in Whitehall and Delhi to avoid the break-up of the administrative and economic unity which they had spent a century in perfecting, can believe that they set out to create Pakistan. But the theory deserves to be recorded, because it enshrines, as amber does a fly, the memory of the deep and painful shock caused to the Hindu leaders of the Indian nationalist movement when they gradually discovered, between 1930 and 1947, that the Congress was becoming less and less entitled to speak for the majority of the Muslim population of the old undivided India. Nor did the trouble stop there; the contention of some leaders of the Muslim League that the Indian Muslims were a nation in their own right, separate and distinct from the Hindu majority of the population, showed with almost brutal clarity the failure of Mr. Gandhi's and Mr. Nehru's conception of the 'religiously neutral' State to win the confidence of the Muslims.

15

There are, of course, many people in India who are too well informed to believe that Pakistan came into existence through a sinister
British plot. But even they cannot entirely rid themselves of the feeling
that partition ought to have been—and, indeed, could have been—
avoided if some of the then leaders of the Congress had played their
cards a little more skilfully. This feeling that Pakistan need not have
emerged at all is important politically, because it shaped the Indian
attitude, and influenced Indian behaviour, towards Pakistan, not only
in the early critical days when the national outlooks on either side of
the new frontier were in process of formation, but also in later years.
As we shall see, the Indian outlook evoked a corresponding reaction
in Pakistan, apart altogether from the specific quarrels which emerged
to worsen relations between the two neighbours.

From the Pakistani point of view, Pakistan seems an inevitable
resultant of ancient history and modern needs—a resultant in which
British policy has been a complicating, not an initiating, factor. In
West Pakistan, in particular, the memory of the past is strong; many
of the leading families trace their descent to soldiers and administrators who came in the train of conquerors through the northern
passes; no one forgets that until the break-up of the Mughal Empire,
Muslims ruled a Hindu country for many centuries—and, but for the
British, might easily be ruling it still. In East Pakistan, racially so
different, the ancient tradition of Muslim rule is very much alive, and
remains today among the strongest bonds with the Western wing.

With the memory of this imperial heritage behind them, it is easy to
understand why Muslims in general adapted themselves less readily
to the régime of the East India Company than did the more flexibly-
minded Hindus. The failure of the sepoy insurrection of 1857 hit the
Muslims very hard, for, as the former ruling class, they had most to
gain if the Mughal Empire had been effectively revived; accordingly,
they were suspected by the British of deep-seated hostility. The upper
classes understood only two professions—warfare and administration:
the British kept them out of both for several decades in favour of the
Hindus, who readily learned English, acquired western culture, and
made themselves as indispensable to the new rulers of India as they
had become to earlier conquerors.

Muslims of birth and breeding, the natural leaders of Muslim
opinion, had thus little reason to love the British, although warm
friendships, based on a common love of sport, and upon a certain frank
outspokenness which both peoples share, sprang up between in-

16

A tribal jirgah on the North-West Frontier

A Khattak Dance on the North-West Frontier

Camel caravan in the Khyber Pass

Inside a rifle factory in tribal territory (Kohat)

dividuals. The way to better understanding between the Muslims and the British was pointed out by Sir Sayyid Ahmed (1817–98) who has been called 'the first Pakistani'. He deplored the prevalent tendency among contemporary Muslim religious leaders to preach undying hostility to Britain and the British. He urged his community to fit themselves, by education and by conscientious service of the State, to play their full part in the new régime, as they had done under Mughal rule.

It was an uphill fight at first, but he won it: the British and the Muslims drew more closely together, without upsetting the relations between the British and the Hindus. The Anglo-Oriental College, which he founded at Aligarh in 1875, became the main centre of western learning for Indian Muslims, who were taught there to take pride in acquiring a culture which blended the Mughal tradition with a modern outlook. Many of the men whom I met at Aligarh as students, when I visited it as Allahabad University Inspector during the First World War, have later risen to great prominence in Pakistan.

As the nineteenth century drew to a close, the 'wind of change' began to blow across India, as it is blowing across Africa today. At first it touched the Hindus, whose cultural heritage makes them receptive to new ideas. The Indian National Congress was founded to press for parliamentary government and for a larger share for Indians in the higher administrative cadres. Some educated Muslims were attracted by the idea of representative institutions on the British model, and joined the new movement; but many, like Sir Sayyid Ahmed, held aloof, because they saw that parliamentary government, based on universal suffrage, might eventually condemn the Muslim community to the position of a permanent minority. On the other hand, an important section of Muslim opinion—and one to which Mohammad Ali Jinnah himself belonged at the outset of his career— urged the necessity of Hindu-Muslim co-operation to get rid of the British. This section of opinion grew more influential as nationalist ideas spread among the intelligentsia of both communities: and it was strengthened when the new province of Eastern Bengal and Assam, which had been liked by the Muslim majority it contained when it was set up in 1905, was annulled in 1911 because of Hindu agitation against it. This convinced the Muslims that political agitation could be effective: they began to think that parliamentary government was destined to come, in spite of British reluctance, and to seek means of fortifying their position. Already, in 1906, they had sought and gained from the

British separate representation, through their own electorates, on all local, provincial and central elective bodies, and had set up the Muslim League to protect their interests.

Before very long, however, as western ideas spread among the leaders of the Muslim community, the feeling grew up that the British, even if they honestly desired to protect Muslim interests—which many Muslims had begun to doubt—would be powerless to do so for very long in face of the increasing agitation for Indian self-government. The Muslims were further alienated from the British when Britain's ally, Italy, attacked Turkey—the last surviving Muslim State among the Great Powers; and when the adherence of Turkey to Germany in the First World War brought British forces (including Indian Muslim soldiers) into conflict with Turkish troops. The two famous brothers, Muhammad Ali and Shaukat Ali, headed a strong agitation against British policy. In such circumstances, it was natural for the Muslims to turn away from the British and towards the Hindus: Jinnah was able to persuade the Muslim League to try to reach an understanding with the Congress. This was effected in 1916, when the Lucknow Pact, which conveyed Congress acceptance of separate Muslim electorates, provided an illustration both of Jinnah's great negotiating skill, and of his instinctive readiness to rely on constitutional guarantees by the Hindus as a means of securing Muslim rights.

The Muslims and the Hindus came more closely together than ever before in 1919, when the Muslims were offended by Britain's share in the break-up of the Turkish Empire, and nationalist leaders of both communities were shocked by Britain's Draconian suppression of serious rioting in the Punjab. It was an uncomfortable time for Englishmen who, like myself, had many Hindu and Muslim friends: it got worse when Mr. Gandhi, grasping the opportunity to unite Hindus and Muslims on a common platform against a government which he deemed 'Satanic', took the lead in launching a non-co-operation movement to oblige the British to concede the Muslim demand that the Khilafat should be maintained intact in Turkey. Mr. Jinnah, while condemning British policy wholeheartedly, refused to countenance this kind of movement, which was characteristically Hindu, rather than nationalist, in ideology. He felt that only dis-illusionment awaited the rank and file of the Muslim community; and that Hindu-Muslim co-operation in constitutional progress would be made more difficult. All too soon he was proved right.

A horrible thing happened in 1920; simple-minded Muslims were persuaded by interested persons that India had ceased to be a place where Islam could be practised and had become *dar-al-harb*—a land of strife which good Muslims must leave. In the Punjab, the North-West Frontier Province, Sind and, to less extent, elsewhere, several thousands sold their property for a song to their Hindu neighbours, and marched off with their families to seek refuge in Afghanistan. Many hundreds perished by the way. The movement was peaceful and orderly. It was impossible to stop these misguided folk by force; it would have taken three Army Corps, which the British had not got. I was attached to the Supreme Government at the time, organizing what was to become, perhaps, the first official Department of Public Relations ever established; and it became my duty to try to convince those who could influence Muslim opinion of what we in Delhi and Simla knew to be a fact—that Afghan Government officials, naturally alarmed at this mass-influx, were turning back the unhappy emigrants at the point of the bayonet. Mr. Jinnah was a tower of strength in striving to stem the migration; so too were other enlightened Muslim leaders like Sir Muhammed Shafi and Sir Fazl-i-Husain. Eventually the truth spread, and the movement was halted; but not before the Khyber Pass, as I saw with my own eyes, was littered with corpses. The Government helped the survivors to return to their villages; but few Hindus would give back the property which had been acquired so cheaply; and Muslim resentment, as Mr. Jinnah had foreseen, began to turn from the British and against the Hindus.

Communal bitterness was further increased by a savage rising of the Moplah community in South India against their Hindu landlords. The trouble began in agrarian unrest, but soon assumed the form of a Holy War, with forcible conversions to Islam and wholesale massacres as its feature. At first, general Muslim sympathy with the Moplahs encouraged anti-British feeling when the rising was forcibly suppressed; but the sufferings of the Hindu victims, widely publicized, aroused resentment against the Muslims among the Hindu community as a whole; and Muslims were attacked in a number of localities. The Muslim-Hindu alliance which Mr. Gandhi had created began to break down; and when he suddenly called off the entire non-co-operation campaign because a mob of his supporters had murdered the occupants of a police-post at Chauri-Chaura, the Muslims, with their grievance about the Khilafat still unremedied, thought they had been betrayed. Their disillusion was completed when Mustafa Kamal Pasha, 'Ataturk', creator of the new Turkey, decided in 1923 and 1924 not only to divest himself of the burden of ruling the Arab lands (including the Holy Places), but also to abolish the Khilafat itself altogether.

Disappointment; conviction that they had sacrificed more than the Hindus in the non-co-operation movement; and the feeling—whether justified or not—that they had been made use of by Mr. Gandhi and other Hindu political leaders, began to draw the bulk of the Muslim community together in a new sense of solidarity. On the Hindu side, also, religious sentiment took an anti-Muslim turn: movements like *Shuddhi* and *Sangathan* were started to 'reclaim' for Hinduism certain sections of the population which retained Hindu customs while nominally following Islam. Communal hatred grew, although Mr. Jinnah, with his usual courage, continued his efforts to reach a new understanding with the Hindus as the basis for a campaign aiming at full self government and dominion status for India. He headed the party in the Muslim League which advocated entry into the legislatures: he himself became a member of the Legislative Assembly, in which he and I sat together for several years. I was privileged to have many talks with him, and I became familiar with his ideas. There were on the other side men such as Motilal Nehru, Tej Bahadur Sapru, and C. R. Das, who, like Jinnah, believed in Hindu-Muslim unity; but the bulk of both communities did not share their statesmanlike views, and anti-Muslim feeling became very strong in the Congress. Motilal Nehru's own conciliatory outlook was overborne in 1928, when a committee which he headed produced a draft constitution for the future independent India which rejected separate Muslim electorates and any claims for weightage. Jinnah was greatly disconcerted, and put forward a scheme embodying the safeguards which he thought that his community required. But his own side did not back him—he had at that time little contact with the masses—and the Congress showed no sympathy with his ideas.

It was during this period, I am sure, that he began to re-think his position on what the future of the Muslims ought to be. I sat with him through the sessions of the Round Table Conference in London (1930–2); and his disillusion about the prospects of the Muslims receiving a fair deal from the Congress became visibly stronger as the proceedings went on. He was particularly affronted by the claim put forward by Mr. Gandhi in 1932 that the Congress represented India, and he—Mr. Gandhi—the Congress. Believing that there was little he could do to strengthen the Muslim position, Jinnah retired from politics and practised as a barrister in London for the next two years. In 1934, however, he yielded to entreaties and returned to India to organize a revived and more vigorous Muslim League. This was eventually to provide him with the Party machine which he needed for his campaign; but until the idea of Pakistan began to arouse the enthusiasm of the mass of Indian Muslims, the League's influence remained limited to the Muslim *élite*.

While high-level negotiations on the new constitution for India— ultimately embodied in the Act of 1935—were going on between the British and the Hindu and Muslim leaders, a new movement was growing up among the Muslim masses. Communal rioting had become a relatively common occurrence; a sense of insecurity was shaping the Muslim outlook. It was the famous philosopher-poet Iqbal who first gave concrete expression to Muslim hopes and fears when, presiding over the Allahabad Conference of the Muslim League in 1930, he put forward the demand for an autonomous Muslim State. The idea spread; and although for some time Jinnah himself remained un-convinced, it began to attract increasing attention from the Muslim community.

Initially, it was far from winning general acceptance, especially from Muslim leaders whose cast of mind had been shaped by British Liberal tradition. But between 1930 and 1940, it gradually bit more deeply into the Muslim consciousness. This was due in part to the increasing gulf between Hindu and Muslim political ideas about how the power which the British were steadily handing over was to be shared: but there were other forces at work also. Many educated Muslims who were not convinced by what was soon to be called the 'two nations' theory, were seriously concerned about how they would fare in a future India dominated by a Hindu majority.

Some years after Pakistan had become an accomplished fact, I asked a prominent Pakistani industrialist what his own view was about why things had happened as they did. He said: 'For a long time, I per-sonally thought Pakistan an unsound idea; but gradually I became convinced that it was the only way of giving Muslim interests a fair chance. To my mind, the trouble was social rather than religious. Hindus and Muslims each have their own social system: people on each side are clannish, tending to stick together. Hindus had the monopoly of such key-pursuits as banking and finance: they kept Muslims out. In other branches of commerce, textiles for example, Muslim business men found entry difficult. Much the same thing held true of the administration: there were few Muslims in high positions. So Muslim business men and Muslim officials who had many contacts, used their influence to mobilize opinion in favour of the creation of a homeland for Muslims, where Muslims as such would not be handicapped, and would have a fair field for their energies. But from the point of view of the Muslim masses, it was the religious factor which counted most.'

Jinnah's own instinct, when he returned to India in 1934, was to build up the Muslim League into a strong movement, representative of the entire Muslim community, which would be formidable enough to secure from the Congress the kind of constitutional safeguards which would assure Muslim interests in a self-governing India. The task was not easy. There were a number of different groups among the Muslims; and Muslim leaders in the Provinces where there was already a Muslim majority took little notice of the League. But in the first election campaign (1937) under the new constitution laid down by the Act of 1935, Jinnah began to make contact with the Muslim masses, to understand the feelings that swayed them, and to appreciate the rich fund of loyalty to Islam and to the Islamic way of life which they could dedicate to the service of a Muslim leader whom they trusted. He began to realize the importance of enlisting the support of the religious leaders—the *mullahs*, the *pirs* and the *ulema*—in his campaign for creating Muslim solidarity. He saw that good Muslims had become really alarmed at the prospect of Hindu rule. Very soon this alarm was to prove well-founded. The Congress, after winning the elections in eight out of eleven Provinces, refused to share power with non-Congress Muslims; and from that time onward Jinnah grasped the strength of, as well as the justification for, the forces which were gathering behind the demand for a Muslim homeland. He came to see the situation in something like Iqbal's terms. His conversion was completed when he observed the predominantly Hindu character of the type of administration which quickly emerged in the provinces where Congress had gained power; and when he listened to the bitter complaints which arose from Muslims living in those provinces that everything was looked at from the Hindu point of view, with small regard to Muslim susceptibilities.

From 1937 onwards, Jinnah devoted his exceptional talent, unflinching fixity of purpose, and remarkable gifts of organization, to the task of uniting the Muslim community in support of its claim to be considered the third party in the country—the British and the Hindus being the other two. He built up the Muslim League into a powerful machine which eventually established an effective chain of command between himself as President, with his central committee, and the provincial, district, and primary, branches. In the process, his own ideas underwent a further change. Himself a product of a generation of leaders trained in the traditions of Parliamentary democracy, he began to entertain serious doubts about the suitability of this system to Indian conditions, not only because, as he asserted, India contained 'two nations', the Muslims and the Hindus, but also because he had discovered that what the Muslim masses were seeking was strong leadership, and an opportunity to follow the Muslim way of life, not Parliamentary institutions or partnership in a State where they would suffer from the humiliations of perpetual minority. His mind began to turn more and more to the problem of winning acceptance from the British and from the Hindus for the creation of a compact Muslim *bloc* of territory, distinct from the Hindu-majority areas, which could form a Muslim homeland.

Iqbal himself, in advocating the idea in 1930, had suggested that the homeland should consist of the Muslim-majority areas in the Punjab, along with the North-West Frontier Province, Baluchistan and Sind —in fact the modern West Pakistan. In the succeeding ten years, many other people put forward schemes with territorial additions and supplements, mostly intended to incorporate all the Muslim-majority areas then inside the British Raj into a Muslim Federation. This could come together with a corresponding federation of Hindu states to set up an All-India Federation, endowed with powers too limited to permit the inevitable Hindu majority to prejudice Muslim interests. These schemes all brought in the Muslim-majority part of Bengal— now East Pakistan: and the name Pakistan itself (the 'land of the pure') gained increasingly wide currency. In 1940, the Muslim League, at its meeting in Lahore, resolved that the North-Western and Eastern zones of India should be grouped into autonomous States—a resolution which is usually regarded as the formal endorsement of the idea of Pakistan. At the time, no one was very clear whether or not there should be two Muslim homelands, one in the North-West and one in the East; whether the two should be co-equal partners in a new State; or whether they should be linked at the top in a kind of all-India federation with the Hindu provinces.

The Second World War was raging, and the British were anxious to stabilize the position in India. The Congress was pressing for the immediate transformation of the Viceroy's Executive Council into a national Cabinet composed of representatives of the main political groups. At the same time it bitterly opposed, of course, any suggestion that the unity of India should be broken up by the establishment of a homeland for Muslims. The British were reluctant to concede the Congress demand, partly because they thought that it would weaken the administration at a time when maximum strength was needed for the war, and partly because it was difficult without elaborate alteration of the 1935 Constitution, to make a Cabinet representing the major political parties responsible to the legislature. They were also impressed by the growing strength of the Muslim demand that the Muslim League, as well as the Congress, should be recognized as a party to all negotiations. When Sir Stafford Cripps came in 1942 with proposals for a provisional central government giving considerable power to Indian party leaders, but without full Cabinet responsibility, it was apparent that the British had awakened to the possibility that there might have to be not one, but two, Successor States; even so, Muslim sentiment was affronted by the overmastering importance which Britain seemed to be attaching to Congress views about the future of India. The fact was that the British were still trying to hold India together by finding a formula which would safeguard Muslim rights inside a single polity.

The Congress leaders, believing that they were in a strong position, and wearying of British hesitation, adopted the 'Quit India' resolution in August 1942. The Muslim League, which had not been consulted, held aloof—it was not prepared to see power handed over to the Congress. Disorders broke out: Mr. Gandhi and some of the other Congress leaders were imprisoned. Some wise men on the Hindu side, led by C. Rajagopalacharia, tried to arrange a Congress-League *entente* on the basis of a recognition of the Muslim claim for Pakistan; but when Gandhi and Jinnah met in 1944, no agreement could be reached because the two leaders did not really speak the same language. Jinnah insisted upon unambiguous precision in any arrangement: Gandhi disclaimed his ability to tie down the Congress to specific engagements, further arguing that even if the Muslims were conceded a homeland of their own, they would still be, not a separate nation, but a part of the Indian family.

Jinnah's opinions were by this time both strong and fixed; he sensed that nothing short of independent nationhood would satisfy the bulk of the Muslims. In taking up this position, he was in advance of some of his own immediate followers—for example, Liaquat Ali Khan, who tried to reach an understanding with Bhulabhai Desai for Congress-League parity in an interim Government. Jinnah firmly repudiated the whole idea, just as he firmly repudiated, in 1945, the idea that the Muslim League could allow the Congress to nominate Muslim Congressmen to the seats reserved for it on the reconstituted Executive Council which Lord Wavell, the Viceroy, was trying to set up. Again and again, the British tried unsuccessfully to bring the Congress and the League together in a plan which would somehow bridge the gulf between them and enable India to retain the political and economic unity which the Raj had built up.

In Britain, some people who had the professional responsibility of following in detail, and trying to explain to the public, what was going on in India, not infrequently failed to do justice to Mr. Jinnah at this time. It was all too easy to attack him as an obstructionist, as a man who was determined—almost perversely as it seemed to some—to hold up the transfer of power from British to Indian hands, which most people in Britain knew to be essential. While vigorous campaigns were being conducted in Britain, and also in America, by the Congress and their sympathizers, it was sometimes rather difficult for people outside India to understand what lay behind Mr. Jinnah's political moves. Personally, I was in a fortunate position because I had been in contact with him, both directly and indirectly, for a number of years, so that I had come to grasp clearly what he was fighting for. *The Times* consistently warned British public opinion that it would be dangerous to underestimate the strength of the movement which he was heading for the creation of a separate Muslim State.

This point of view was amply justified by the success of Mr. Jinnah and the Muslim League—which he now controlled completely—in the new elections which were held in 1945. The League's propaganda campaign among the Muslim masses, aided by religious leaders and Muslim students from Aligarh and other Universities, had gathered impetus, and the great majority of Muslim seats were captured. The success of the Congress in the Hindu-majority provinces was equally complete: and the division of interests between Muslims and Hindus became sharply defined. The Congress declared its opposition to any partition of India: the League pledged itself to resist any unified constitution, and demanded Pakistan. The British Labour Government, anxious to get on with the task of handing over power, despatched a Cabinet Mission in 1946 to try and find a way out of the *impasse.* We in Britain followed with considerable anxiety the complicated negotiations which the Mission initiated between March and May of that year. The details of these negotiations, and of the claims put forward by the Congress, the League, the Sikhs, the orthodox Hindus, and other interests, would fill an entire book. It is sufficient to say here that after much difficulty, the Mission devised a scheme which was intended to hold India together in a federal union with powers confined to foreign affairs, defence, and communications. With the exception of these powers, the Muslim-majority areas were to enjoy autonomy, and to group themselves as they wished. Meanwhile a provisional national government was to be set up, and a constituent assembly was to be convened. Most people in Britain were, I think, pleased by this plan; both the League and the Congress had made concessions; and it seemed quite possible that the autonomy of the Muslim-majority provinces could be harmonized with union at the summit.

The Cabinet Mission had rejected the idea of Pakistan *per se,* but had been obliged to concede the substance of it. Mr. Jinnah, sensing that things were going his way, was quite content for the moment to assign to the future Indian Union the powers already mentioned; he could afford to wait and see if the Congress leaders had really reconciled themselves to Muslim autonomy and to the grouping of the Muslim-majority provinces in the way that the Cabinet Mission had proposed. Difficulties soon broke out over the formation of the interim Government: Lord Wavell invited six Hindu Congressmen (including one Depressed Class representative); five members of the Muslim League; a Parsee; a Sikh; and an Indian Christian, to take office. Congress insisted on its right to nominate a Muslim, and when this was not conceded, refused to join. The Viceroy, who had announced that if one of the major parties declined to participate, he would go ahead without it, had second thoughts, and adjourned the negotiations, instead of inviting Mr. Jinnah and the Muslim League to carry on. Mr. Jinnah, somewhat naturally, accused the Viceroy of breach of faith, and suspected that the British were ready to appease the Congress at the expense of the Muslims. This suspicion was in fact ill-grounded; in Britain, where the danger of ignoring the wishes of the Muslims was more and more realized, the Viceroy was passably criticized for making a mistake.

It was now the turn of the Congress leaders to have second thoughts; they agreed to take office with Mr. Nehru as Vice-President of the Council. In Muslim eyes, this was the beginning of Hindu Raj, since the League still held aloof: and when Mr. Jinnah proclaimed August 16th as 'Direct Action Day', on which Muslims must, while conducting themselves peacefully, show themselves alive to the political situation, the response of the community was immediate and whole-hearted. Unfortunately, the accompanying demonstrations served to spark off the growing tension between Hindus and Muslims in spheres far removed from the high level of political negotiations. What amounted to open hostilities between Hindus and Muslims broke out in Bengal, Bihar, and U.P.; horrible massacres took place on both sides. Fortunately, the disturbances were suppressed before they resulted in wholesale civil war; but they underlined the risk that this might easily occur.

Rather belatedly, Lord Wavell began negotiating with Mr. Jinnah and the League for their entry into the provisional Government. Jinnah's position was now so strong that he was able to secure the key-ministry of Finance for Liaquat Ali Khan; the portfolios held by other staunch League members were Commerce, Health, Posts and Air, and Legislative. But friction soon broke out inside the Council between Hindu and Muslim members, ostensibly over such things as Budget details, but in reality because of a growing cleavage between Hindus and Muslims all over the country. The League and the Congress differed in their interpretation of the grouping-plan designed by the Cabinet Mission to ensure Muslim autonomy: when the British endorsed the League's view, the Congress members of the Executive Council threatened to resign. It was becoming more and more clear to us in England that even the 'link at the summit' suggested by the Cabinet Mission had become impracticable, because of the complete refusal of Congress and the League to work together: and that unless arrangements were soon made for the partition of the Raj between them, civil war was inevitable. The Labour Government acted promptly, announcing that Britain would make over complete power not later than June 1948, and sending out Lord Mountbatten as Viceroy to effect the transfer, but with orders to preserve, if he could, the 'link at the summit'.

Mr. Jinnah had managed things with such consummate skill that even many Congress leaders now thought that Pakistan and partition represented the sole hope of avoiding catastrophe. He did not get on well with Lord Mountbatten—a man of equal force of character; but this mattered less to him at the time because things were going broadly as he wanted them to do. Mr. Nehru, who became a close friend of the Viceroy, found himself obliged by circumstances to agree that there should be two Sovereign States as successors to the British. The Labour Government accepted the principle of partition, and endorsed a plan worked out by Lord Mountbatten to give effect to it by 14th August 1947 instead of June 1948. The breathless speed necessary to secure this result is often blamed for the tragic disorders which accompanied partition; but it seems clear that Lord Mountbatten was convinced that unless he took instant advantage of the acceptance— grudging though it were—of the plan by the British Government, the Congress and the League, and gave none of them any time for second thoughts, Hindu-Muslim antagonism would convulse all India in civil war, of a type which the Army and the Police were too thin on the ground, and, indeed, too riven by Hindu-Muslim tension, to deal with.

It would be unfair, moreover, to ignore another factor in the situation. Both the League and the Congress were anxious for the British to hand over power: each side honestly believed that when this had once taken place, it would be fully competent to deal with any disorder that might occur. Congress and League leaders were alike inclined to resent British fears of widespread disturbances as a reflection on their own competence to rule their respective countries. This atmosphere severely limited the possibility of taking precautions of the kind which some experienced British officials felt to be necessary; it explains why the horrible communal massacres which broke out after partition, particularly in the Punjab, did such fearful damage before they were brought under control. In certain other matters, also, the sensitiveness of leaders on both sides to any suggestion that they might prove unequal to their new responsibilities was to have unforeseen consequences. The distinguished British jurists who presided respectively over the commission which was set up to draw the new frontiers and the arbitral tribunal appointed to deal with claims, were assured again and again by their Congress and League colleagues that all points of difficulty would be jointly settled with complete amicability between the future India and the future Pakistan when once the irritant of British rule was removed. For example, when the new frontier line gave to India the headworks controlling the water from the Ravi and Sutlej rivers which irrigated Pakistan's eastern canal colonies, the British Chairman was rebuked by both sides for even suggesting that some precise agreement regarding the supply of water to Pakistan was desirable. This was a reflection, they said, upon the common sense of Hindu and Muslim states-men! And yet this very question soon gave birth to the long and dangerous dispute over the division of the water-resources of the Indus basin which brought the two countries to the verge of war, and was only settled after years of painstaking effort by international agencies.

During the hot weather of 1947 these, and many other consequences, of partition were mercifully veiled in the future. The procedural plan for the creation of the two new Dominions was keeping pace with the time-table: partition was almost an accomplished fact: and the only remaining trace of the 'link at the summit' for which Britain had so long worked would shortly be the Joint Defence Council, set up to deal with the problems arising out of the sharing of military supplies and the division of the armed forces. Mr. Jinnah had indeed suggested that it might be desirable to retain the services of Lord Mountbatten as Supreme Governor-General, with co-ordinating functions between the two new Governors-General shortly to be appointed for India and Pakistan respectively, so that the division of the assets of the former British Raj according to principles already agreed on, might be carried through equitably and smoothly; but the British Government and the Congress thought the plan impracticable. In the event, Lord Mountbatten was invited by Mr. Nehru and his colleagues to stay on as Governor-General of India—a move which was distrusted by the League leaders because of the personal friendship between the Viceroy and Jawaharlal Nehru. Mr. Jinnah, after a good deal of hesitation and real reluctance, accepted the office of Governor-General of Pakistan at the pressing insistence of the League leaders. His health, never robust, had suffered severely from the protracted campaign for a Muslim homeland which he had led to final victory. He would have liked to rest, at least for a time. But he was indispensable: he was Quaid-i-Azam, the Great Leader who, in the eyes of millions of Muslims was their Man of Destiny. In addition to being Governor-General, he was also President of the Constituent Assembly, and of the Federal Legislature which was the Assembly's other aspect.

His decision to hold office was criticized both in India and in Britain by those who did not appreciate his position. To them, he seemed only a professional, rather autocratically-minded, politician, ill-fitted both by experience and by temperament for the self-abnegation which the post of a constitutional Governor-General, or of the President of a Legislature, necessitates. But to those who, like myself, knew him better, it was clear that he was making a final sacrifice of all real prospect of recovering his health to the cause with which he had identified himself. He was thinking not only of the necessity of holding together a new country, full of diverse forces and conflicting interests: he was thinking also of the people of Pakistan, of the masses of unconsidered folk to whom his name had become a legend. Their need was leadership, not a constitution which might look nice on paper but which took little account of their real requirements. In England, while he still had many months of life before him, he had told me of his conviction that the future of Pakistan depended, not upon the politicians of the Muslim League, but upon the ordinary Pakistani men and women: and that whatever constitution was finally adopted, strong leadership, by someone whom the people trusted, would be essential. It was in this spirit, I knew, that he was taking up his new office. As long as he lived, he was determined to give the people of Pakistan the guidance and control which he knew they needed, and, indeed, demanded, from him.

Thus it was that the new country of Pakistan came to birth on 14th August 1947. It stemmed mainly from the differences between the Muslim and the Hindu ways of life which the previous history of both communities had engendered: its precipitating cause was the British decision to hand over the power they had mostly taken from the Muslims to all the peoples of the sub-continent. Such power had never been shared in the past between Muslims and Hindus: the Muslims had been dominant until both were subjected to a third force—the British. When the British threw in their hand, and it became clear that authority would vest where the counting of heads might set it, the Hindus failed to convince the Muslims that they would receive a fair deal under Hindu majority rule. Accordingly, the Muslims, led by a man of genius, struggled for, and obtained, a homeland of their own.

Chapter 2

FIGHTING FOR LIFE

To most Pakistanis, the creation of their country seems a miracle, the direct gift of God, the crown of an effort which, without His help, must have been doomed to failure. Again and again, in talking to them, I have come across this deeply-held conviction, sometimes even expressed in terms which recall the Psalmist's invocation: 'Except the Lord build the house. . . .' This firm faith in Divine guidance is fundamental to the Pakistani outlook: it serves as a rallying-point for everything that is strongest and best in the national character. It proved its potency in the years prior to 1947, when it united a variety of interests in pursuit of the common objective of a Muslim homeland, and ensured, for the time at least, their continued co-operation even when that objective had been successfully achieved.

The materials out of which the new nation fell to be constructed were varied indeed. Like Pakistan herself, the Pakistani administration was a thing still to be built up, a jigsaw puzzle of separate fragments. For while India inherited a working machine of government, Central and Provincial, with only a few parts missing here and there where the withdrawal of Muslim territory and Muslim personnel had caused a gap, Pakistan started with nothing but bits and pieces. Some of the pieces themselves were of high quality, but these were few in relation to the rest.

First there was the handful—it was no more—of thoroughly experienced men, generally with the background of an Oxford or Cambridge College and an Inn of Court, who represented the solid if small Muslim element in the Indian Civil Service, on the Bench, at the Bar, and in the learned professions. Not many of them had taken an active part in political life, but their experience of responsibility made them invaluable. Next were the more numerous, but still pitiably small, band of well-trained Muslim officials who held senior—but rarely the most senior—posts in All India Services such as Police, Accounts, Forests, and Engineering. Below them again were the minor Muslim officials of the former Provincial Services; men with useful training, but with little practice in responsibility.

It was round these three classes that the new administrative machinery of Pakistan had to be built up. Their numbers were inadequate: most of them had insufficient practical experience of the tasks which awaited them. Many had to be promoted over-rapidly, because senior posts must be filled: recruitment for junior ranks had to be extemporized out of rather haphazard material until a new Public Services Commission could be appointed and set to work. On the whole, it was remarkable that, in the face of appallingly difficult problems, the extemporized machine worked as well as it did in the early months after partition.

So far as concerned the Defence Forces, Pakistan was more fortunately situated. For almost a generation, the India Armed Services had afforded an excellent career to young men of breeding and intelligence, the cream of whom received higher training not only at Indian military academies but also at Sandhurst and other famous British nurseries of martial skills. While Muslims were only occasionally successful during the British Raj in entering the highly-competitive Indian Civil Service, they showed a marked aptitude for soldiering. By the time partition came, considerable numbers of them had reached field rank, and were ready for high command in the Army, the Navy and Air Force. In certain respects they were the *élite* of Pakistan; they were not only soldiers, but also potential statesmen and administrators —as the events of 1958 were later to show. Their morale and efficiency were high; they commanded professional skills of which any country could be proud. They were accustomed to work cordially with their British colleagues on terms of personal friendship as well as of equality. While they had taken no share in the campaign for Pakistan —the British tradition that the armed forces ignore politics had become an instinct with them—they looked forward to having a country all their own to defend. The task of creating a Pakistan Defence Force out of the Muslim elements in the former Indian Army, Navy and Air Force was faced with real enthusiasm.

Pakistan was fortunate to start with such excellent material as her new soldiers, sailors and airmen: it was also lucky for her that there was plenty of cantonment accommodation for them in the West Punjab and the North-West Frontier Province, where the old Indian Army had always been thick on the ground. The new Pakistani forces inherited, along with parade-grounds and buildings, the tradi-

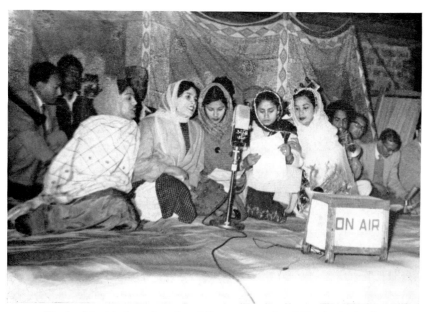

Kashmiri girls broadcasting folk songs on Azad Kashmir Radio

A view of Saidu Sharif, capital of Swat State

Passenger bus descending the Malakand Pass

Hiking in the Khagan Valley, a favourite tourist resort

tions connected with these historic cantonments and these messes of many famous regiments—traditions which it has been their pride to maintain ever since. But the early difficulties of reorganization were enormous; the regiments of the former Indian Army were first broken up into Muslim and Hindu elements and then regrouped in each country. I have been assured on good authority that in October 1947 —more than two months after partition—there was not a single complete military unit at the disposal of the Pakistan Government. Moreover, the new Indian Government steadily refused to part with the share of arms and equipment in the Indian arsenals which had been allotted to Pakistan: and when Field-Marshal Auchinleck, as Supreme Commander, tried to insist on Pakistan being given what was due to her, the Indian Government demanded his removal from the scene, along with his headquarters organization. These points will be worth remembering when the time comes to consider the problems which the Pakistan Government had to face almost immediately over Kashmir and the North-West Frontier.

Outside the ranks of State servants, there were numerous other elements which were to play their part in the new nation. Very important, because of the extensive local influence they exercised, were the great landowning families of West Pakistan. They had few counterparts in East Pakistan, where holdings were smaller, feudal traditions almost forgotten, and landowning a matter of business investment rather than a badge of inherited status. But in West Pakistan, they still counted for much. Some landlords had entered politics, first under the encouragement of the British, who found them very likeable because of their love of sport and of country life. Under Mr. Jinnah's lead, most of these had become pillars of the Muslim League, in which they exercised great influence: they had also been prominent as Cabinet Ministers and Members of the Legislatures in Muslim-majority provinces. They were the main available material for building political life in Pakistan. Some few of them were interesting themselves in commerce. Others were content to live in almost baronial magnificence, surrounded by sturdy retainers and obsequious tenants. But whatever pursuits they followed, they had one thing in common—a strong vested interest in an agrarian system which conferred upon them prestige and power at the expense of their tenantry.

There were a few—very few—families of major industrialists, like the Isfahanis, the Adamjees, the Rahimtoolas, the Haroun Jaffers. The heads of these families by sheer ability and acumen had won their

c   33

place in the commercial hierarchy of India, and had, in some cases, maintained their position for several generations. They dealt on equal terms, not only with the greatest of the Hindu business magnates, but also with the modern commercial combines of Western Europe and America. Experienced, far-sighted, and judicious, they were to prove strong pillars of Pakistan's developing economy. But their numbers were fantastically small in a country whose population was estimated in 1947 at about 80 millions.

While all these classes—administrators, soldiers, landlords, industrialists—were good Muslims, glad to find themselves in a land of their own, where they were free from the fetters of Hindu social and religious exclusiveness, they were for the most part content to view Pakistan in terms which were practical rather than idealistic. A new nation had to be built up on modern lines: many pressing problems must be faced. Most of these men took it for granted that Pakistan would ultimately frame for herself her own polity according to some such western conceptions as those with which their life under the former British Raj had familiarized them, rather than along the traditional Islamic lines. Meanwhile, there was much to be done into which religious idealism scarcely entered.

But there was yet another element in the new Pakistani nation to whom Islamic religious idealism was important not only because it was supported by the influence of the *pirs* and the *ulema*, but also because it held out hopes of a new and better kind of life. This element, potentially the most powerful of all, was the mass of the people. It was on them, as Mr. Jinnah himself had recognized, that the future of the country ultimately depended, rather than on the handful of administrators and politicians who had thrown in their lot with him. It was they, the ordinary Pakistani men and women, who had given him the support which had made the League so powerful. Without this support, neither his own genius, nor the backing of the Muslim *élite*, could have brought Pakistan to fruition. These millions upon millions of humble folk, who ranged in economic status and physical characteristics from the prosperous farmers of the Punjab canal colonies and the indomitably-independent villagers of the North-West Frontier, to the marginally-subsisting share-croppers and fishermen of the poorer parts of East Pakistan, had two things in common which bound them together in spite of all differences of race, physique and surroundings. In the first place, they were country folk, far removed from the realm of high politics and the sophistications of city life. Secondly they looked to find in Pakistan, not only a land where good Muslims would be free from exploitation by Hindu cleverness, Hindu wealth, and Hindu weight of numbers, but also a land where the principles of Islam would prevail, where oppression of the poor by the rich would be forbidden, and where the social justice which their Faith enjoins would guide their new rulers. This instinctive identification of Pakistan with a 'new deal' by the masses of East and West is critically important. It accounts both for the astonishing surge of national energy which was released in Pakistan during the months after August 1947, when everyone was full of hope for the future; and also for the angry disillusion which grew to so dangerous a pitch among the masses during the later years when leadership faltered. It was to furnish the dynamic impulse behind the remarkable achievements of the Revolutionary Government which came to the rescue of the country in October 1958.

The loyal support of the masses of the people was crucial in the early days of Pakistan, because no effective administration existed for the country as a whole. The new Central Government set up in Karachi by Mr. Jinnah was obliged to extemporize from day to day in order to hold together the fragments of territory for which it had become responsible. Sind was a relatively undeveloped province under the British. It had one good port, Karachi, and very little else that could meet new and urgent requirements. The buildings which had accommodated a small-scale provincial government were entirely inadequate to the needs of the Central administration of a great country. Officials lived where they could—in tents, in shacks, in one-roomed cottages; they carried on their work by night as well as by day. The records and files which should have come to them from Delhi when partition took place often failed to arrive, or arrived incomplete, owing to the disruption of communications with India which followed the flights and the massacres of refugees. There were no telephones, no typewriters, no stationery, no office equipment—practically everything which ought to have come either did not arrive, or arrived too late to be useful.

For the time, the local administrations in East Pakistan, Sind, Baluchistan, the North-West Frontier Province, and those western districts of the Punjab which partition had brought to Pakistan, carried on as best they could, grappling with their own local problems with such small assistance as was all that the Karachi administration, with the best will in the world, could afford them.

35

One thing it could do, however, which was of immediate service. Mr. Jinnah appointed experienced British officials as Governors of the North-West Frontier Province, West Punjab, and East Pakistan, and a very able Sindhi as Governor of Sind. He insisted that they kept in close touch with him personally through fortnightly letters: he gave them direct instructions himself. What did it matter if these Governors acted rather as agents of the Quaid-i-Azam, and sometimes short-circuited the Ministries of the provinces where they presided? The Quaid-i-Azam himself exercised powers unfettered by the constitutional limitations of an orthodox Governor-General, even as enlarged by the discretionary powers laid down in the 1935 Act, which was taken as the new State's temporary legal framework. He could even pass orders to the Prime Minister and the Cabinet. The people wholly approved. He dismissed the pro-Congress Ministry in the North-West Frontier Province, which had been suspected of working for the creation of a separate Pathan State ('Pakhtunistan')under its Chief Minister, Dr. Khan Sahib and his brother, Abdul Ghaffar Khan, 'the Frontier Gandhi'. Baluchistan—then a Chief Commissioner's province—was brought under what amounted to Mr. Jinnah's direct control. He dismissed the Premier of Sind on charges of maladministration. It was the goodwill of the people as a whole, and their enormous respect for Mr. Jinnah, now their own Governor-General, which held everything together until the new nation began to find itself.

Without a sense of dedication on the part of the leaders and of hopeful faith on the part of the led, the fervour of which transcended all obstacles of distance, race, and surroundings, Pakistan could never have taken shape. The organizational difficulties which had to be overcome might have appeared at first sight insuperable. West Pakistan—the original homeland of Iqbal's vision—was separated from the portion of Bengal which partition made into East Pakistan by a thousand miles of Indian territory as the crow flies, and by more than thrice that number of the sea-miles involved in the circumnavigation of peninsular India. At no previous period in the world's history could a country divided into these widely-separated wings have aspired to united nationhood, for the bare elements of a common administration would have been impossible to construct. Mr. Jinnah had been rebuked at one stage by his political opponents for demanding a land-corridor across India which should link West and East Pakistan. To do him justice, he soon realized the difficulties, political and administrative, which the creation of such a corridor would entail, and accordingly he ceased to press for it. In the event, he came to see that the development of radio communications, and of man's conquest of the air, had by 1947 proceeded sufficiently far for a seeming miracle to be achieved: the two wings of Pakistan could be linked by radio-telephone as easily as a man dials a neighbouring town: while modern air travel would make light of distance.

From her earliest beginnings, Pakistan has been obliged by her very circumstances to become 'communications-conscious', as befits the first nation in the world to depend upon the radio and the air-link as the very sinews of her being. Today, communications between the East and the West wings have been so far perfected that Pakistanis— and others—take them for granted. Except during certain days in the monsoons, or under abnormal atmospheric conditions, it is as easy for an official or a merchant in Dacca to speak to his opposite number in Rawalpindi, Lahore, or Karachi as to ring up a friend in Sylhet or Chittagong. Air services, thanks to the efficiency of the Pakistan International Airlines Corporation, which looks after all domestic as well as all foreign routes, are now so highly developed that Pakistanis fly between Karachi, the Punjab, the Himalayan territories and the North-West Frontier with as little hesitation as a British suburban 'commuter' travels between his home in the Green Belt and his office in the City. Moreover, people 'commute' between East and West Pakistan almost automatically as occasion arises. A day's work can be done in Karachi or Rawalpindi, now Pakistan's capital: a swift journey by jet plane enables the next day to be spent in Dacca: a second night flight returns the traveller to his office, with no working hours wasted. It has, of course, taken time to bring Pakistan's domestic air-services, to say nothing of her east-west communications, to their present well-regulated efficiency: in the early days, strenuous efforts had to be made to create them from nothing and to keep them in being.

East-west communications in particular, had to be given high priority, for more reasons than one. Mr. Jinnah early realized how much remained to be done before the peoples of East and of West Pakistan could achieve the understanding upon which their joint future depended. East Pakistanis, with the exception of small communities like the Maghs of Chittagong and the tribes of the Hill Tracts, are Bengalis by race, whose speech, culture and habits are more closely akin to those of their neighbours in West Bengal—now become a State of India—than to those of the Punjabis, Sindhis, Baluchis and Pathans who inhabit West Pakistan. Fortunately for the unity of Pakistan, East Pakistanis, also, have traditions of Muslim rule; and before Pakistan came into existence, they remembered with regret the short-lived province of Eastern Bengal and Assam which had revived Dacca into new dignity—recalling its prominence in Mughal days—as a capital city. But in British times it had been often remarked, not without truth, that a Bengali Muslim and a Bengali Hindu as a rule understand each other better, and have more in common, than a Bengali Muslim and a Muslim from the country which is now West Pakistan. Certain it is that in East Bengal most of the Government officers, most of the lawyers, almost all the doctors and schoolmasters, nearly all the considerable landowners and most of the heads of business firms, were Hindus, whose 'spiritual home' was Calcutta rather than Dacca. The dependence of East Pakistan's entire economic and administrative structure upon the Hindu element was a factor of cardinal importance at the time of partition.

Very large numbers of Hindus decided to leave East Pakistan and to go to West Bengal, while Muslims in roughly equivalent numbers left West Bengal for East Pakistan. The decision in each case seems to have been a matter of choice rather than of necessity; although Pakistanis think that India brought pressure upon the Hindus to withdraw in order to embarrass the new régime. Those Hindus who opted to remain in East Pakistan felt—and were—perfectly safe there. Possibly because the peoples affected were all Bengalis, the migrations were unmarred by the massacres and terrorism which stained the corresponding movements into and out of West Pakistan. In East Pakistan, Hindu real property, which could not be carried away, remained unmolested: a large house with its contents would be left in the custody of one old woman, and no one interfered with either. Not a single Hindu temple was desecrated. From the first, the local authorities did their best to reassure the Hindus who remained that they would be well treated: indeed indulgence was carried to remarkable lengths. Hindus who had transferred their families to Calcutta were permitted to remain, and even to hold official positions and elective offices, in East Pakistan, while remitting their salaries to their wives and children. A similar arrangement was common in the case of Hindu business men.

After partition, some 9 million Hindus remained in East Pakistan: but these were predominantly the lower-income groups. The leaders of the community, the men who had occupied senior posts in the administration, who had dominated finance, commerce and industry, who had almost monopolized medicine, teaching, advocacy and the other learned professions, mostly departed. The Muslims who had migrated from West Bengal, being mainly of the cultivating and small shopkeeping classes, could not replace them. The change-over left crippling gaps in every branch of the local economy; for an astonishingly high proportion of the 40 million Muslims in East Pakistan were wholly lacking in the kind of experience which would be needed to run the country. The result was that some quite unsuitable persons found themselves suddenly promoted to positions of authority because no better material was forthcoming. Things were all the worse because few Muslims from East Bengal had entered the former All-India Services, so that all the difficulties which West Pakistan was encountering in creating a new administrative machine were found, in aggravated form, in the Eastern wing. The only thing that the newly-established Central Government in Karachi could do was to send a good British Governor, and some trained men, whom it could ill spare, to help East Pakistan.

The East Pakistanis had rallied enthusiastically to Mr. Jinnah, and were prepared to accept any arrangement that he approved; but they were not happy about the influx of officials from the Western wing. These officials did not know Bengali: they insisted that Urdu was the national language of Pakistan, and they were not always tactful in pointing out the administrative inexperience of the people whom they had come to help. The East Pakistanis, conscious that they make up more than half the total population of Pakistan, that their wing produces the bulk of the revenue of the country, and being besides, justifiably proud of their own culture and their own language, were sensitive to any suggestion that their wishes did not count for as much as the wishes of the people of West Pakistan. The mere choice of Karachi as the new capital seemed likely, they thought, to give West Pakistanis an advantage: being closer at hand, would not West Pakistanis be able to look after their own interests with the Central Government better than the more distant East Pakistanis? And what, after all, the East Pakistanis complained, was West Pakistan? It was a strange mixture of separate races and heterogeneous administrations—the Western Punjab, the North-West Frontier Province, the hill territories, some Princely States, Sind and Baluchistan. What a contrast to East Pakistan, where the people were mainly all of one race and culture, and where there were experienced and adroit political leaders with long training in the testing atmosphere of the former Bengal legisla-

Railways
International frontiers
Divisional boundaries
Kashmir Cease-fire line
Land over 1000 metres

0   50   100   150   200
Miles

AFGHANISTAN

Miran
Wana
Dera Is
Fort Sandeman
Chaman
QUETTA
Quetta   Loralai   Dera G
Sibi
Dalbandin   Kalat
BALUCHISTAN   Jacobabad
KHARAN   Sukkur
Khuzdar   Khairpur
IRAN   Larkana   KHAI
Panjgur   Dadu   T
MAKRAN   •Bala
HYDERABAD
Gwadar   Hyderabad   •Um
KARACHI

W

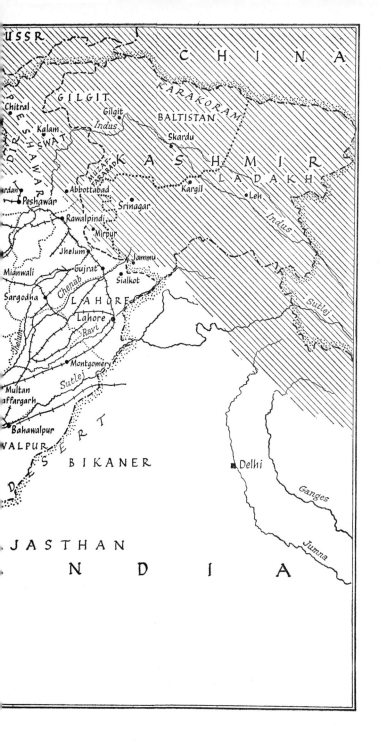

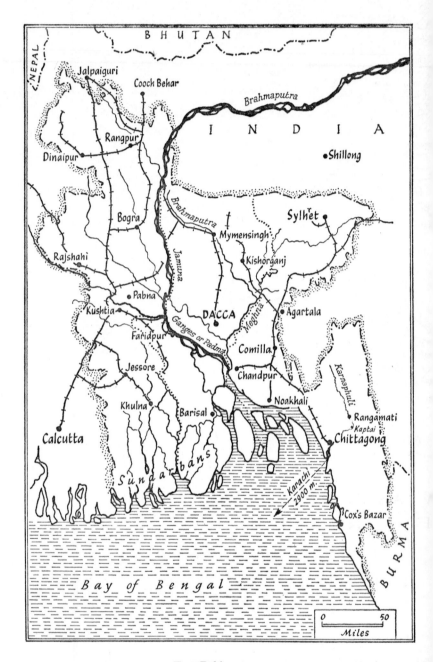

East Pakistan

ture! Nor was the feeling on one side only. The West Pakistani officials complained that they were being treated as intruders, that they received inadequate co-operation, and that the East Pakistanis were not only unable to do anything for themselves, but, in addition, were deeply resentful if someone else tried to help them. West Pakistanis thought the East Pakistanis clannish and incompetent, more proud of being Bengalis than of being Pakistanis, lacking in the national, as distinct from a provincial, outlook which Pakistan now required from her citizens. East Pakistanis considered West Pakistanis frequently overbearing and often uncultured.

The mere fact that each wing did the other far less than justice in these mental images perhaps mattered less in the long run than the opportunities for friction and misunderstanding to which these attitudes of mind gave rise. The position was not serious so long as Mr. Jinnah lived: he criticized each side for its intolerance, and used his great influence to make both realize that they were Pakistanis first and foremost. He did all in his power to make communications between the two wings quick and easy: he gave East Pakistanis their full share in Cabinet and other appointments: he insisted that the interests of East Pakistan should rank equally with the interests of West Pakistan in the plans and policies of the Central Government. In this effort to bridge the gulf his lead was largely successful for the first few months of Pakistan's existence. Moreover the difficulties, particularly the economic difficulties, which shortly arose between Pakistan and India, had the effect of drawing the two wings more closely together to meet a crisis which for some time threatened them both. But when Quaid-i-Azam departed to his rest, and the problems of West Pakistan not only multiplied, but were also aggravated by the quarrels with India over Kashmir and the division of the water-resources of the Indus basin—which naturally tended to preoccupy the Central Government —the rift between West and East widened.

No foreigner who toured East Pakistan at regular intervals, as my wife and I did, in the years between 1955 and 1958, could fail to sense the resentment felt both by the leaders and by the people of East Pakistan at what they regarded as their subordination to, and as the neglect of their interests by, a Central Government largely preoccupied by the pressing problems of West Pakistan. On the other hand, there was a marked tendency at high levels in the Central Government to look on East Pakistan as a problem child, full of tiresome factions, undisciplined and parochial in its outlook, unable to manage even its

43

own local affairs with reasonable efficiency. As soon as West Pakistan became unified into a single administration, the Central Government proved even more responsive to its pressure (to the relative neglect of East Pakistan) than ever before.

Today, all this has changed for the better. In the matter of East-West tension, as in so many other delicate problems, the Revolutionary Government set up in October 1958 has effected, as we shall see later, a salutary transformation. By giving the East Pakistanis tangible proof that their interests really do count, and that their land is looked on as being in all respects as important as West Pakistan, the new Government has carried on the work which Quaid-i-Azam began, to the great benefit of the country as a whole. President Ayub Khan, soon after he took over power, gave a pledge to the East Pakistanis that he would not send outsiders to rule them. He has kept his promise. East Pakistan has now an East Pakistani G.O.C., an East Pakistani Chief Secretary, and an East Pakistani Chairman of the new Eastern Wing of the Pakistan Industrial Development Corporation. The new Constitition gives East Pakistan substantial local autonomy with its own railway system and makes Dacca both the second capital and the permanent seat of the National Assembly. Further, expenditure on development works in East Pakistan under the Second Five Year Plan now annually exceeds the total revenue derived from the Province. While differences of outlook can still be discerned between the East and the West wings, each has now a better understanding of the other; initial resentment is yielding to mutual comprehension. It was noticeable that when some students in Dacca and Rajshahi Universities rioted in February 1962 —misled partly by Communist propaganda from Calcutta and partly by the influence of a hard core of Hindu East Pakistanis who have never reconciled themselves to becoming Pakistani citizens—the ordinary public remained unmoved; and the authorities, secure in popular support, were able to treat the unruly youngsters with great clemency. A real sense of partnership between East and West Pakistan is now growing, thanks largely to the confidence which both sides feel in a régime which works impartially for the common good of both.

During the years from 1947 to 1949, these later and more healthy developments lay far in the future; and it seemed almost inevitable that the kind of difficulties which pressed hard upon the new Central Government would drive it to focus its attention mainly upon West Pakistan. These difficulties were so varied, and at the same time so inter-connected both in time and in nature, that they can almost be considered as particular aspects of a single problem which time alone could solve: Was Pakistan to survive or not? That this question received a triumphantly affirmative answer was due entirely to the efforts of the Pakistanis themselves. But the upsurge of nation-building energy which accounted for their success, and the self-sacrifices ungrudgingly rendered by so many elements in the population, were not wholly, although they were very largely, due to the general will of Pakistanis to preserve the Muslim homeland which Mr. Jinnah had secured for them. A powerful element in the stiffening of their determination to survive as a nation was their strong reaction to the attitude of India.

Mention has been made on an earlier page of the acceptance—albeit reluctant—by the the Congress leaders of the creation of Pakistan as the quickest expedient for securing a British withdrawal, and as the only practicable alternative to widespread civil war. But at the time of partition many of these leaders—as I know from talking to them—looked on Pakistan in their heart of hearts as a purely temporary aberration, as something which prudence had obliged them to acquiesce in merely for the moment. Hardly any of them expected Pakistan to last for very long. Her continued survival without initial collapse came as a shock: more lately it has given rise to those deep heart-searchings—to which reference has already been made—about who is to blame for Pakistan's original emergence, and about whether Pakistan need ever have emerged at all. During the first months of Pakistan's existence, no such speculations arose in India: it was almost taken for granted that Pakistan would, before long, find her position impossible and would approach India, hat in hand, with a plea to be allowed to join the Indian Federation. Given this premise, it is hardly surprising that India, where she did not deliberately increase Pakistan's early difficulties, did nothing at all to alleviate them. Many Pakistanis remain firmly convinced that India deliberately engineered the withdrawal of Hindu key-men to precipitate Pakistan's collapse. In Lahore and Lyallpur, they say, there was an exodus, which looked concerted, not only of men of substance in business and professional life, but also of clerks, minor officials in every Department of Government, nurses, orderlies, schoolmasters, and medical staff. Even prosperous Sikh farmers are said to have left their land on the assurance that they would be able to return in six weeks, when Pakistan collapsed. In East Pakistan, as we have seen, the withdrawal was even more complete. Whether this exodus was deliberately organized or not, I am quite sure that it would be difficult to overestimate the unifying effect upon Pakistanis of the successive manifestation of Indian unfriendliness, which only served to stiffen their fixed determination to ensure the survival of their country at any cost to themselves.

There can be little doubt that India relied mainly on Pakistan's economic difficulties to bring her to her knees. When the idea of Pakistan was adopted by Mr. Jinnah and the Muslim League as the goal of their efforts, economic experts, not only in India but also in many Western countries, were almost unanimous in deciding that a country so constituted could not conceivably prove economically viable. They argued that Pakistan had nothing but some good raw materials, particularly jute, cotton and hides: and that the handling of all these was entirely under Indian control. The developing pattern of undivided India had dictated that while primary materials came from the country ultimately earmarked for Pakistan, all the factories, all the industrialization, all the marketing, were located in the country which would remain India. These economic authorities took East Pakistan as one example of their assessment of the situation. True, the soil, though terribly over-settled, can grow anything: the forest wealth is great. But economically, the entire region was organized as a kind of hinterland of Calcutta: and it was in Calcutta that jute, the main crop of East Pakistan, was processed, marketed and its world-price fixed. It was there that grading took place, and it was there that the standards of quality on which the export trade depended were enforced. How, it was asked, could East Pakistan survive when cut off by a new international frontier from West Bengal and its jute-mills? Nor could West Pakistan be in a position to give effective help, these same authorities maintained: its own economy depended mainly on food crops and cotton. There were scarcely any mills to spin and weave the cotton: most were located in India. And in food crops, as the past years had shown, there was rarely much surplus for export. How then could Pakistan hope to engage in international trade, and without international trade, how could she survive as a nation?

The manner in which these confident prophecies of disaster came to be belied is now a matter of the record: but a vivid impression of the frame of mind in which Pakistanis faced the seemingly-impossible economic problems, can be gathered by questioning them. In 1955 I remember finding, in reminiscent mood, a high Pakistani official of the Ministry of Finance; a man who was carrying on the work of two successive British financial experts, Sir Archibald Rowlands and Sir Jeremy Raisman, whose names are still greatly honoured in Pakistan today. 'To some extent', he told me, 'the phenomenal growth of industrialization which you now see was forced on Pakistan by India's attitude in the early days. We had nothing except our primary crops like jute and cotton: even these were handled by India. In East Pakistan, it was the Calcutta Marwaris who financed, moved, and marketed the jute. After partition, they ceased to come, expecting that our jute cultivators would be forced either to accept absurdly low prices or to face ruin. We had to set up our National Bank of Pakistan at once to take over the financing of the crop: Government had to build mills to handle the jute. Cotton was in a better position: but the mills which private enterprise was setting up had to be helped to find new international connections. It was a struggle for sheer survival, so far as we were concerned: we had to change our entire economic pattern and to make our trade flow into new channels. We were very lucky in one thing. Under the British Raj, financial skill was very rare among Muslims. But at the time of partition, as it so happened, there were among us some men of exceptionally great financial experience, such as Ghulam Mohammad, Chaudhury Mohammad Ali, Mohammad Shuaib. In addition, we had some very good British advisers. These men pulled us through. But we certainly should not have tackled this enormous task of rapid industrialization so whole-heartedly unless India had obliged us to do so. We offered her a customs-union so that the economic pattern which had grown up under the British could survive partition: she refused. Later, she came to us with a similar offer, but we in turn refused: we had become meanwhile too strong to need it. I doubt if even now Indians realize how easy it would have been to kill our economic progress by kindness. Industrialization', he concluded, 'was in any event necessary: we had to undertake it to avoid helpless dependence upon outside sources: and we needed it because it provides the only hope of raising the living standards of our people to a reasonable level. But we could have made many of the changes involved in turning ourselves from an importing country into an exporting country far more easily if India had been willing to enter into friendly arrangements. Since she was not ready to do this, we had to manage as best we could, and build up our industries to compete, rather than to co-operate, with hers.'

As I have already pointed out, India's attitude, although it unquestionably helped greatly to stiffen the determination of Pakistanis

47

of all walks of life to preserve their country's independence at any cost, was perfectly intelligible from India's own point of view. She did not expect Pakistan to survive: why should she help to prolong the process? Especially as the Hindu-Muslim bitterness which had convulsed the British Raj during the concluding five years of its existence had rapidly begun to find new and even more sinister expression in the shape of Indo-Pakistani hostility after partition.

Much has been written about the frightful massacres on each side which took place after the publication, on 18th August 1947, of the Boundary Commission's award defining the Indo-Pakistani frontiers in the Punjab and Bengal. Pakistan is still sore about some features of this award; in particular she criticizes the allocation of the Gurdaspur and Batala *tahsils*, in spite of their Muslim majority, to India—a decision which linked the State of Jammu and Kashmir to Indian territory and thus facilitated India's later occupation of that State. But at the time, Pakistan's dissatisfaction was restrained when compared with the blazing anger of the Sikhs in the Eastern Punjab. Furious at the partitioning of their historic homeland, they determined to free the entire East Punjab from the Muslim element in the population. The movement of between 7 and 8 million people—Hindus to India and Muslims to Pakistan—must inevitably, in the prevalent condition of Hindu-Muslim tension, have led to tragedies which the few troops available for the duty of patrolling short portions of the frontier would have been powerless to control: but Pakistanis maintain that the atrocities—'killing first and looting only afterwards,' as they described the process to me—inflicted by the Sikhs on their terrified Muslim neighbours, and on refugee trains carrying Muslims to Pakistan, partook much more of the nature of deliberately-organized massacres than did the individual cases of looting and violence which Hindus fleeing from Pakistan had to endure in return.

One of the reasons why deaths and suffering among the refugees were so frightful was that in the districts in which they had to move on both sides of the border, the local authorities had had no opportunity to take breath, as it were, before the crisis was upon them. Disorganized by the partition, short of staff owing to the defection of Hindus and Muslims respectively, the machine of local government collapsed under the strain. Nor were the Central Governments of Pakistan and India in much better case to assert their authority: communications broke down: communal fury, fanned to white heat by the tales—which lost nothing in the telling—of the sufferings endured by Hindus at the hand of Muslims and by Muslims at the hand of the Hindus, seriously affected discipline not only in the police and other civil cadres, but in certain cases even among the troops as well.

That the local authorities on both sides honestly did their best to protect the refugees fleeing through their respective jurisdictions need not be doubted—there are many instances in point. But very often, they were quite helpless when confronted by mob violence inflamed by communal passions. This fact was brought home to me very vividly, when, some years later, I was talking to a member of a Muslim family formerly settled for generations in Patiala State, whom I encountered at Skardu in Baltistan—of all unexpected places—where he was engaged as an engineer in building new roads for the development of that beautiful, but until lately neglected, country. Many years before, when I was Foreign Minister of Patiala, I had known him as a child: he had been a playmate of my own children. He told me that he and his family, who were substantial property owners, widely respected by everyone, owed their lives to the fact that they and their dependants occupied their own separate *mohalla* (quarter) in Patiala City. This they fortified, and defended tooth and nail against frenzied attacks from the Sikhs and the Hindus, who, in spite of all the efforts of the Maharaja of Patiala to restore order, were rounding upon every Muslim they could find and killing at sight. At long last, the Maharaja was able to arrange a safe-conduct for them to leave: even then they had to run the gauntlet of the persistent attacks directed against refugee trains passing between Amritsar and the border. In the event, they owed their lives to the chance that they reached Amritsar at the same time as a train containing a batch of fully-armed Muslim troops on their way to Pakistan. The troops cleared the station platform of the mob which had already begun to pull Muslim refugees out of the carriages to butcher them: the two trains moved off together and crossed the Pakistan border in safety.

Tales equally terrible are told on the other side: and it requires little effort of the imagination to picture the effect of such atrocity-stories—inevitably magnified by being passed from mouth to mouth —upon the post-partition relations of India and Pakistan. In both countries, there sprang up a fierce demand for open hostilities: it says much for the good sense of both Governments that would-be trouble-makers were firmly discouraged. Even so, at this very time when the true interests of Pakistan and India called for the closest co-operation between them if the initial difficulties facing both were to be surmounted, bitterness, hatred and suspicion poisoned the atmosphere.

As though some malignant deity had decided that the tragedies which accompanied the migrations between India and Pakistan were insufficient to ensure their mutual enmity, a fresh source of friction was shortly forthcoming in the emergence of bitter disputes over their competing interests in certain of the Princely States.

During the life of the British Raj, the Princely States had not been part of British India. They had remained bound to the British Crown, and to the Crown's representatives, by a complicated relationship originally based on ancient treaties, engagements, and understandings of various types—relics of the long series of wars and alliances incidental to the growth of British power over India. These compacts permitted them varying degrees of internal autonomy subject to broad supervision by a special department of the Supreme Government. The British were under an obligation to protect them; they, on their part, were pledged to loyalty. In all, they numbered more than 560: but only some thirty were of viable size individually. Occupying as they did just under one-half of the area of the sub-continent, with a population nearly as numerous as that of Pakistan today, they might have emerged as a 'third force' or even as a separate Dominion, if they could have decided to pool their resources under effective leadership. But for more than a century, the policy of the British had been to prevent political combinations between them: and although this policy had been modified after the First World War, and the Chamber of Princes had been set up to foster co-operation for the general good, the legacy of the past, ancestral feuds, and Hindu-Muslim antagonisms, proved a fatal barrier to working unity. A place had been found for them in the All-India Federation contemplated by the 1935 Act: but the personal authority exercised by the Princes over their subjects, and their close ties with the British Crown, were disliked both by the Congress and by the League, so that the Federal scheme never matured. When the time came for the British to hand over power, all they could bring themselves to do was to restore to the States the independence which had been anciently surrendered to the British Crown, and leave them to make the best terms that they could with India and Pakistan. In effect, the Princely States were abandoned to their fate by the Power which they had supported so loyally. In theory, the right of each Prince to decide the future allegiance of his State was secured to him: in fact, most were bound hand and foot by economic interests, by geographical location, and by the weakness which sprang from the isolation forced upon them by their individual relationship with the British.

India, faced as she thought by the risk of Balkanization, acted with Bismarck-like vigour and ruthlessness in the person of V. J. Patel, the formidable Congress Party Manager. In the course of a few months, nearly all the hundreds of States which patchworked Indian territory had been virtually incorporated into the Union. Patel used the threat of force unmercifully to gain these objectives: and when the Muslim Nawab of Junagadh—a maritime State easily accessible by sea from Karachi—decided to join Pakistan, Indian troops were sent to afford his Hindu-majority subjects an opportunity to override his decision by a plebiscite. Pakistan, not unnaturally, was annoyed, and protested at this unconstitutional act. Junagadh would have been little use to her —it was India's violation of principle which was disquieting. Pakistan herself had no such problem with the States as confronted India: the twelve States which lay within her borders were largely Muslim, rulers and subjects alike. They gladly joined her: and she was very ready to permit time to complete, painlessly and gradually, the inevitable process of final assimilation into her polity. From the very beginning, Pakistan has treated the rulers and chiefs within her territory with courtesy and consideration: and it is typical of her attitude towards them that when Queen Elizabeth II visited Pakistan in 1961, a special reception was arranged so that they could pay their respects to the Sovereign to whom they had formerly owed allegiance.

The principle of permitting a plebiscite of State subjects to override their ruler's choice as between India and Pakistan—a principle which India had supported in Junagadh, as well as in the smaller dependencies of Manavada, Babariawad and Mangrol—was to furnish a weapon against herself in the crucial dispute in which both countries were shortly to be involved over the State of Jammu and Kashmir. About this dispute, many bitter words have been written and spoken by protagonists of each side. It has brought the participants to the very verge of formal hostilities on several occasions: it has defied the best efforts of the Commonwealth, of the United Nations, and of innumerable would-be peacemakers to compose it. It is not my intention here to add to the number of the many exhaustive—and perhaps exhausting—studies which have been published about the Kashmir problem: all I shall try to do is to give the general background against which my own personal experiences of it are set.

In the time of the British Raj, I travelled a great deal in the State of

Jammu and Kashmir, partly studying the people and the country, partly doing some work, mainly of an advisory character, for the Darbar, as the State Government was then called. It was an extraordinary State in several respects, more than 80,000 square miles in extent, but made up of quite separate and distinguishable bits held together at the top by a handful of Hindus who ruled many times their number of Muslims. The Princely House was Dogra Rajput: most of the State functionaries were Hindus, prominent among them being the Kashmiri Brahmins who have long been famous—Mr. Nehru himself is one of them—for their intellectual and administrative ability. This small ruling class governed—and governed rather harshly—a population of just over 4 million which was nearly 80 per cent Muslim, with considerable Hindu and fractional Sikh and Buddhist minorities.

Administratively, there were three main divisions. The first, Jammu Province, is a beautiful, hilly country, the original seat of the Dogra Dynasty; the locality from which Maharaja Gulab Singh, in the era of the Sikh Wars, had sent out his troops to conquer the other areas which gave the State its present shape. Although Jammu has never been as famous as Kashmir proper, the rulers always insisted on calling themselves Maharajas of 'Jammu and Kashmir', to underline the fact that Jammu, with its Dogra soldiery, was the real source of their power. Next is Kashmir, properly so called, with the famous Valley, six thousand feet above sea-level, which is one of the paradises of the habitable world. The climate resembles that of Switzerland—a marvellous thing to find in Asia—except that the winters are shorter. The lakes, the mountains, the flowers, the fruit, the trout-streams, the magnificent Mughal pleasure gardens; the city of Srinagar with its seven bridges and its wooden houses with their carved fronts leaning over the winding canals, draw visitors from all over the world. So attractive are the surroundings that before partition, some European officers, on their retirement from service, settled down to live and die amidst all this beauty; ('where', as one Maharaja told me, with a twinkle in his eye, when warning me against following their example, 'the elevation makes many of them notably eccentric before long.')

The third division of the State is the Frontier Districts: Ladakh bordering on Tibet; Baltistan and Gilgit bordering on Sinkiang. The Valley, and the pleasure-resorts higher up in the mountains, were a kind of show piece, to which visitors' money brought the appearance, at least, of reasonable prosperity. The traditional Kashmiri handicrafts of wood carving, carpet weaving, sericulture, shawl-making, papiermâché work, and embroidery flourished on the tourist trade. But if one left the beaten track and went farther afield, the picture was very different.

Some of these Frontier Districts, for example Ladakh, are fascinating in their austere beauty. The journey from Srinagar to Leh, before the days of air services and jeep-transport, took quite a lot of preparation, for it meant marching day after day with camping equipment and pack ponies through almost deserted country over high passes and along very poor roads. On some old maps, Ladakh is called 'Little Tibet'; and it is easy to see why, because the people, the praying-wheels by the roadside, the long-robed lamas, the monasteries which own the cultivable land, look wholly Tibetan, with nothing Indian about them. It seemed to me that the State authorities did nothing much for Ladakh and the Ladakhis: they were largely left alone, although there was a detachment of State troops to keep order. In Baltistan things looked a good deal worse. This is a beautiful country, at that time accessible only from Srinagar by a road through Kargil, overshadowed by the ice-wall of the Karakorams towering up to heaven; a land where Nanga Parbat dwarfs majestically even the innumerable—and unnamed—peaks surrounding her. Here the population is Muslim; the country itself struck me even some decades ago as possessing promising possibilities of development as a tourist centre. It has abundance of game, big and small, fertile valleys, wonderful fruit and flowers, water-power sufficient for local hydro-electric installations, and some of the finest mountaineering in the world. But nothing was done for the people—hardy and naturally cheerful mountain-folk, who looked poor and miserable, plainly overawed by the garrison of State troops occupying the ancient Askandria Fort at Skardu. The Maharaja owned the land; the people were tenants-at-will, entirely at the mercy of high-handed State officials and receiving nothing in return for the heavy taxes they paid.

In all these Frontier Districts, I found the brightest spot at Gilgit, where a British political agent kept watch, for the Government of India, over the districts bordering the strategic frontier with Sinkiang —districts which include the small semi-independent States of Hunza and Nagar. The political agent had his own small enclave of territory: his own police force of Gilgit Scouts, with their pipe-band, their proudly trotting tame markhor as regimental mascot, and their Black Watch tartans. Inside the enclave there was a hospital, there was a school, there was a general air of contentment and prosperity. Outside there was a battalion of State troops supporting the same type of Darbar rule as could be seen in Skardu, and very little else.

Visiting Jammu and Kashmir State several times during the 'twenties' and 'thirties', as I did, it became clear to me that in spite of the efforts of the Maharaja to keep things just as they always had been, changes were coming. Two separate 'popular' organizations emerged to demand limitations on the Maharaja's autocratic power. The first was founded by a certain Sheikh Abdullah, a graduate of Aligarh. He was promptly imprisoned, but the resulting agitation induced the British to press the Maharaja to appoint a commission of enquiry; and eventually a State Legislature, partly elected, was set up. Sheikh Abdullah, who had at the beginning championed Muslim rights, became an admirer of Mr. Gandhi, a personal friend of Mr. Nehru, and an adherent of the Congress, so that his movement took on an avowedly secular and 'nationalist' guise in accordance with the Congress programme in India. But about the same time, the Muslim League began to work in Jammu and Kashmir, with a programme similar to that which it had put forward elsewhere. Under the leadership of men like Chaudhuri Ghulam Abbas, it made considerable headway, for the situation of the Muslims in Kashmir was precisely of the kind that the League was striving to provide against elsewhere. It was a great pity that these two movements could not work together, as Mr. Jinnah tried to persuade them to do. Some people feel that Mr. Jinnah may have made a mistake in trying to force Sheikh Abdullah to merge his movement into the Muslim League, for although on the long-term view Mr. Jinnah was perfectly right, as Sheikh Abdullah came to realize all too shortly, the immediate consequence was a split which reproduced in Kashmir the same cleavage of opinion which was developing in the rest of the sub-continent. As soon as partition looked inevitable, Sheikh Abdullah and his National Conference Party thought that the State should join India: the Muslim League's local organization, the Muslim Conference, considered that it was Kashmir's natural destiny to join Pakistan.

The Maharaja himself, with a curious anticipation of the conclusion to which the mind of many of his then subjects would eventually, after much tribulation, be turning, disliked the idea of joining either India or Pakistan: he once told me that he hoped Jammu and Kashmir would become a kind of Asian Switzerland, under the joint protection of her two great neighbours, friendly with both, but a part of neither. It was for this reason, I personally think, that he evaded all the efforts of Lord Mountbatten, as well as many other people, to persuade him to give a firm decision one way or the other. Unlike many other Princes, he was entirely free to make up his mind: he had been specifically assured by the Viceroy that his accession to Pakistan, if he chose this course, would not be regarded by India as an unfriendly act. Most British observers, I believe, expected him eventually to decide in this way, because all the natural lines of communication between Jammu and Kashmir and the outside world ran through Pakistan, and the entire commercial life of the State was keyed to her, while the only land link with India was the road through Pathankot and the Muslim-majority *tahsils* withdrawn from Pakistan by the Boundary Commission's award. But any such plans as the Maharaja may have had in mind for resisting the competing pulls in the direction of India or Pakistan which his own subjects were organizing, eventually came to nothing because the entire Muslim population of the State were at least agreed on one thing, namely that they were sick and tired of his rule.

The story of what happened in the Frontier Districts of the Gilgit Agency and Baltistan is worth telling, not only because it is less known than the more widely-publicized events which took place farther south, but because it illustrates so clearly the prevailing mood of the people. Some years after partition, I revisited the Frontier areas which I had known in the days of the Darbar, and I talked to the men who had taken part in the struggle which had changed the whole face of the country. It was strange to reach Gilgit and Skardu by air from civilization in an hour or two, instead of by riding for days on end on a hill pony. It was good to learn that many of the tracks along which I had toiled so painfully only a few years earlier were now 'jeepable' for mechanical transport. It was at Gilgit that I came on the beginning of the story of the transformation of the Frontier Districts.

Just before partition, the British withdrew their political officer from the agency, as they were withdrawing his colleagues from similar positions in other Indian States, in favour of the Maharaja's authority. A Dogra Governor was sent from Srinagar to take over. But the Gilgitis had their own ideas: they politely put under house arrest the British Officers of the Gilgit Scouts, as well as the new Governor, and proclaimed their independence of Srinagar. They were joined by the Muslim element in the local battalion of State troops: the Sikh element in the same battalion was made prisoner and sent safely and humanely under escort out of the territory—largely, it is said, through the influence of the British Officers, whose advice was followed. Thus the revolutionary *coup* was wholly peaceful: not a life was lost. The Gilgitis then asked the Pakistan Government to send them someone to take charge, as they wished to join Pakistan. A single officer arrived. He found everything in perfect order, with the Treasury intact; while the British officers and the Dogra Governor were being treated as honoured guests, fraternizing daily with their captors at polo in the narrow, stone-walled enclosure at Gilgit. This ground has seen many village-against-village contests in the Gilgiti national game, a 'free-for-all' in which the men and the ponies are incited to renewed efforts by the fierce music of hill-pipes, and of drums whose skins are kept taut and resonant by small fires kindled on the walls.

From that moment onwards, the former Gilgit agency has been an acknowledged part of Pakistan. India protested bitterly; and a little later, when 'special undeclared warfare' (to employ a convenient Japanese euphemism) broke out in Kashmir, Gilgit came under bombardment from Indian Air Force planes. The town is very difficult to hit from the air; each unsuccessful attack was greeted with derisive tunes from the Scouts' Band, who played their liveliest airs to keep up the spirits of the townsfolk. This annoyed the Indian pilots, and, on one occasion, after dropping their bombs, they returned (unexpectedly as they hoped) to deal with the insolent musicians. But the Gilgitis were not caught napping: as General Iskander Mirza told me with glee some years later. He was in Gilgit at the time, and he had posted a couple of the very few machine guns which Gilgit possessed to protect the Band from just such a low-level attack. When the Indian planes flew in to deliver their fire, those machine guns gave them such a hot reception that they were glad to retire—once more to the accompaniment of derisive tunes. They never tried the trick again. The Gilgit Scouts are proud of this episode; they still retain their pipe-band and markhor mascot which figure on all formal occasions.

Local notables still gather at the agency, with its magnificent garden and priceless heritage of carpets and rugs bequeathed by British political agents of past years. A few years after Gilgit had been incorporated in Pakistan, my wife and I had the opportunity of attending one of these gatherings, and of meeting the Mirs of Hunza and Nagar, the Governor of Yasin, and other important personages. The occasion was a conference called by the Development Commissioner to enlist further support for the Village AID (agricultural and industrial development) movement which was already making encouraging headway throughout the area. In talking to a good many of the notables present—there were about a hundred of them—I gathered one outstanding impression: all were fully alive to the new opportunities for progress which the incorporation of the territory in Pakistan is affording to them. The Mirs of Hunza and Nagar told me that their states, notably fertile and productive if small, are even more prosperous than before because of the channels of employment now opened to their sturdy, warlike subjects in the Gilgit Scouts, the Northern Scouts (a new force, locally recruited, to patrol the frontiers) and the regular Army of Pakistan. The two rulers appeared to feel that their importance was appreciated, their freedom respected, and their friendship valued. In return, their allegiance to Pakistan, and their devotion to her cause, have become a matter of pride to them.

Their host on such occasions is the Pakistani Political Resident, who dispenses hospitality with traditional ceremonial and frank cordiality. His authority is no longer limited, as was that of his British predecessors, to the small Agency *enclave*. Under Pakistan's rule, a great upsurge of development is taking place throughout the entire area. Roads, schools, hospitals, dispensaries are springing up: welfare work is spreading through the countryside: the people look prosperous, cheerful, and well fed. They find excellent opportunities for employment in Pakistan, where their happy, hard working disposition and ready response to kindly treatment make them very welcome. The change of atmosphere from Darbar times is as complete as it is impressive: and the fact that it has resulted from only a very few years of Pakistani rule would be hard to credit if I had not seen the transformation with my own eyes. Now that the people are encouraged to do things for themselves, to take advantage of new opportunities, and to co-operate with a Government which earnestly seeks their welfare, enterprise and hope have replaced apathy and despair. Such are the fruits which the revolt of Gilgit against Srinagar has brought to its people.

The Independence movement in the Frontier Districts was not confined to Gilgit: it spread also to Baltistan. Some hardy spirits from Gilgit made their way to Skardu by hazardous mountain paths: they found the Baltis ripe for revolt. Arms and ammunition were smuggled in: a daring band scaled the nightmare heights—hitherto considered inaccessible to all but the eagles—which command Askandria fort; they raked the *enceinte* with machine-gun and rifle fire until the garrison was forced to surrender. The entire Muslim population rose as one man, proclaimed its independence of Srinagar, sent emissaries to Gilgit and thence to Rawalpindi petitioning for arms to defend themselves, and asking to be allowed to join Pakistan. The Pakistan Government accepted their allegiance, and encouraged them; but could give them little direct assistance beyond allowing unofficial leave to one or two young Pakistani officers, who volunteered to help the Baltis, and organize their defence—if they could get to them. This was by no means easy, because the ordinary route to Skardu lay from Srinagar *via* Kargil, and the Darbar had, of course, closed the road. But by tracks known only to the local inhabitants, more arms, and some trained volunteers, reached the Baltis—just in time. The Darbar despatched a strong punitive expedition to re-occupy Askandria fort and reconquer Baltistan. But a body of Baltis, with incredible hardihood, ill-clad and wearing only rags on their feet, armed just with a rifle and a handful of cartridges apiece, made a forced march across the snow-bound, 13,000-feet high, Deosai plains. When they could march no farther, they lay down and slept by sections in the snow; those on the watch arousing the sleepers before frost-bite could set in, and, in their turn, snatching some rest. Descending unexpectedly on the Kargil-Skardu road at Gol, after this amazing march, they achieved a complete surprise, ambushing the punitive expedition and inflicting such fearful casualties upon the Darbar's troops that hardly any survived to return to Srinagar. After this, the Baltis remained unmolested; before long, the Pakistan Government arranged an air-lift between Rawalpindi and Skardu, thus linking Baltistan to friendly territory.

When I revisited Skardu some little time after these events, it was no longer by road and hill pony from Srinagar and Kargil, but by air from Gilgit. The Gilgit-Skardu direct flight 'over the hump' is rarely possible, because of its exceptional danger. If cloud closes down, it is the end; for no aircraft can fly blinded between the enormous peaks among which it must wind its way as a ship avoids rocks and sandbanks in a dangerous channel. But on the day on which my wife and I were due in Skardu, the Gilgit sky was cloudless: our pilot decided that he could risk the 'direct hop' instead of returning to Rawalpindi and taking the regular route up the Indus Valley. My wife was the first woman to make this trip: as long as we live, we shall neither of us forget the majesty and beauty of the great ice-wall of the Karakorams, glittering in the sunshine, which almost blotted out the sky above as we climbed painfully across the massif. In a matter of minutes, the small dark cleft of the Indus Valley in which Skardu nestles was below us: we slipped down between towering mountain-walls to land on the airstrip. It is characteristic of local conditions that instead of spending twenty-four hours in Skardu as we had intended, we were weather-bound there for five days.

This gave us a good opportunity to look round. I found that the whole situation had changed since Darbar times. The Baltis, free from Dogra oppression, had 'found themselves' as a people. Agriculture was flourishing; schools were multiplying, an admirable hospital, linked to a chain of dispensaries in the surrounding valleys, was doing first-rate work under a devoted band of Pakistani doctors. The Baltis were singing again as they went about their work! And everyone I spoke to had nothing but praise for the 'new deal'. Skardu town even has electric light, provided by 'spare' current from the hospital generators. Every scrap of equipment, and supplies of every kind, had to be transported by air from Rawalpindi along one of the most dangerous routes in the world; the toll of aircraft was high. But Baltistan's isolation had vanished with the oppression which had characterized it; her people could come and go freely, finding new opportunities and fresh careers in the Police, in the Northern Scouts, and in the developing industries of Pakistan. The work done by the Pakistani officers of the various services who volunteer for duty in Baltistan is beyond praise; and as the country flourishes, the Baltis themselves feel that the great days of their ancient heroes, like Raja Alishah Khan and his beloved Queen, Mindok Gailmo, Mother of the Land, have come again. The progress has been steady and continuous. A new road now links Baltistan to the outside world, and helps to supplement, in the summer at least, air communications. Basic democracies on the Pakistan model—of which more will be written in a later chapter—have been introduced and are flourishing. Water channels and irrigation dams are spreading prosperity; there are now sixty-four co-operative societies which deal with the supply of goods and services to outlying areas. Pakistan is doing a splendid job in the whole of this once-neglected country, and finds her reward in the sincere attachment of its inhabitants.

While Gilgit and Baltistan were asserting their right to self-determination in this unmistakable fashion, thus bringing most of the northern territories of the State of Jammu and Kashmir to Pakistan, dramatic events were taking place in the areas to the south and west.

To the east of the Jhelum river, where it forms the boundary be-

tween the State and the old British division of Rawalpindi, lies a
stretch of difficult, mountainous country, whose hardy Muslim menfolk have been accustomed for generations to seek their livelihood
across the border in the Indian Army and Police. Some of them had
their homes in the State district of Muzaffarabad—a locality which
had a bad name at the Maharaja's Court because it was remote, lacked
amenities, and was officered by State servants who had, for one reason
or another, been virtually banished there because they had fallen into
disfavour. Others came from the principality of Poonch, whose Hindu
ruler belonged to a junior branch of the Maharaja's family, but who
possessed the good sense to guide his spirited subjects with a light
rein. Early in 1947, the Raja lost his position, and the oppressive
Kashmir system of taxation was introduced into Poonch. The tough
soldiers and policemen, some on leave from India, some retired from
service, rebelled. State troops were despatched by the Darbar to bring
them to heel; but the Muslim sepoys deserted to join the rebels.
Strong forces of Dogras, clansmen of the Maharaja, were rushed to the
district, and bitter fighting broke out. The Dogra troops behaved very
brutally, burning down whole villages on mere suspicion of rebel
sympathies. But the rebels were too strong to be terrorized thus: very
soon they succeeded in setting up their own government in their home-
country, which they called 'Azad' (free) Kashmir. Their first aim, like
that of the Gilgitis and Baltis, was to throw off Darbar rule: their next,
to maintain their position against all attack. They looked to Pakistan
for help: but while all would have preferred to join her rather than
India, if the only choice lay between them, there was a body of
opinion which hoped for an autonomous Kashmir. They soon
mustered 30,000 fighting men, under the experienced command of
officers like Major-General M. Z. Kiani, a veteran of Subhas Chandra
Bose's Indian National Army, and Brigadier Akbar Khan. They
bought arms and ammunition from wherever they could, including
the rifle factories in the tribal belt of territory between the frontiers
of the old British Raj and Afghanistan. They found sympathizers in
every quarter of the North-West Frontier Province.

The Maharaja, having lost control first of Gilgit, next of Baltistan,
and finally of Muzaffarabad, Mirpur, and all Poonch except the
capital town—where a Dogra garrison still held out—made a determined effort to assert his authority over the remainder of the State.
Since the allegiance of the bulk of his Muslim subjects was very
doubtful, he began to arm the Hindus in Jammu, and to attract mili-

tant Sikh and Hindu elements from across the Indian border to help them. The Muslims of Jammu and Kashmir provinces were subjected to a reign of terror: thousands were massacred, either in their homes or as they were fleeing to Pakistan or to Azad Kashmir territory. Altogether, nearly half a million left Jammu Province, which, as a result, was converted from a Muslim-majority to a Hindu-majority area. Thus, in consequence of the Maharaja's systematic persecution, the flame of Hindu-Muslim enmity flared up in Jammu and Kashmir State no less fiercely than in the Eastern Punjab. This situation had one unexpected and tragic consequence—it gave the impression to some of the many warlike and turbulent tribal elements on the North-West Frontier that, with the departure of the British a 'free for all' fight, with plenty of loot as a reward, lay open to everyone who had the courage to enter it.

To explain what happened next, I must outline the situation on the North-West Frontier, and set out the problems which this situation posed for Pakistan.

Chapter 3

THE NORTH-WEST FRONTIER

'When God had finished making the rest of the world,' say the Pathans, 'He took all the odd pieces left over, and threw them down sideways to make the North-West Frontier country.' It is through this grim barrier, with its narrow passes and winding defiles, that innumerable invaders, from the Aryan-speaking migrants at the dawn of recorded history down to the fierce warriors of Ahmed Shah Durrani, have stormed their way to the conquest of Hindustan. To keep the gates of the north securely locked and barred against incursions from Central Asia was always a major preoccupation of the British as it had been of the Mughals, and of countless other Muslim Powers, before them. After 1947 responsibility for carrying out the task of guarding the marches came to vest in Pakistan. The difficulties which beset this task must be briefly outlined.

The British, to cope with the problem of defence, had created the North-West Frontier Province, with a separate administration of its own, specially streamlined to meet the requirements of the terrain. The Province fell into two divisions; the settled districts, which were directly administered like any other part of the British Raj; and the tribal territories, forming a belt between the settled districts and the frontier of Afghanistan, which were not administered at all. This tribal belt of warlike Pushtu-speaking peoples had successfully resisted for centuries all attempts to subdue them. Until fifty years before the end of the British Raj, they lived in a kind of no-mans'-land between India and Afghanistan, owing allegiance to neither, and raiding both impartially. Each country competed with the other for influence in the area. The situation profited neither; and in 1893, after careful and long negotiations, an agreement was concluded between the great Amir Abdurrahman of Afghanistan and the British, which demarcated a definite international frontier by splitting the tribal belt vertically from north to south. The Durand Line (named after Sir Mortimer Durand, the British negotiator) was freely accepted by both sides, and became one of the best-defined and most clearly recognized frontiers in the world.

The Afghan and British Governments differed radically in their treatment of the portions of tribal territory which the Durand Line allotted to each. The Amir Abdurrahman, a mighty warrior, whose grim humour and heavy hand have become legendary in his country, carried his rule with fire and sword right up to the Durand Line, incorporating the tribal areas into his kingdom. His ruthless methods forced the turbulent tribesmen into a submission which, so long as he lived, was real enough for all practical purposes, especially as he was careful to interfere as little as possible with tribal institutions; while as a good Muslim himself, he was able to enlist the remarkably strong influence of local *pirs* and other religious leaders in support of his authority. After his death, the grip of his successors over the tribal areas gradually relaxed, and the allegiance of the tribesmen to Kabul, although nominally unchallenged, became too tenuous to count for much as a force for law and order, except where it was backed up by the presence of garrisons of regular or irregular troops stationed at strategic points.

By contrast, British policy was marked for a long time by uncertainty and hesitation. One school of thought (the 'Forward') advocated the enforcement of British authority up to the Durand Line in emulation of what the Afghans had done; but the British were not Muslims, so that the whole formidable religious influence of the *pirs* and *mullahs* was against, not for, them. The country is extraordinarily difficult to penetrate, especially for forces with heavy modern equipment; its inhabitants are bold, warlike, marksmen from childhood, and highly skilled as guerrilla fighters. Thus the 'Forward Policy' soon proved too expensive in lives and money to be practicable: it had few advocates by the time I arrived in India. The logical alternative would have been for the British to keep out of tribal territory altogether, and establish a defensive cordon on the edge of the settled districts. But the tribesmen, who had been accustomed for centuries to eke out the resources of their stony, barren country by raiding the plains, could not be controlled by any sort of Maginot Line, no matter how scientifically sited and constructed: the border was too long and too vulnerable. In the event, a kind of compromise was evolved, which I myself watched in action: strategic roads were built, at great cost in blood and treasure, to open up tribal territory: and to connect strong points, heavily garrisoned, with each other and with the massive forces

63

maintained in the plains. The tribesmen—except those who supplied the well-paid labour for building roads—hated them as a symbol of British authority and as channels along which strong punitive forces could penetrate tribal territory to avenge raiding. But except in the case of particularly turbulent tribes, such as the Wazirs and Mahsuds, with whom agreements were ineffective because the authority of the tribal *maliks* (chiefs) was limited by almost anarchic conceptions of individual liberty, a kind of loose order, governed by tribal custom, was gradually established under British influence. This was achieved partly by paying to local chiefs generous subsidies to ensure the general good behaviour of their tribes, and partly by the excellent personal relations which successive British (and more recently, indigenous) political officers cultivated with the tribal leaders and their immediate following. Armed levies, locally recruited, were well paid to guard the roads, along which the 'peace of the Raj' prevailed. But when I first knew the Frontier at the time of the 'Kaiser's War', any British officer (or, for that matter, any stranger) who stepped off the metalled surface, was fair game for the ever-lurking sniper, who, although he might present the outward appearance merely of an innocent-looking shepherd or a teen-age village youth, had always his rifle ready to hand to take a 'pot-shot' at the unwary.

It was a curious system, liable to unexpected breakdown if an influential *pir* chose to incite his local followers to embark on a Holy War (with hope of loot) against the infidel British; or if the tribes persuaded themselves (or were persuaded by others) that British strength was strained either by political unrest in the Raj or by the pressure of external enemies. Moreover, any British officer serving on the Frontier, or even any one of the heroic medical missionaries who toiled to relieve widely-prevalent diseases like ophthalmia and tuberculosis, was always exposed to the risk of sudden assassination by some individual fanatic, confident in the expectation of an immediate translation to Paradise if he slew an Unbeliever. Yet those who served on the Frontier loved this land, where every man carries a rifle as naturally as a Westerner carries a watch; they would hear nothing against its hardy, upstanding, turbulent people, with their love of sport, their boundless hospitality, and their capacity for warm friendship as well as for deadly enmity. And in normal times, the curious, makeshift system did work: indeed, when the border was more or less tranquil, it became a kind of game, in which each side adhered to certain well-known rules—the breach of which meant death. It was no uncommon thing to find three brothers of a tribal household, one of whom would be serving the British loyally as a soldier, while the second harried them as leader of a raiding band, and the third made a comfortable livelihood as an informer in the pay of both sides, carrying news of British intentions to the tribes, while giving to the British advance intelligence of real (or imaginary) future forays. But peace always hung upon a hair: it was no country for gentle and unwarlike souls.

There were certain constant factors in a situation which might vary from day to day—almost from hour to hour. The first, and most important, was the passion for freedom animating the tribes themselves—a passion engrained into them by centuries of defiance of all authority other than their own tribal custom. To this they adhered with almost savage intensity, particularly approving of its sanction of the blood-feuds transmitted murderously from generation to generation, and of its rigid insistence upon equality between man and man. They fiercely resented any external control—and, in particular, the control asserted by the infidel British. They were often restive even against the traditional authority of their own chiefs, when it was used to restrain the forays against their neighbours which formed a part of the pattern of their lives. The second factor was the formidable influence of the anti-British religious leaders, who not infrequently combined a local reputation for sanctity with the prestige attaching to successful robbery under arms. The third factor was the persistent incitement of the tribes by Afghanistan to defiance of British authority. The ruling house in Kabul disliked the gradual, if intermittent, advance of British influence toward the Durand Line, and lost no opportunity for fanning the latent anti-British feeling among the tribesmen to a blaze. A number of religious leaders received lavish subsidies and flattering favour from the Afghans: many of the tribal *maliks* drew regular payment from Kabul as well as from Delhi, keeping both sides 'sweet' with great ingenuity and complete cynicism. Trouble-making by the Afghan authorities was all the more easy because men 'wanted' in British India could often find refuge across the frontier with a section of their own tribe living on the Afghan side; and from this Alsatia they were able to organize new forays into British territory. As the Afghan Government saw the time approaching when the British would hand over power, it began to question the agreement of 1893, and to assert a claim to a new international boundary as far east as the River Indus. This claim was firmly rejected by the British; the Afghan Government then began to support the idea of a separate Pathan State ('Pakhtunistan') carved out of the British sphere. It was confident that before long it would be able to incorporate a State of this kind in its own territory.

The independence movement which spread through the rest of British India had its repercussions on the characteristic situation of the North-West Frontier Province. The Pushtu-speaking peoples in the settled districts were, of course, fully in favour of getting rid of the British and managing their own affairs; and since they were all—with the exception of a few Hindu merchants and professional men—Muslim, no question of the need for protecting Muslim rights against a future Hindu majority ever entered their heads. It was therefore natural for leading men in the North-West Frontier Province to join the Congress movement, which promised them freedom, and to participate in Congress-directed campaigns against British rule. Mr. Gandhi visited the Province, where his personality and reputation made a considerable impression: but his gospel of non-cooperation and passive resistance was given a strictly local interpretation by those who met him.

In particular, the Red Shirt movement, started by Abdul Ghaffar Khan, the 'Frontier Gandhi', mentioned on an earlier page, although nominally peaceful in its objectives, became a powerful instrument of political pressure when it recruited several hundreds of burly Pathans armed with formidable staves. It gave the local British administration some bad moments, in particular on the occasion when it announced a mass-march on Peshawar to protest against British 'oppression'. But the much-publicized demonstration was defeated by a ruse which is still described with chuckles of mirth up and down the Frontier. Among the political officers then stationed nearby was that same Iskander Mirza, whose later exploit at Gilgit has already been recounted. Knowing that the Red Shirts, like all Pathans, would never set out on their early-morning march until they had consumed vast quantities of freshly baked Frontier bread, washed down with quarts of green tea, he induced the cooks at their camp to mix masses of a very strong purgative with the rations. The march started in fine style, with much shouting of slogans and brandishing of staves; but before long first one, and then another, of the marchers fell silent, broke ranks, and hastily retired into a field from the view of his companions. As time went on, men fell out in increasing numbers, and it was only a weak and very hollow-feeling band of stragglers who at length crawled wearily into Peshawar.

Yet in spite of occasional set-backs of this kind, the Congress point

of view was firmly entrenched among the political leaders of the
North-West Frontier Province; and for some time the Muslim League,
whose main appeal was against future Hindu domination (which no
Pathan thought possible, in his own area) made small headway. In
1947, the Province was under a Congress-supporting Ministry headed
by Dr. Khan Sahib, Abdul Ghaffar Khan's brother. The Ministry
was undoubtedly in touch with some of the anti-British elements in
tribal territory: and it is said that through its agency Congress money
came into the hands of the Faqir of Ipi, a politico-religious figure of
some local prominence who had long been a nuisance to the Frontier
Administration, and had received arms and money from Axis sources
during the Second World War. Abdul Ghaffar Khan seems to have
thought that there was a real chance of setting up an independent
'Pakhtunistan' with the help of the Congress, of anti-British leaders in
tribal territory, and above all, of the Afghans: but Dr. Khan Sahib
was more level-headed. He would not join the Muslim League; but
as the emergence of Pakistan became more and more certain, he realized
that if the people of the North-West Frontier Province had to choose
between joining India and joining Pakistan, nothing that he could do
or say would prevent them from following the call of religion and
turning their backs on India and the Congress organization. When, in
accordance with the Congress-League agreement, a referendum was
held on 20th July 1947 in the North-West Frontier Province, the
decision to join Pakistan was taken by an overwhelming majority. Dr.
Khan Sahib remained nominally in power until Pakistan came into
being. Mr. Jinnah had earlier asked Lord Mountbatten, as Governor-
General, to dismiss him because the Provisional Government of
Pakistan suspected him of working for a separate Pathan State. But
the British Cabinet, to whom the matter was referred, declined to
permit this action. It had to wait until Mr. Jinnah himself, as Governor-General of Pakistan, ordered the Governor to dismiss the Congress Ministry on August 22nd. Dr. Khan Sahib was succeeded by
Abdul Qayum, a former Congress leader who had joined the Muslim
League, and had won a considerable reputation for energy and force-
fulness. Before long, many former adherents of the Congress also
joined the Muslim League, and gave Abdul Qayum a majority in the
Legislature. Abdul Ghaffar Khan, unlike his brother, refused to
realize that a separate Pathan State would be, in the changed circumstances, not only impracticable but useless. He continued his activities
until he was placed in detention.

The emergence of Pakistan laid the foundation for changes which were to transform the whole situation in tribal territory. But during the first few weeks and months of her existence, the attitude of the tribesmen hung in the balance. In the process of splitting up the Indian Army which accompanied partition, the Hindu elements had to be withdrawn from the garrisons of the strong points in tribal territory, notably Wana and Razmak. The Pakistan Government came to a notable decision—these advance posts were to be given up. In part, this decision arose out of a realistic appreciation of the fact that the armed forces of Pakistan had yet to be organized, and that there would be very few resources to spare for the manning of these outlying positions; but another and more idealistic argument was also involved in taking so bold a step. Mr. Jinnah and those around him believed that British policy had made a mistake in looking on the tribesmen as an extraneous, largely hostile, element, to be excluded so far as possible from the life of the settled districts. By contrast, the new Pakistan Government proposed to treat the tribesmen as friends, and, indeed, as potential Pakistanis. The first step in this process was, plainly, to win their confidence and to make them feel that their traditional liberty would be respected. This entailed the withdrawal of the garrisons which the British had installed at strategic points. In the middle of December 1947, Razmak was abandoned to the Mahsuds, in whose territory it had stood as a focus of passionate tribal resentment for a quarter of a century. The process of withdrawal proved to be entirely peaceful and unmolested.

Opinion in tribal territory, I learned later, was a good deal puzzled by what was happening. For a long time, no one believed that the British had really departed. 'The British have not been defeated,' the tribesmen reasoned: 'Why should they give up their authority? No one goes like that!' They were confirmed, as they thought, in this opinion, because they still saw British officers, military and political, about—for a number of them had decided to continue in service under Pakistan. Moreover, when the first Pakistani Brigadier came to the area—it was Brigadier Ayub Khan, later to be Commander-in-Chief, and subsequently President of Pakistan—his fair complexion, tall stature, and typical Sandhurst bearing caused them to mistake him for an Englishman. Little by little, however, the Pathans on the Pakistan side of the Durand Line began to realize that the authorities now governing their neighbours in the plains were no longer the infidel British, but fellow Muslims: and to discover that when men from tribal territory came to Peshawar and other lesser urban centres, they were received, not with suspicion, but with welcoming goodwill.

Pakistani political officers, and British political officers who had opted to continue their service under Pakistan, laboured hard to convince the inhabitants of tribal territory that Pakistan desired their friendship. They had to contend not only with the natural suspicions of the tribesmen themselves, but also with the persistent propaganda of the Afghan Government and of leaders in Afghan pay, such as the Faqir of Ipi. Afghan agents insisted that Pakistan could not last, and was bound to break up: that the confused situation following the withdrawal of the British offered the Pathans a golden opportunity of creating an independent Pathan State of their own (to be carved, of course, out of Pakistani and not out of Afghan, territory). But Pathans are shrewd people, not easily deceived: they noticed the contrast between Afghan words and Pakistani deeds. Before long, Pakistan's policy of 'trust' began to pay dividends, small at first, then considerable. Some of the most influential of the Afridi *maliks* were persuaded by Abdul Qayum to take up town property, in Peshawar and elsewhere, which had been abandoned by Hindus going to India. Their example was soon followed: the tribesmen found that opportunities for employment in the settled districts—and indeed elsewhere in Pakistan—lay open to them for the asking; and that such employment was more profitable than raiding—especially as the religious justification for periodical forays no longer held good. True, the Faqir of Ipi still preached a Holy War at the instance of his Afghan paymasters; but his exhortations began to fall on deaf ears, and his nuisance-value was greatly diminished when Meher Dil, the leader of his war-band, made his peace with Pakistan and came over with a couple of hundred well-armed warriors. Other religious leaders of less questionable integrity cast their influence firmly on the side of friendship with Pakistan and her new rulers. Slowly but steadily, the atmosphere in tribal territory changed.

I saw the process for myself when, after only a few years of Pakistani administration in the Frontier areas, I re-visited some of the places that I had known under the British Raj. This time my wife could accompany me everywhere—a proceeding which would have been frowned upon, with good reason, in the old days. What impressed me particularly was the breakdown of the old barriers between tribal territory and the settled districts: men from tribal areas were to be seen everywhere, driving public-transport vehicles with terrifying *élan*, working on roads and in the fields, keeping shops, and making up the bulk of the labour force for the construction of big projects like the Warsak Dam—of which more later—and the magnificent new University Quarter outside Peshawar. Many of the important *maliks* of the tribes near the Khyber seemed now to have their town houses: and when the political agent of the Khyber area holds his periodical *jirgas* (tribal assemblies) to explain Government policy, to hear grievances and to settle disputes, a goodly proportion of the tribal notables arrive by car or by motor omnibus from Peshawar. What was even more striking was the changed attitude of the tribes towards foreigners. When my wife and I went through the once notorious Kohat Pass— the scene of some gruesome shootings and kidnappings of British people in the old days—on our way to Parachinar, the Adam Khel *maliks* were waiting to receive us on the road. To my surprise—and momentary consternation—I saw my wife disappear from sight down a narrow alley under their guidance. But all was well: we were sumptuously entertained with biscuits and green tea, treated as honoured guests, and conducted over the famous rifle factory, where passably efficient and outwardly exact copies of British .303 and other rifles are produced, entirely by hand, in considerable numbers. Not only were we shown with pride, and invited to try, the finished products, but my wife was allowed, on her request, to begin the process of drilling a rifle barrel from a bar of cold steel. The factory proprietors and the 'hands' crowded round to admire the unusual spectacle of a 'white memsahib' doing, for once, a piece of useful work: our visit ended with warm handshakes and expressions of mutual esteem.

It became increasingly clear to me, as we covered more and more of the Frontier areas in our travels, and as we gathered information from political officers and tribal leaders, that Pakistan has wrought in these areas a revolutionary change which is no less dramatic than, if slightly different in kind from, that which she has effected in Gilgit and Baltistan. It is true that the tribal Pathans had no need, like the Gilgitis and Baltis, to liberate themselves from oppression—they were free already. But they were cordoned off, as it were, from progress by the British belief that they were generally intractable, and thus best left alone, with ample subsidies to keep them quiet, and with strong deterrents against misbehaviour in the shape of entrenched garrisons and the threat of punitive expeditions. All this is changed. What has happened now is that Pakistan has been thrown open to them, just as England became open to the Scots from the time of the Union. The notoriously keen business acumen of the Pathans finds full and profitable fields for its employment. They exercise a virtual and lucrative monopoly in the local transport of goods and passengers by lorry and by bus—which has led, in turn, to an entire change in their attitude towards roads, of which they now demand more and more. They take up land in the distant new canal colonies made possible by the extension of irrigation in the east and south, and by reclamation schemes, such as those operating in the former Thal desert. They have entered the wholesale as well as the retail market in a large range of commodities, and are to be encountered as traders and men of business from Peshawar to Karachi. They have become geared, as it were, into a progressive and developing economy, to which they themselves can contribute an impulse which is the more valuable because it is pristine, unspoiled, and dynamic. For the first time in all the centuries of their turbulent history, the tribesmen of the Frontier areas are acquiring a vested interest in economic progress, and, along with it, a dawning appreciation of the practical advantages to be derived from law, order, and personal security. It was gratifying to hear from the Pakistani officers engaged in this constructive work how valuable they are finding the roads which the British had built at the cost of so many British lives. 'We owe much', they told me, 'to what you did while you were on the Frontier—you gave us the foundations on which we are building now.'

It is not only in commerce and industry that the Pathans are making themselves felt in Pakistan. Even before the end of the British Raj, selected individuals had entered the armed forces, the police, and occasionally, the political service. Such men now occupy very high positions: their example has stimulated others. Sons of tribal *maliks* are obtaining commissions in the Defence Forces in increasing numbers, after receiving their education, through an extensive and liberal system of scholarships, in the splendid new University of Peshawar, which has arisen on the foundations originally laid by the Islamia College of British times. The demand for education is rapidly growing in tribal territory: boys who go to school and to college are demanding educated wives as their companions in the new and attractive careers which Pakistan offers. Hence there is a surprising demand for girls' schools: tribal notables find that their daughters are unacceptable, without education, as brides to desirable young men. Even tribes like the Mahsuds, classed by the British as one of the most intractable among Frontier peoples, are asking for more girls' schools than can readily be staffed by the available teachers. Throughout the tribal areas, the last eight years have seen the growth in the number of school-going pupils from 2,000 to 20,000. And the whole process of development and progress seems to gain, not lose, impetus as time goes on. Radio telephones and wireless receivers—of which many Frontier villages possess one—together with improved roads and frequent motor-bus services, are breaking down the isolation which helped to keep the Frontier tribes backward and bigoted.

Although the progress which can be observed in the Frontier areas is impressive testimony to the success of Pakistan's policy towards their tribal inhabitants, no one can claim that everything there has already become mere sweetness and light. There is plenty of the old Adam left—perhaps fortunately, because it is evidence of that continued Pathan dynamism which is now so valuable a contribution to the make-up of Pakistan. The passengers who cram the motor-buses which career dizzily—if miraculously without accident—along the narrow, twisting mountain roads are all armed to the teeth: the rifle is as ubiquitous as ever, even if it is now often used as a walking-stick or as a prod to urge a donkey to mend his paces. The watchtowers on the heights which overlook the Warsak Dam are reminders—even though they are now mostly untenanted by pickets—of days not so long ago when tribesmen not lucky enough to be included in the labour gangs crept up to empty their rifle-magazines at their more favoured fellows. Infinite tact had to be used to ensure that the Afridis working on one side of the dam and the Mohmands working on the other were broadly keeping pace with each other—if one tribe had been left obviously behind, fighting would immediately have broken out. But the diplomacy of the political officers and the bluff friendliness of the Canadian engineers who, under the Colombo plan, have achieved the completion of this great hydro-electric project for the benefit of the whole north-western region, eventually overcame every difficulty: and now the tribesmen, even those who did not build it, take a proprietary pride in the dam.

The change which has come over the North-West Frontier is all the more creditable to Pakistan because she has by no means had things all her own way in her dealings with the tribesmen. The anti-Pakistan propaganda campaign of the Afghan Government has never ceased; indeed it has been intensified since the time when Afghanistan began to realize that Pakistan, far from breaking up, as both Kabul and New Delhi confidently expected, is here to stay. The Congress Party, supreme in India, could hardly have been expected to view with indifference the elimination of its one-time supremacy in the North-West Frontier Province: and the rapid deterioration of Indo-Pakistani relations so soon after partition increased the temptation to add to Pakistan's difficulties. Inevitably, Indian money joined Afghan money in fomenting the campaign for an independent Pathan State among all who could be induced to listen. Some tribal leaders, already committed, like the Faqir of Ipi, were possibly stimulated to fresh efforts: but others fell back upon the well-tried tactics of demanding subsidies from Kabul by promising 'trouble' of a kind which they had not any intention of creating. The Pathan sense of humour derived considerable enjoyment from the situation. One tribal leader related with pride how he had obtained a handsome sum from the Afghan Government by promising to burn down Peshawar University—a promise which he had not the slightest desire to fulfil because both his sons were receiving their education in that institution. To cap the story, he told me that he had gone to Kabul again, and had there claimed a further reward for doing the job. He had later experienced, he said, the supreme satisfaction of hearing his invented fairy-tale solemnly broadcast as a fact from Radio Kabul. Whether this latter climax was added for my benefit—Pathans are incorrigible leg-pullers—I could not determine. But it became quite clear to me from a number of other conversations on the same topic that while there are tribal leaders who regularly go to Kabul to collect subsidies ('after all, Sahib,' one said, 'it's only Indian or Russian money—why shouldn't we take it?'), there are very few indeed who care to imperil their new and excellent relations with Pakistan, from which they benefit so substantially. It is true that they will explode grenades at a harmless distance, and loose off some ineffective rounds over the roof of the residence of some Pakistani political agent; but when remonstrated with, they will cheerfully say: 'But, Sahib, we took very good care to do no damage to anyone!'

Perhaps the best illustration of the broad success of Pakistan's policy was furnished a little while after my visit by the events which took place in Bajaur during the autumn of 1960. North of the Malakand Pass—which it commands—lies the territory of the Nawab of Dir, at that time a hide-bound old gentleman who had been notorious as long ago as British days because of his medieval methods of rule and the backward condition of his subjects. A great reactionary himself, he found grave cause of offence in the progress achieved by his neighbours in Swat and Chitral under Pakistani encouragement. He turned a deaf ear to every suggestion of improvement: he would permit no schools, no village AID, and no hospitals in his territory—although he kept a veterinary surgeon to look after his dogs; his attitude towards economic development was shown by the severe beating-up administered to a visiting Japanese forestry expert. The Afghan authorities, knowing his discontent, gave large sums to him and his favourite (second) son, who held the subordinate appanage of Jandol, buying their friendship, and opening the way for the use of Dir territory as a base of future operations. The Pakistan authorities, although thoroughly ashamed that such a 'black spot' as Dir should exist in their country, made allowances for his age and turned a blind eye to the Nawab's misdeeds for a long time, in the hope that his attitude could be changed for the better by kindly remonstrances and friendly treatment. Eventually, however, circumstances forced their hand.

Among Dir's feudatory chieftains in the Bajaur area is the Khan of Khar, who planned to develop his own territory by building a road to connect it with civilization. As it happened, this programme involved him in a dispute with the Utmanzais, who demanded an excessive price for passage through their area. Hearing of this friction, the Afghans decided to complete their preparations for an advance into Dir by frightening the Khan of Khar from his allegiance to Pakistan. They threatened that if he did not fall in with their plans, they would, when they came to Dir, 'take tea in his house, kick him out, and walk down to the Indus by way of the Malakand Pass'. The ¨han, an independent-minded man, who had had his own di⸍ ⸍ences with Pakistan, but had no intention of playing the Afghan game, remained unmoved by the threat, which he reported to the Pakistani authorities. He added the information that the Afghans were assembling a force of irregulars on the Bajaur border; and that if the incursions proved successful, they were proposing to send in regular forces; to occupy Dir as 'liberators' with the good will of the Nawab; to proclaim the establishment of 'Pakhthunistan' as an independent State, and to appeal to the United Nations for its recognition.

The Pakistan Government was inclined at first to think that the Khan of Khar's report was somewhat highly coloured, although it watched the situation in Bajaur as closely as possible. Before it could take any action, Bajaur was in fact invaded by a powerful *lashkar* from Afghan territory. The Khan, taking advantage of fierce local resentment aroused by the looting and rape perpetrated by the invaders, soon gathered an unexpectedly large force, amounting to some 2,000 rifles, from his clansmen and neighbours. He fell upon the invaders, attacked them tooth and nail, and sent them scurrying back over the border with losses which he estimated at 500 dead and several thousand wounded. He invited the Pakistan Government to send observers to check his claim, which was, in fact, confirmed from other sources. The significant thing is that he did all this without any support from Pakistani forces—the whole thing had happened too quickly for help to reach him in time. It would be difficult to find a better illustration of the determination of the people in tribal territory to deal drastically with any attempt to interfere with their friendly relations with the Pakistan Government. The Khan of Khar had no intention of allowing Kabul to substitute itself for Rawalpindi. To complete the story. Immediately afterwards, as might be expected, Pakistan sent some Scout platoons by air-lift to Dir: the old Nawab and his second son were removed. The elder son became the new Nawab; and under his more enlightened rule, schools and hospitals have started, and a real effort is being made to improve the living conditions of the people— as I observed when I visited Dir territory in the spring of 1961. The Afghan authorities, reluctant to lose face, continued their probing tactics in Bajaur throughout the year: a certain Badshah Gul distributed on their behalf radio sets tuned to Kabul and lavish supplies of ammunition. But so little was done by the recipients in return that soldiers—said by the Pakistanis to be Afghan regulars out of uniform —were sent into Bajaur to make more serious trouble. But the tribesmen again resisted them; the few places where Badshah Gul found shelter were attacked from the air after the inhabitants had been warned to leave: and things settled down. Soon afterwards, according to Pakistani sources, Afghan regular troops entered Bajaur: they too were expelled. Later in 1961, Afghan propaganda was further stepped up, and when Pakistan closed her consulates in Afghanistan because local hostility made the work of the staff impossible, and asked Afghanistan to take corresponding action, Kabul broke off relations with Rawalpindi. When I was again in the neighbourhood of Bajaur in 1962, I found everything quiet. Afghanistan may well have been banking on the hostile reaction which any occupation of Bajaur by Pakistani ground forces would have evoked from local opinion; but the Pakistani political officers were far too experienced to fall into such a trap. The ground forces were promptly withdrawn; in their place came doctors to give medical aid, teachers to start schools—there are now forty in Bajaur—and skilled technicians with electric pumps to help the Bajauris to raise to the surface the plentiful subterranean streams until now unutilized. Six of the sons of the local Khans are now being educated at schools in Pakistan; there are 500 boys studying on Government scholarships. To provide local employment and to link up this area with civilization, more than forty lorries and trucks have been distributed. The recipients are taught to drive, and given licences to ply for goods and passengers. This not only gives them a good livelihood but also a definite stake in the economic development of their remote area. I do not think that Afghanistan has now much chance of stirring up trouble in Bajaur again.

For the purposes of this narrative, the record of Pakistan's dealing with the peoples of the North-West Frontier has been carried from 1947 up to the time of writing. It is now time to revert to the period when serious initial difficulties had to be overcome before the civilizing process could be fairly set on foot. These loomed very large during the early months of Pakistan's existence: indeed the fighting in Jammu and Kashmir nearly upset her whole Frontier policy almost before a beginning could be made with it.

The last chapter described the anti-Muslim drive by which the Maharaja of Jammu and Kashmir designed to reassert his crumbling authority; and the resulting establishment of Azad Kashmir as an independent unit by the Muslims of Poonch, Mirpur, and Muzaffarabad. Emissaries from the new administration, set up at that time by one Sardar Mohammad Ibrahim, a leader of the movement, found their way into tribal territory to purchase rifles and to enlist help. By the time that they arrived, in the autumn of 1947, a number of the more adventurous souls were already excited by rumours of atrocities inflicted upon the Muslims of the Eastern Punjab by Sikh fanatics; they were planning, in face of the attempts of Pakistani and British political officers, to persuade them to settle down to peaceful and friendly relations with Pakistan, to march into the plains to attack their hereditary enemies the Sikhs. The news of the fighting in Jammu and Kashmir brought home to the tribesmen—as nothing else had done—the fact that British authority had really withdrawn for good: they felt certain that under the British Raj, disturbances on such a scale as this would never have been permitted. Since the British had gone, what was there to stop men of spirit embarking upon a Holy War against the oppressors of Islam—with good prospects of loot? Revenge upon the Sikhs must wait: Jammu and Kashmir seemed to offer easier prey—and larger spoils.

The Pakistan Government was thus faced by a situation of appalling difficulty. Its sympathies were, naturally, with Azad Kashmir in its struggle against the Maharaja. Many Pakistanis have told me that they believed, at the time, that the establishment of Azad Kashmir was the beginning of a process which would eventually bring the whole State to join Pakistan, in spite of the Maharaja's efforts. They could not understand why their Government did not support Azad Kashmir with all its armed resources, for they did not know how pitifully inadequate those resources were. The Pakistan Government took a longer view. The last thing that it desired was the declaration of a Holy War in the tribal areas, which might set something like 200,000 truculent and uncontrollable warriors from tribal territory in movement across the North-West Frontier Province on their way to fight either the Dogras in Jammu and Kashmir or the Sikhs in India. The threat to law, order, and civilized administration inherent in such a mass movement was too serious to be contemplated. Yet on the one hand, as has been made clear on an earlier page, Pakistan's army, lacking formed units and still in process of regrouping after partition, was in no case to stop such a move; while on the other hand, any show of force, however perfunctory, in restraint of a Holy War, would have imperilled the entire relationship, still in the early, delicate stage, between Pakistan and the tribal areas. In the event, the efforts of the authorities and of the political officers prevailed. No Holy War was declared; the great mass of the tribal warriors abandoned any idea of interfering in Kashmir, and began to settle down in amity with Pakistan. But it was impossible, in the excited political atmosphere of the time, to prevent the emissaries of Azad Kashmir from carrying on their recruiting campaign, with which so many people in the North-West Frontier Province sympathized, even though they had been dissuaded by the authorities from joining in it. This campaign eventually enlisted some 2,000 men, including a number of known bad characters, from among Mahsuds, Wazirs and Mohmands, who set off in October 1947 to try their luck in the fighting in Azad Kashmir.

No doubt because of the notorious atrocities which these raiders perpetrated, and of the unexpectedly disastrous consequences to Pakistan, India, and Kashmir itself which their invasion set in train, a bitter controversy has raged over who is really to blame for the whole affair. India, later, roundly accused Pakistan of encouraging and assisting the invaders; Liaquat Ali Khan retorted that his Government had done all in its power, short of war, to discourage the movement. I am myself sure that this statement is true, because I know from my own enquiries that the main objective of Pakistan's policy at the time—an objective to which even the fate of Kashmir yielded precedence—was the establishment of peaceful conditions on the North-West Frontier. But the Pakistan Government, with all its energies engaged in the task of building up an administration from scratch, and with no force to speak of at its disposal, could not prevent individual sympathizers, some of them no doubt in quite high official positions, as well, also, as leaders and members of local branches of the Muslim League, from quietly speegdin the invaders on their way with food, transport, petrol, money and equipment of various kinds.

In contrast with the Azad Kashmir forces, which, though poorly equipped, were well-officered, under strict discipline, and mainly concerned to defend their own homeland area from attack, the tribal invaders were wild, ungovernable, and animated by two simple incentives—religious fanaticism and the desire for loot. They more or less by-passed the bulk of the Azad Kashmir forces, whom they were supposed to help, pushing up from Abbottabad towards Baramula and Srinagar, burning the (friendly) towns of Domel and Muzaffarabad *en route*, and brushing aside the feeble efforts of the Maharaja's troops to stop them. They killed, raped, and looted indiscriminately, claiming Muslim as well as Hindu victims. At Baramula, they destroyed St. Joseph's Convent, killing two English people, Colonel Dykes and his wife, and wounding some of the nuns. This naturally caused a great sensation, made headlines in the Press, not only of India, but also of the outside world, and brought the Pakistan Government, which was in no way to blame, into undeserved discredit. A Pakistani officer who was serving at the time as a volunteer with the Azad Kashmir forces, and who had rushed to Baramula post-haste when he heard that the convent was being attacked, told me that the tribesmen had no real intention of molesting Europeans, but were wandering about, helping themselves to pots of jam and other food, when Colonel Dykes tried to turn them out of the convent at the point of his pistol. Indiscriminate firing then broke out, and tragedy followed. This was on 25th October 1947. Had the *Lashkar* pushed on from Baramula, there was little to stop it. But being wholly unaccustomed to discipline, the tribesmen threw away, time after time, the advantages which they might have reaped from their formidable fighting powers because they refused to pursue a retreating enemy until they had totalled up, and divided with meticulous care, every scrap of plunder. Thus they lost their opportunity of reaching Srinagar.

Chapter 4

TRAGEDY IN KASHMIR

By this time the Maharaja, realizing that he was at the end of his resources, telegraphed to New Delhi for help. He was told that no assistance could be sent unless he acceded to India. Accordingly, he signed his formal Instrument of Accession on October 26th. This Lord Mountbatten accepted, with the proviso that 'it is my Government's wish that, as soon as law and order have been restored and the soil cleared of the invader, the question of the State's accession should be settled by a reference to the people'. An air-lift was hastily extemporized, largely by the use of civilian planes assembled at Delhi to evacuate Muslims to Pakistan; and Indian troops arrived in Srinagar on October 27th, just in time to halt, at the very edge of the air-strip, an advance party of the tribal invaders. No one in New Delhi took the trouble to inform Pakistan of what was happening.

It seems doubtful, in retrospect, whether India's action served anyone or anything except her own policy and the Maharaja's waning authority. There were enough Muslim leaders, Muslim troops and Muslim police in Srinagar to protect the city and its inhabitants from the tribesmen, if they had been allowed to do so: but men like Chaudhuri Ghulam Abbas and other leaders of the Muslim Conference—the local branch of the Muslim League—together with substantial bodies of Muslim troops and Muslim police, were held in confinement by the Maharaja's orders. But when he himself fled to Jammu on October 26th, there was nothing to prevent the organization of a Kashmir force to defend the city except the presence of the Indian troops, who assumed the task of keeping order. Sheikh Abdullah had been let out of prison at the end of September, probably because the Maharaja wanted to gain the support of his National Conference party. Sheikh Abdullah promptly renewed his ties with Congress leaders in New Delhi; and after the Maharaja's departure he set up in the Maharaja's name an interim administration, with India's support, pledged to religious neutralism and a non-communal policy on the Indian model.

This turn of events took Pakistan wholly by surprise. Even now, after all the years that have passed, Pakistanis cannot speak of this time without bitterness. It appears to them that India by a sudden *coup* through the instrumentality of the discredited Maharaja, and wholly against the mass-opinion of the Kashmiri people, set up an administration in Srinagar which was markedly unfriendly to Pakistan; and did this without any notification to, or consultation with, the Pakistan Government. Taken wholly by surprise, Mr. Jinnah at one moment thought of sending into Kashmir whatever troops could be collected: he was persuaded, however, by General Gracey, his British Commander-in-Chief (who realized Pakistan's unreadiness if war should break out with India) to hold his hand until Field-Marshal Sir Claude Auchinleck, as Supreme Commander with responsibilities both to the Indian and Pakistani armies, could be consulted. The Quaid-i-Azam then gave a statesmanlike lead which, if it had been followed by India, would have solved the whole problem. On November 1st he suggested that Lord Mountbatten and himself, as Governors-General, should issue an immediate cease-fire order: if it were not obeyed everywhere in Jammu and Kashmir, Pakistani and Indian troops should co-operate to enforce it. Both Governors-General should, when fighting had ceased, jointly take over the administration of Jammu and Kashmir and organize a plebiscite which would enable the Kashmiris to decide their future for themselves. Quaid-i-Azam, because of the supreme power which he exercised, could pledge himself to such an agreement. Lord Mountbatten was bound, he thought, to refer it to the Indian Cabinet. They rejected the plan out of hand: all Lord Mountbatten found himself able to do was to suggest that a plebiscite should be held under United Nations auspices. After some hesitation, Pakistan agreed, provided that Kashmir was placed under impartial administration and that all outside forces were withdrawn until the plebiscite was held. Mr. Nehru accepted in principle the idea of a plebiscite under United Nation's auspices; but made his acceptance valueless in Pakistan's eyes because he would not agree to the immediate withdrawal of Indian forces, and because he insisted that Sheikh Abdullah's administration represented the will of the Kashmiri people. It was from this moment that the Kashmir dispute actually began to run its tragic and unnecessary course, the initial stages of which were marked by quite severe fighting.

This fighting continued throughout 1948. Indian troops had

originally come to Srinagar by air-lift, and from Srinagar they pushed down to Uri, driving back the tribesmen, who, sated with loot, gradually filtered back to their own territory. But in Indian eyes, the Azad Kashmir forces were equally obnoxious as rebels against the Government of a State which had acceded to India: they and their territory became the next objective. No mere air-lift could have coped with the requirements of any operations undertaken against them. Pathankot became the Indian Army railhead; and many observers have found substance in the Pakistani complaint that the entire Indian campaign would have been impossible but for the allocation of Gurdaspur to India by the Radcliffe award. At first sight, the sides seemed very unevenly matched: the Indian troops possessed the latest military equipment; while the Azad Kashmiri forces had only rifles, and these, too, in very short supply. But the Indian lines of communication were long; the Azad Kashmir forces were fighting on their own ground—very difficult ground too—of which they knew every inch. In the type of guerrilla fighting which followed, Indian superiority in equipment was largely offset by the courage, determination, and resourcefulness of men—and women—who were defending their own homes. The women, indeed, played a great part in the campaign, not only in tending the wounded, but also in carrying up ammunition under fire to their menfolk. Among those whose reputation made them national heroines was Nasira Siddiqui, who had taken a prominent part in the former political movements aiming at protecting the Muslims of Kashmir against the Maharaja's oppression. She won a decoration for gallantry under fire, was seriously wounded, and is now the much-respected wife of Major-General M. Z. Kiani, who, when the fighting was over, rose to high civil employment in Pakistan Government service.

When I visited Azad Kashmir a few years after the fighting had ended, I found that the local military leaders were still in very buoyant mood. They explained to me some of the ruses they had employed in building up their control of the country south of the Pir Panjal range. For example, the capture of Mirpur, held by a Dogra battalion and 1,500 armed civilians, at the hands of a force which had only 103 rifles between them, was effected by sheer bluff. An enormous body of villagers was collected, and mustered at a safe distance, so that the garrison believed themselves confronted by overwhelming numbers, and surrendered. I heard, also, how the deficiencies in arms and equipment were made good by daring and well-planned raids on the Indian supply lines. The Azad Kashmiris claimed that they had not lost permanently an inch of ground; that they had fought the Indian army to a standstill; and even that the cease-fire, when at last it was arranged between Pakistan and India, came at the very moment when the local forces were mounting a counter-stroke which would have cut off three Indian divisions. They also told me that on several occasions, they had been restrained from pushing home their successes because of their respect for Pakistan's view that if the Indian troops lost too much 'face', the upshot might be a full-scale inter-Dominion war—which no one wanted. I must leave it to military experts to decide how far these claims are justified; what I myself can testify to is the fighting spirit of the Azad Kashmiris and their conviction of the justice of their cause, which in their eyes is the defence of the freedom of their country against Indian aggression.

As the Indian forces advanced towards Azad Kashmir territory, thousands of Kashmiris fled before them and sought refuge both in Azad Kashmir and in Pakistan. If Azad Kashmir's resistance had collapsed, the number of these refugees would have multiplied enormously beyond the power of the Pakistan Government to deal with them. It was for this reason, I was told, that some Pakistani regular troops were stationed, early in 1948, just inside Azad Kashmir territory to give the local forces confidence; they were ordered to take no part in the actual fighting against Indian units. Before very long, however, as the struggle grew more intense, Pakistani regular forces were obliged to play a more active role in defending Azad Kashmir territory. It was due to one such 'holding action' by General Hajji Iftikhar Ahmad (later Chairman of the Pakistan Industrial Development Corporation) that important components of its territory were saved for Azad Kashmir. In addition, a number of Pakistani junior officers and N.C.O.s. seem to have been allowed leave to volunteer for the Azad Kashmiri forces, so that these latter, as their equipment improved and their discipline tightened, were not infrequently mistaken for Pakistani regulars by the Indian troops opposing them. This misapprehension led the Indian Government to underestimate the strength of the armed opposition to Indian rule in Kashmir which existed independently of the Pakistan Army, and would survive the withdrawal of Pakistani regular forces from the State. When the mistake was realized, India was no longer willing to withdraw her own forces in the proportion necessary to facilitate the plebiscite.

It was a strange type of fighting in which the professional

soldiers of India and Pakistan became shortly involved. A number of the commanding officers on each side were old comrades in arms: some had been at Sandhurst or Dehra Dun together. It was no uncommon thing, when the front line was quiet, for a visit to be paid to the officers' mess in the opposing lines. More than once, indeed, men who had served in the same regiment, but in different companies, found themselves face to face: and I was told many stories of the revival of old friendships in the midst of the strife. This type of professional *cameraderie*, although it puzzled and sometimes dismayed the Azad Kashmiris, who were fighting with the most deadly seriousness, unquestionably helped to prevent the operations in Kashmir from resulting in formal hostilities between India and Pakistan.

In October 1948 the Indian Army at last succeeded in relieving beleaguered Poonch; but in the rest of Azad Kashmir territory there was stalemate, which could only be resolved if the area of operations were enlarged to a scale involving open warfare between India and Pakistan. Such a contingency seemed unthinkable to the professional soldiers on both sides: they determined to prevent it, and they succeeded, first, because neither country desired to push matters to extremes, and next because the Security Council, as we shall see, had sent a Commission to India and Pakistan with instructions to arrange a cease-fire. Thus neither India nor Pakistan would lose anything by taking the initiative. General Bucher, commanding the Indian forces, sought and obtained from Mr. Nehru permission to send a telegram on 30th December 1948 to General Gracey, his opposite number on the Pakistani side, suggesting a cease-fire. After consulting his own Government, General Gracey agreed at once; and the details were quickly arranged between the forces on both sides. The then existing positions along the borders of Azad Kashmir territory were crystallized into a *de facto* international boundary on 1st January 1949.

Before the fighting came to an end, India had set on foot, early in 1948 the lengthy, and so far inconclusive, reference of the Kashmir situation to the United Nations, which has been the source of so much controversy on either side. She reported, under Article 35 of the Charter, a situation—for which she blamed Pakistan—likely to endanger international peace. Indians have subsequently criticized their Government for not indicting Pakistan for formal aggression: but this criticism overlooks the fact that New Delhi would have been hard put to it to supply the necessary evidence. India no doubt expected Pakistan to be serverely censured. But Pakistan retorted by accusing

The Cease-Fire Line in Kashmir
(by permission of *The Times*)

India of conniving at the massacre of Muslims inside and outside
Kashmir. After much argument, the Security Council appointed a
five-man commission, which was instructed to arrange a cease-fire and
to prepare the way for a plebiscite. It reached India and Pakistan in
the summer of 1948, before the fighting had died down: and it found
the statesmen of both countries angry with each other, not only because of Kashmir, but also because of disputes over refugees, over
canal waters, over trade difficulties, over the division of the British
Raj's assets, and over the clash of interests on the North-West Frontier connected with the 'Pakhtunistan' chimera. But the Commission
suggested the possibility of a solution of the problem by stages: after
the cease-fire, Pakistan should withdraw her own regular forces, and
effect the withdrawal of everyone else who had come into Azad Kash-

85

mir from outside to fight: India should then withdraw the bulk of her own forces: local authorities under the supervision of the Commission should administer their own territories until a plebiscite could be arranged. Both sides accepted; Pakistan after some hesitation because she feared that the plebiscite might pass into the background. Her fears have proved justified.

In spite of all the efforts subsequently made by the United Nations and by well-wishers in Commonwealth countries—the sorry tale of which is too lengthy to be pursued here—the Indo-Pakistani dispute over Kashmir remains still unresolved because the plebiscite has never taken place. For one reason after another, India has never seen fit to allow it: her official line seems at the moment to be that circumstances have so changed with the lapse of time that there is nothing to hold a plebiscite about, because Jammu and Kashmir State has become a part of the Indian Republic. Indian troops are in Kashmir territory in great strength: no political opposition can flourish under the present administration, which overthrew and imprisoned even Sheikh Abdullah because he turned his thoughts towards Kashmiri independence and unity. But Pakistan has never ceased to press—and probably will never cease to press until her objective is achieved—for the necessity of giving the Kashmiri people a genuine opportunity of freely determining their own political future for themselves, either through an impartially-conducted plebiscite or through some equally efficacious means.

It is the Kashmiri people for whom one must feel most sorry, when one visits them, divided as they are by the cease-fire line, which, patrolled by United Nations observers, cuts village from village and sometimes house from house. Not all the former State of Jammu and Kashmir is unhappy. The Gilgitis and Baltis have made their own decision to cut their ties with Srinagar, and, as I have seen, they are certainly not regretting it. But in Jammu and in the Valley of Kashmir, where the Indian-supported administration exercises authority, I found the position less cheering. Since Sheikh Abdullah became Prime Minister in 1947, this administration has encountered many vicissitudes. It has been allowed to hold elections—in defiance of an undertaking given in the Security Council—and to secure the return of an Assembly composed of its own supporters. Gradually Indian-occupied Kashmir approximated to the position of any other State in the Indian Republic. But the time came when Sheikh Abdullah, friend of Mr. Nehru's though he was, began to kick over the Indian traces which were fastening his country more and more securely to New Delhi. He began to talk about a plebiscite, to claim special status for Kashmir, and to exhibit signs of increasing independence of thought. Retribution was ruthless. In 1953 he was overthrown, imprisoned, and replaced by Bakshi Ghulam Mohammad, a hard-bitten realist who considers—so I clearly gathered—that India is the better bet for Kashmir because she has more money to spend on the country than has Pakistan, and is quite ready to spend it freely. Under his firm rule, supported by large numbers of Indian troops—they are so thick on the ground to the west of Srinagar that the country looks like one great cantonment—Indian interests are secure. I found it very difficult to discover what ordinary men in the town and the villages are thinking and feeling—they will not talk freely. There are too many pressures upon them: the Indian garrison, the State Police, and a kind of Youth Vigilance Corps, are ubiquitous. At the same time it is easy to see that a great deal is being done for them on the material side: money is being well spent on new irrigation-works, particularly on lift-irrigation; on new hydro-electric projects; on improved agricultural methods; on better communications; on more schools and colleges; and on the revival of traditional handicrafts. The tourist trade has begun to flourish again, as more and more wealthy Indians are discovering the beauties of the Valley. Money is plainly pouring in from one source or another; and the material condition of the people is far better than it was under the rule of the Dogra dynasty. But is this enough? I somehow sensed that it is not.

In Azad Kashmir I myself have never seen Pakistani troops about at all. The territory is protected by its own—Azad Kashmiri—forces. These are locally recruited; some regiments have the occasional officer borrowed from the Pakistan Army: but most of the officers, too, are locals. There is a high proportion of men trained in the old Indian Army: and the lent Pakistani officers have spoken to me in the warmest terms of the bravery and discipline of the Azad Kashmiri troops. Possibly because of the absence of foreign forces, and of the general atmosphere of 'freedom' which prevails, it is very easy to find out what people are thinking. Opinion seems to follow certain marked lines of cleavage. The original inhabitants of Poonch, Mirpur, and Muzaffarabad are so thankful to be free from Darbar rule that they are, by and large, ready to carry on as they are for the time. I was told that one reason why so many men from this part of the world were formerly obliged to seek work outside the State was that, under

Darbar regulations, no fruit-growing was allowed—presumably to avoid competition with more favoured areas—and taxation was so onerous that crops were seized while they were still standing. Nothing whatever was done for the people; and since the only officials on the spot were those who had fallen out of favour at Court, the entire area had been shamefully neglected. This has now changed completely; and the locally-born section of the Azad Kashmir population feel that their lot has become much better.

The total area of Azad Kashmir extends to between four and five thousand square miles; but the population, even when swelled by the refugees, is fewer than a million strong. Before the new administration took over, communications were almost confined to the main Jhelum Valley road which traverses the area; and most of the food and other requirements of life came from outside. Azad Kashmir is now cut off from the more fertile areas of the State by the cease-fire line, which can be traversed only by the white jeeps of the United Nations corps of observers: and in spite of all that has been done by the present régime, it will be some time before Azad Kashmir becomes fully viable. Without the help which Pakistan has given so generously, much less would have been accomplished than the progress which now impresses the visitor who knew the area in Darbar days.

The improvement, indeed, is cumulative: every year that I have come to Azad Kashmir I have noticed visible signs of steady and un-spectacular, but definite, advance. More is being done for the whole area than has ever been done before. In addition to the extension of metalled roads, new pony tracks are linking outlying villages together. Strenuous month-in month-out work is needed to make good the enormous damage caused every year by monsoon water, which cuts into the shifting hill-sides and carries entire roads down thousands of feet into the river below. Drinking water is being piped from mountain springs to villages which have no water-supply of their own: irrigation is being extended: seed farms for the supply of better fruit and vegetable seeds and cuttings are multiplying. The Village AID movement has taken hold well: the villagers themselves often find as much as 70 per cent of the labour and money involved in new community projects, while contributions of 50 and 60 per cent are quite common. Village-level workers go in increasing numbers to the Village AID Training Centre at Lala Musa in the Punjab: they come back with techniques and methods which are beginning to transform village life in Azad Kashmir. Medical relief is extending fast, and dispensaries have been set up at all important centres. There is a splendid new Women's Hospital at Muzaffarabad. But perhaps the most noticeable improvement which has taken place lies in the enormous extension of education. In Darbar days, this was virtually non-existent: I only remember seeing one or two schools in the whole area. Now, few villages are beyond the reach at least of a primary school: on every road I met cheerful youngsters, hurrying along with their alphabet-boards in their hands or their books on their heads. There are three well-attended colleges for higher education. Economically, the future, too, seems bright. Great undertakings are on foot which will, when completed integrate the whole area in a planned development. The Mangla Project for a dam, power-station and a reservoir of 100 square miles centring on the headworks of the Jhelum canal system—a project already approved and in process of construction—holds the promise that Azad Kashmir will eventually cease to rank as a backward tract, and will profit greatly both from extended cultivation, and from the scientific exploitation of bauxite and other natural resources which will thus become possible.

Yet, in spite of all that is being, and has been, done in Azad Kashmir to redress the neglect and oppression of Darbar days, the country is, by and large, a place which saddens the visitor because he cannot fail to observe a cleavage of opinion among those living there which follows the line of their birth and origin. Unlike Gilgit and Baltistan, Azad Kashmir has a high proportion of embittered exiles, who have flocked to it for refuge from the areas ruled by the Indian-supported Government in Jammu and Srinagar. If it were the home only of local men and women who now, for the first time, feel that they are free to improve their lot with intelligent and sympathetic help from those in authority over them, the picture would be cheerful indeed. But Azad Kashmir is, also, the abiding-place—temporary, they hope and pray—of many who have lost their all rather than submit to the sacrifice of their freedom: of many whose lot was once cast in more fertile and congenial surroundings: of many to whom the isolation and remoteness of their present refuge stand in distasteful contrast with the busy, cosmopolitan life to which they have been accustomed in the Valley of Kashmir. These men and women cannot settle down, as the original inhabitants are settling, to the promise of better things. For them, Azad Kashmir is merely the means to an end; the improvements which fill the indigenous inhabitants of the area with new hope leave them unenthusiastic. For them, nothing can ever be right until the people of Jammu and Kashmir are set free to choose their own political destiny through a plebiscite, conducted without fear or favour, under international auspices.

Azad Kashmir, in fact, has a dual aspect. As the scene of steady and successful effort to improve the lot of those who are native to the area, it merits real admiration, justified by achievements which are undeniable. As a symbol of the determination of the Kashmiri people to preserve their freedom against desperate odds, it calls rather for sympathy and understanding, because the difficulties confronting it are so great. Among an important section of the population, and that the most vocal, restlessness and frustration prevail, as they assuredly must prevail wherever displaced persons congregate together. Nor is the general atmosphere improved by the fact that there are large numbers of refugees who cannot find room in Azad Kashmir, but have been obliged to settle in the Rawalpindi district. The Pakistan authorities have done all in their power to help these people, but, perhaps because they are not Pakistani subjects, but Kashmiris who cannot live in even an outlying part of Kashmir territory, they feel even more rootless and frustrated than their fellows in Azad Kashmir. There is much coming and going over the Azad Kashmir-Pakistan border, just as there is much coming—but not going—into Azad Kashmir from Indian-occupied Kashmir. This continual movement, in its turn, is a potent source of restlessness.

Thus in Azad Kashmir there are two main sections of opinion—the locals and the refugees—each with its own spokesmen and leaders. Both sections are united in one thing—the belief that they are upholding the right of the entire Kashmiri people to freedom and self-determination. The refugees are, as might be expected, much the more bitter of the two. Again and again I have been asked by them to explain why it is that world opinion—and Commonwealth opinion—permits India to evade her pledge about the plebiscite; why the Security Council cannot take action to oblige her to do so. Why, they ask, does Pakistan try so hard to damp down their anger and to prevent the renewal of fighting? Why should the rights of the people of Kashmir suffer because Mr. Nehru has found in Pakistan's foreign policy, and in the supply of American arms to her, the justification for postponement after postponement of the plebiscite? Why do not the other Commonwealth countries expel India from their midst because she refuses to abide by the decisions of the Security Council and continues to occupy Kashmir? It is questions like these that reveal the deep emotions which rack Azad Kashmir. They find further expression in the conviction, the strength of which seems to me to vary from time to time, that not even Pakistan—and most certainly not India—ought to have the final say in what the future of Kashmir should be. The desire for an independent Kashmir which I have heard expressed on many occasions is largely, I think, emotional; because the wiser heads at least know that a Kashmir free to choose her own path cannot dispense with the help and protection which could be acceptable only if they came from Pakistan.

It cannot be emphasized too strongly that Azad Kashmir, unlike Baltistan and Gilgit, is not a part of Pakistan. Pakistan would undoubtedly intervene to protect Azad Kashmir from invasion, if the Azad Kashmiri forces proved unequal to the task of defending their territory. Further, Pakistan helps the Azad Kashmir administration with food (the area is a deficit one, and will remain so until the new development-schemes fructify): with money: and with the services of lent officers. Some of these latter are experts in such lines as police organization, forestry and engineering: others are liaison officers with the Pakistan Government charged with the duty of ensuring that the subventions which Pakistan provides are properly spent upon the objects for which they are given. By and large, there are very few Pakistanis: the main work of governing is carried on entirely by Kashmiris. The administration of Azad Kashmir has been careful not to give itself the appearance of permanent location in Muzaffarabad by setting up there the outward appurtenances of a Government—even a Government in exile: it lives in a few converted private houses under what are almost ostentatiously 'camp' conditions. It spends next to nothing upon the comfort of its officers: everything that comes in, either by way of revenue, or in subventions from Pakistan, must be spent on raising the living standard of the people. To do anything else, it thinks, would lend support to the idea, now apparently favoured by India, that the State of Jammu and Kashmir has been irrevocably divided by the cease-fire line into two separate entities. Although the administration headed by Mr. K. H. Khurshid as President is now seeking international recognition as the only legitimate Government of the parts of Jammu and Kashmir under Indian occupation—a step which it has been induced to take by the example of the Algerian Nationalists—it still regards itself primarily as a caretaker of Kashmir interests until the time comes when the Kashmiri people are free to set up a Government of their own choice in the twin capitals of Jammu and Srinagar. The Azad Kashmir administration has, for the same reason, opposed the setting up of formal representative institutions—these, too, might give an appearance of permanence which it considers undesirable. For some time the administration was responsible to the Muslim Conference Party—the original resistance organization—but there are now district and municipal councils, and Basic Democracies have been introduced on the lines of which Pakistan—as will be seen in a later chapter—has so successfully pioneered. President Khurshid sought and obtained from the Basic Democrats an endorsement of his policies, and he has now a State Council of twelve members which forms the uppermost tier of the structure. This system gives the people of Azad Kashmir a real 'say' in the running of their local affairs, and justifies a recent change in the title of their administration, which is now termed 'The Azad Government of the State of Jammu and Kashmir'. The Government of Pakistan accepts this position, and uses its influence to see that the scales of office are held fairly even between the representatives of the Poonch-Mirpur-Muzaffarabad people and the representatives of Kashmiri exiles who belong to other areas.

This has not always been easy; and the rather frequent changes-over of Presidents and Ministers in Azad Kashmir have been seized upon by Indian critics as proof that the whole administration is a mere puppet creation of Pakistan. But my own observations have convinced me that this is far from being the case: the men who control Azad Kashmir are Kashmiri patriots—some of whom, indeed, show small gratitude to Pakistan, and little appreciation of her long and sustained efforts to secure for Kashmiris their right to settle their own future. It is never easy, human nature being what it is, to accept benefits gracefully at the hands of others; to do this is doubly difficult for the heart-sick, frustrated exiles in Azad Kashmir. The surprising thing, to me at least, is the way in which personal rivalries and jealousies are usually subordinated to the main task—which all recognize—of developing this once-neglected area into an example of what can be achieved by imaginative and enlightened administration in the face of great difficulties.

One powerful factor in sustaining the morale of the Kashmiri people, whether in Azad Kashmir or outside, has been the Azad Kashmir Radio. Ever since 1948, the devoted staff of this organization has been broadcasting its patriotic programmes, with Kashmiri folktunes carrying topical words, with Kashmiri choruses, and with Kashmiri talks. The original single mobile transmitter which operated from Trarkhel—whence the entire Valley of Kashmir can be covered—has grown into a compact system, with its own training schemes, its own engineers, its own outside staff, and its own producers. The up-to-date studios in Muzaffarabad, where there is a 1-kilowatt transmitter, are linked by land line to a 10-kilowatt relay station at Trarkhel. In Azad Kashmir alone, there are more than 10,000 receiving sets, and the messages and letters which come across the cease-fire line are evidence of many eager listeners in the territory which India controls. Competent, keen, and wholly convinced of the justice of their cause, the staff of Azad Kashmir Radio make a notable contribution to Kashmiri faith that justice must at last prevail.

The actual cease-fire line which cuts off Azad Kashmir from the territory which is in Indian occupation conveys a vivid impression to the visitor of the general artificiality of the present *de facto* arrangements. It has been drawn quite arbitrarily: it merely follows the forward positions of both sides when fighting came to an end. It cuts off villages from their pastures: it sometimes even separates a peasant from his field. The only good thing that one can say about it is that it is broadly respected: it does in fact keep the armed forces themselves apart. To the villagers it is a great nuisance, because it stops all through-traffic along main roads: but it is crossed by mountain paths which are not always strictly patrolled, and a certain amount of coming and going is winked at by the authorities—at least on the Azad Kashmir side. My impression, after visiting both fronts, is that the Azad Kashmir forces do not stop any genuine peasant who has good reason—for example, the recapture of a straying animal—from crossing into their territory: and, on the Azad Kashmir side, cultivation goes on undisturbed right up to the line. It seemed to me that the Indians are more strict, perhaps because their troops, being outsiders themselves, find it more difficult than the Azad Kashmiris to distinguish between a 'local' who merely wishes to go about legitimate business, and a stranger who may be an enemy agent in disguise. When I was there last, the Indian authorities were not allowing cultivation—as contrasted, perhaps, with mere grazing—within two or three miles of their line, and the deserted fields and abandoned hamlets were a sad sight. There was talk at the time of settling some Sikhs, or similar hardy souls whose loyalty to India could be relied upon, to cultivate the vacant holdings; I do not know whether this has now been done or not.

There are not quite such comradely relations between Azad Kash-mir forces and Indian troops as existed between the 'professional' soldiers of the Indian and Pakistani armies at the early stages of the fighting. Everyone is very much on the alert; shots are sometimes exchanged, although the United Nations observers are vigilant, quick to localize any 'incident' and to keep it from spreading. Yet nothing could have exceeded the kindness which each side in turn showed to my wife and myself when we visited front line troops on the spot.

As it happened, we were in Azad Kashmir first. We drove along the road from Domel, which so many travellers in the old days have followed, as they journeyed from the heat and dust of Rawalpindi to the freshness and flowers of Srinagar. On our way, we met difficulties which are perhaps worth describing, because they are so characteristic of what the Azad Kashmir authorities are continually encountering in their efforts to improve communications. The road was deeply pock-marked by, and dotted with, enormous boulders dislodged by a heavy thunderstorm which had broken during the night before: mud and shale were slithering down the steep hillside, crossing the metalled surface, and plunging into the Jhelum river hundreds of feet below. We pressed on across rivers of mud, shale and running water, with occasional rocks—fortunately small—still falling round us, until we reached a point where the road was completely blocked by an enormous fall. Our situation was uncomfortable, because the hillside was still slipping, large stones, mud, and shale were coming down the whole time, behind us as well as in front of us: anyway, there was no room to turn the car. Fortunately, a lorry with half a dozen policemen came up; they cheerfully lent a hand. But the long, heavy, American car was awkwardly placed, and resisted their efforts. Finally an Army lorry arrived with Azad Kashmiri engineers on their way to dynamite the obstruction: troops and police together lifted the car bodily and turned it round so that we could retreat until the road was cleared. We were so glad to reach a spot where the hillside was more stable! As soon as the landslip was blown clear, we resumed our journey.

After passing Chenari, where the headquarters of the forces then on the line was located at the former rest-house, in which travellers between the Punjab and Srinagar in old days often stayed, we came to the road-barrier at Chakothi, where we showed our passes and found a young Azad Kashmiri subaltern waiting to escort us to the forward position. He had come from Srinagar originally. As the sun suddenly gleamed through the dark clouds which had been filling the landscape with gloom, a golden light, uplifting to the heart, softened the rugged lines of the surrounding hills, flooded them with colour, and transformed the whole scene into life and warmth. 'What a lovely country you have!' I remarked. Sadly he replied: 'My country is in enemy occupation!' Soon we left the car, and followed a footpath which led us directly to the rear of some low buildings, plainly part of a farm. Vegetables were being grown in plots, and peasants were working, quite unperturbed, in nearby holdings. Skirting these, we found ourselves on a track leading to a sandbagged look-out post, which commands a turn in the main road where a broken bridge lies in fragments at the foot of the narrow ravine which it once spanned. A jeep track takes off from the road on our side of the bridge foundations, winds its way to the bottom of the ravine, crosses a small stream, and then ascends the other side, where the sandbagged outposts of the Indian Army are in plain sight. This track is used, we were told, by the United Nations observers, who pass freely from one army to the other.

No one else can do this: constantly-manned machine-guns command the ravine on each side, and an air of grim vigilance prevails. When my wife and I were helped on the parapet so that we could look across, there was a visible stir on the Indian side: and in a matter of moments half a dozen pairs of binoculars were trained on the unusual sight of an English woman in the opposing lines. My wife gave a friendly wave or two with a head scarf to those who were scrutinizing us—this was enthusiastically returned: she then remarked to an Azad Kashmiri officer: 'We shall be on the other side in a month or two, we will wave across to you then with the same scarf!' He replied: 'Madam, that would be very kind of you, but I am sure you will never get there. In all the time we have been posted here, we have never seen a civilian, let alone a lady, on the Indian side.' My wife said: 'Well, look out for us, anyway!'—which he promised to do. After we had spent some time at the look-out post, we were escorted back to the forward mess, set up in one of the farm buildings we had passed, where we were warmly welcomed, and entertained to tea, by a group of officers, mostly Azad Kashmiris, but with one or two Pakistanis. The mess was comfortably furnished: there was an air of homely, pleasant hospitality and good comradeship which did not conceal an efficiency which was not the less impressive because it was easy and natural. It seemed to us that Azad Kashmir is fortunate in the quality of her young defenders.

Three or four months later we did, in fact, reach the other side of the ravine, by the courtesy of the Indian Government. Everything on the Indian side was noticeably smart and military: it was a world of professional soldiers with no civilian dilution. Long before we reached the line itself, we were impressed by the strength of the supporting forces, by the variety of the mechanical transport, by the Aldershot-like atmosphere which prevails. The headquarters where we were given lunch might have been found in any large military station with British traditions: a good solid building, with none of the temporary look of a camp, containing offices, a well-furnished dining-room, a drawing-room provided with current English and Indian periodicals as well as with plenty of books; in fact, all the appurtenances of ordered military life. We saw no other civilians, and no peasants were about; but soldiers were everywhere—obviously in considerable numbers. At the cease-fire line, we had the opportunity, this time, of looking across the ravine to the Azad Kashmir post which we had visited earlier: this side we were facing, not the Indian, but the Azad Kashmiri machine-guns. My wife asked the Indian Major who was escorting us if she might wave her scarf: 'I have a date', she explained, 'with the boys across there!' He assented with a friendly smile. She then climbed on the parapet and began waving vigorously. We watched the binoculars on the other side being trained upon us; a sepoy ran off and returned with a number of officers. They obviously recognized us, for they began to wave back with jerkins, jackets, scarves, and anything else that came to hand. The process was infectious: before long the Indians and the Azad Kashmiris were waving to each other in friendly fashion. The Indian Major even arranged to send our visiting cards over to our former hosts in Azad Kashmir by the hand of a U.N.O. officer whose jeep was due to cross the lines that same afternoon!

Episodes such as this bring home to one, more vividly than oceans of argument, how futile and unnecessary is the tragedy of this divided land, which not only suffers deeply itself, but is a cause of estrangement between the two partners in the sub-continent whose friendly co-operation means so much to the well-being of both.

Chapter 5

PARTING OF THE WAYS

K ashmir is not the only issue which divides countries which ought to be partners. Congress-League jealousies: Hindu-Muslim antagonism: recrimination over the sufferings and, later, over the property of the refugees: disputes over the division of assets bequeathed by the British Raj: competition for influence on the North-West Frontier: conflicts over the alignment of certain Princely States—such are some of the general causes of the discord which from very early days has poisoned—and, unfortunately, still continues to poison—the atmosphere between Pakistan and India. These causes have operated to accentuate certain broad, and quite understandable, differences between the outlooks of each country upon domestic and foreign problems. The unhappy quarrel over Kashmir has already been described: in addition to this, there have been two further major problems round which bad feeling has crystallized. One is the dispute over the water-resources of the Indus Basin: the other is a conflict of interests arising from marked divergencies in the patterns of external relations. The former dispute, potentially as dangerous as any, has now, fortunately, been brought to an end through a process of give-and-take on both sides, which has been stimulated and fostered by long and patient negotiations under international auspices. The story of this dispute from its emergence to its settlement is, I think, worth following, because it may well point the way for the application to other quarrels of the methods of patient, disinterested, conciliation by an impartial agency which were eventually to prove successful.

Even before partition, there had been inter-provincial rivalry between Sind and the Punjab about the sharing, for irrigation-purposes, of the Indus Basin water-resources. Both provinces had land which was crying out for development into prosperous agricultural colonies. This dispute was never settled to the satisfaction of either party: but since both were provinces of an undivided India and were subject, in the last instance, to the over-riding authority of the Raj, the quarrel went no further than bitter memoranda and acidulous noting. Very different became the position as soon as the disputants were independent sovereign States.

The Indus River system consists of the great main stream, which gives the system its name, together with some small tributaries to the west—the most important is the Kabul River—and five very important tributaries to the east—the Jhelum, Chenab, Ravi, Sutlej and Beas. The investigation of this river system, and the 'planned utilization' of its resources, rank among the most impressive achievements of scientific irrigation to be found in any part of the world, and are not the least valuable of the legacies which the British Raj bequeathed to its two successor-States. But British engineers, not foreseeing partition, and engaged on carrying out by stages long-term plans for the development of the area as a whole, naturally first took in hand tracts of land which seemed to lend themselves most readily to immediate colonization. When partition came, development had been carried to a point at which there were in operation twenty-three main perennial canals (that is, canals operating all the year round as contrasted with canals operating only at certain seasons), and eight non-perennial canals, which irrigated between them about 23,000,000 field-acres. The new Indo-Pakistani frontier, setting at naught the plans of the engineers— as political arrangements all too often do—cut through the entire area in such a way as to bring twenty-one perennial canals, seven non-perennial canals, and 18,000,000 field-acres of irrigated land to Pakistan. It was only the balance which went to India. But—and this was the real source of the dispute—India also received, along with some 35,000,000 acres of land in the East Punjab which could only be irrigated in future from Indus system sources, a virtual stranglehold over the upper waters of the rivers which feed Pakistan's canal system. This will be clear from the following explanation.

The Indus and the Jhelum both pass through Kashmir, although the depth of their gorges makes it difficult to take any considerable extractions of water from them before they reach Pakistan. The Chenab passes through Jammu before it enters Pakistan: the Ravi and Sutlej, also, pass through India first. The Beas lies wholly within India. The important headworks at Madhopur on the Ravi, and Ferozepur on the Sutlej, vital for the control of the waters used by Pakistan's eastern canal colonies, fell in Indian territory. Plainly, if India chose to cut off water supplies, the situation of many of Pakistan's cultivators would be desperate. It was for this reason, as we have noticed in our earlier chapter, that the British Chairman of the tribunal responsible for partitioning the British legacy, pressed for definite undertakings from both sides about the future division of the water—only to be rebuked for suggesting that Indo-Pakistani statesmanship would fall so far short of ordinary common sense as to disrupt the operation of the splendid irrigation works based on the Indus River system!

There is no reason to doubt the good intentions either of the Indian or of the Pakistani representatives on this tribunal when they pledged

The Indus Basin River System
(by permission of *The Round Table*)

their countries to work amicably together for the preservation and improvement of the irrigation system which was to be divided between them: but these intentions did not survive the strain which the tragic circumstances accompanying partition imposed upon the equanimity of both India and Pakistan. As fate would have it, it was the East and West Punjab—the very area where Pakistan's water was most susceptible to interference—which saw passions most deeply inflamed because of Hindu-Muslim atrocities. Those who barely escaped with their lives across the border on each side were in no mood to be reasonable. Open hostilities had already broken out in Kashmir: Pakistan was becoming apprehensive about the effects of the Indian occupation of that State upon the supply of water reaching her from the Indus and the Jhelum. In April 1948 her fears about the Indian attitude were sharpened by the action of the East Punjab Government which cut off Pakistan's supply of water at the headworks of Madhopur and Ferozepur. India later admitted that this action was mistaken, and stated that it was due to a technical dispute. But the effect on Pakistani opinion can be gauged from the seriousness of what happened: cultivation on more than a million acres in the canal colonies irrigated from the Bari-Doab and Dipalpur canals was ruined because there was no water available for six weeks.

This particular incident was closed by the personal intervention of Mr. Nehru, after the Pakistan Government had made strong representations: but the compromise agreement intended to reconcile the views of the East Punjab (Indian) and the West Punjab (Pakistani) Governments itself opened the way to fresh disputes. The East Punjab Government claimed the full ownership of the water, but was willing to allow the West Punjab Government to use it on payment of seignorage and of a contribution to the cost of the Madhopur headworks. The West Punjab Government disputed both claims, but recognized the natural anxiety of the East Punjab Government to use water for the development of its own areas. A long legal wrangle took place: Pakistan asserted that under international law, India had no right to interfere with long established user of the water by lower riparian owners, and offered to submit the whole dispute to the International Court of Justice at The Hague. India refused, on the grounds that the dispute was not justiciable because it involved her sovereignty, and was, in any case, *res judicata* because of the East-West Punjab agreement.

Pakistan's situation remained very difficult. Whenever there was a bad monsoon or a water-shortage, she found that her supplies were cut. Further, although *ad hoc* agreement was reached from time to time about the quantity of water that she should receive, much of the promised supplies came to her during the monsoon, in the shape of spates and floods which were useless to her cultivators. The quantities so arriving were deducted from her total quota, so that when her cultivators needed water, she was told that the quota was exhausted. It was hardly to be expected that India would fail to think first of the interests of her own people, who needed water just as much as did the Pakistanis. But the hard fact of the situation was that it was India who decided how much water should cross the frontier. There was a further complication from Pakistan's point of view. In a number of her older colonies, land is falling out of cultivation at a horrifying rate—as much as 100,000 acres a year—because of water-logging and salinity due to the rising of alkaline salts to the surface. Something like 10,000,000 acres need treatment. For water-logging, drainage projects and tube-wells are the remedy: but for salinity, the only known cure is to increase the supply of water far beyond what land in good heart would need, so that the salts can, in the course of time, be washed out. Thus at the very time when Pakistan's need for water was greatest, she found herself entirely at the mercy of India, who was mainly concerned with the pressing requirements of her own cultivators.

The position which resulted was charged with dangerous possibilities: for if men's livelihood is threatened, they will prefer to die fighting rather than to die of sheer starvation. It was an American—Mr. David Lilienthal, of Tennessee Valley Authority fame—who in 1951 first focused international attention on the problem after he had paid a visit to the Indus River system. In a magazine article which was widely circulated in the western world, he pointed out that Pakistan's claim to the uninterrupted flow of water, however legally unassailable, did not in practice settle anything because it left unsolved India's food problem. His own unique standing as an irrigation-engineer of international reputation lent authority to his assertion that the real solution lay in reverting to the British plan of treating the Indus Basin as a unit to be developed as a whole. He suggested that development should be undertaken, with the help of the International Bank, by a joint Indo-Pakistani authority—on the model of the Tennessee Valley Authority—which would be able to utilize, for the benefit of both countries, the high proportion of the total water-resources—he estimated it at 80 per cent—which still ran to waste into the Arabian Sea because it was not used for irrigation.

Mr. Lilienthal, in fact, performed a service for which both India and Pakistan owe him boundless gratitude—he drew the attention of the International Bank to the possibility of financing, as a creative, humanitarian project, a joint authority for the exploitation of the water resources of the Indus River system, and of removing, by this means, the source of a quarrel which was a direct threat to peace. But his unfamiliarity with local conditions led him into two serious errors. First, he did not realize that the divergencies in policy and outlook between India and Pakistan—to say nothing of their bitter quarrels over particular issues—made the sort of co-operation which he envisaged quite impracticable, at least for the time. Next, he failed to appreciate the enormous labour and expense involved in storing up, and turning to useful purposes the 'wasted' water which comes down in the form of floods when the Indus system rivers are in spate. And unless this 'wasted' water could be made available, there was little point in his proposals.

The International Bank offered its services to India and Pakistan to help them to work out a solution: and a long series of conferences took place in Washington, New Delhi and Karachi. To reconcile the divergent points of view of India and Pakistan proved impossible: and in 1953, the International Bank put forward its own solution. It proposed cutting the Indus River system in two, assigning the Sutlej, Ravi and Beas water wholly to India, and the Chenab, Jhelum and Indus water wholly to Pakistan. This plan, of course, entailed bringing water right across Pakistan from the western rivers to replace the water which she had hitherto taken for her eastern canal colonies from the rivers which were in future to belong to India. The Bank suggested that India should meet the cost of the necessary works.

India liked the plan, which would give her the water she wanted where she wanted it. She thought Pakistan ought to be contented with it, too: because the Bank's engineers had calculated that Pakistan would receive no less than 80 per cent of the total water supplies of the Indus River system. But Pakistan hesitated, because no one knew quite enough about the flow of the rivers given to her—they had never been as carefully measured as the eastern tributaries. She asked for an independent opinion by a firm of hydrographic consultants on whether there would be enough water to meet her requirements, present and future. Unfortunately, her hesitation was expressed at a time when feeling over water-supplies was running exceptionally high because two bad monsoons, which had affected the flow of the Sutlej and Ravi, caused India to be particularly short of water, and to reduce drastically the supply to Pakistan. Violent recriminations broke out on both sides. India complained that Pakistan was trying to prevent her from engaging on works like the Bhakra-Nangal project, which would relieve her distressed cultivators: Pakistan roundly asserted that India was trying to starve her out. In East and West Punjab, feeling ran very high. I was visiting both parts of the Punjab at the time, and it was a sad sight to see the dried-up, barren fields on each side of the frontier. Pakistan was, in fact, by far the worse sufferer: her cultivators were both angry and desperate. My own impression then was that had the Bank not been, as it were, seized of the quarrel, and in a position to give both countries some hope of better things in the future, war would have broken out. Even so, I believe it was very fortunate for the preservation of peace that neither India nor Pakistan wanted to alienate American opinion, on account of the generous help which the United States Government was giving to both countries.

The political crisis passed, and the Bank's patient labours took on a fresh lease of life. Before long, the hydrographic consultants who were advising Pakistan reported. They completely confirmed Pakistan's fears. Of the theoretical 80 per cent of total supplies which Pakistan would get under the Bank's plan, almost the whole would in practice be quite useless to her because it all came down in spate in a few weeks, and would be non-existent at the very time when it would be most wanted for cultivation during the rest of the year. Rather ruefully, the Bank found itself obliged to issue in 1956 an *aide mémoire,* in which it admitted that even the proposed transfer by link canals of flow supplies from Pakistan's western rivers to her eastern canal colonies would leave her faced with water shortages in winter which would be too severe and too lengthy to be tolerable. The Bank proposed alternative ways of meeting the situation as thus clarified: either India should keep Pakistan going by giving 'timely water' when it was wanted: or India should pay for the vast storage works which, as it was now realized, would be necessary to supplement the link canals already proposed, and, indeed, already partly under construction.

The effect of this *aide mémoire,* of course, was to throw the dispute into the melting pot again. Neither country liked the first alternative: India, because she wanted the water of her rivers for herself—already, in 1954, she had begun her wonderful Bhakra-Nangal project which was to supply water and power to vast areas in Rajasthan: Pakistan, because she refused to allow water-supplies essential to her cultivators

103

to remain under the control of India—her experiences both in 1948 and in subsequent years were too fresh in her memory. Besides this, what was to happen when she needed *more* water for her own development schemes in the future? Thus the second alternative was the only practicable one.

This, in its turn, was found to entail considerable difficulties. The project of the link canals was tricky enough from the engineering point of view, because they have to be run horizontally, as it were, from west to east, right across the natural drainage system of the Indus Basin. They are always liable to be damaged by flood water. Indeed, one of them, I was informed, which had already been constructed by the Pakistan Government, was breached, and had to be repaired, no fewer than twenty-eight times in the course of the year 1959. In order to stop this happening, some canals must be carried across country on aqueducts, or projected through tunnels, at great expense. And when to the problem of the canals there was added the further problem of the storage dams, for which sites had to be found in terrain which was little suited to their construction and maintenance, the net result was to drive the engineers almost distracted. But they sat down to the job —Indian and Pakistani engineers together: because while the Pakistani engineers were primarily responsible for solving the technical problems, the Indian engineers had to be satisfied that the solutions proposed would involve their country in no more expense than she could legitimately be expected to defray.

Left to themselves, the engineers on both sides were quite capable of working out something satisfactory—many of them were old colleagues from British days. But the final word was not theirs: it rested with the Governments of their respective countries. And in 1956 and 1957 the political atmosphere once more proved unfavourable to agreement. Again there were two bad monsoons: again India reduced Pakistan's quota in proportion to the shortage in her own withdrawals. Again Pakistan complained that this quota was made to include flood water: and that when she needed 'timely water', she was told that her quota was exhausted. India accused Pakistan of deliberately delaying a settlement, and warned her neighbour that after 1962 —fortunately still five years ahead—she could expect no more Indian water: all available supplies would be needed for India's new Rajasthan canal system. Thereupon Pakistan formally complained to the Bank that this ultimatum was a threat to her existence.

Fresh material now became available to increase Indo-Pakistani bitterness as the dispute over the Indus River's water merged with the dispute over Kashmir. The shadow of Kashmir had always, in Pakistani eyes, loomed over the Indus waters question, owing, as we have seen, to the fear that Pakistan's water supplies might be threatened by Indian control over the regions in that State through which the Indus, the Jhelum and the Chenab pass. But at this stage of the Indus waters dispute, the Kashmir quarrel intervened in slightly different form. Pakistan had succeeded in reactivating the Security Council on the Kashmir issue: and though nothing positive finally resulted, India was dismayed to find that an increasing weight of world opinion was ranging itself behind Pakistan's contention that the Kashmiri people were entitled to self-determination through a plebiscite under United Nations auspices. Since India has always prided herself upon her policy of openly supporting the rights of small nations to self-determination and freedom from external control, the kind of criticism which countries whose opinion she respects began to direct against her attitude over Kashmir was particularly galling to her: she blamed Pakistan for her awkward position. Moreover, she found another grievance in the Mangla Project, to which reference was made in the last chapter. But for the resistance offered by Azad Kashmir, the site of the Mangla Project would have lain in Indian-controlled territory. India laid a complaint in the Security Council about the Project, to which Pakistan retorted that the Mangla scheme was not only an essential aid to the developing economy of Azad Kashmir, but was also a pivot of the replacement works which, under the Bank's own plan, would be needed to make up the deficit when no water from the eastern rivers would reach Pakistan's western canal colonies. Again, nothing tangible emerged from the controversy, except that the work of the engineers on both sides was complicated by angry, and often unreasonable, directives from their respective Governments, forbidding compromise and insisting upon demands based more upon considerations of prestige than upon the dictates of reason. But by the middle of 1958, the engineers had succeeded in working out a scheme for the sharing of the waters which looked quite practicable provided that two conditions obtained: namely, that both Governments were willing to consider it on its merits: and that somehow the very large bill could be met.

The engineers had done a good job. Was it to be wasted, as other previous attempts at agreement had been wasted, because the statesmen could not compromise?

Most fortunately for both countries, a new factor entered into the situation at this juncture. In October 1958 the new Revolutionary Government came into power in Pakistan. It was, as we shall see later, a strong, stable, and fearless administration, firmly grounded in popular support. It was able to do what no other Pakistani Government had been able to do since the days of Quaid-i-Azam and Liaquat Ali Khan—it could lead public opinion firmly along the line which it knew to be advantageous to the country. It began to devote serious attention to the settlement of the Indus waters question as part of a wider policy of improving relations with India. It dealt severely with trouble-makers and religious fanatics who preached hostility to India. On the Indus waters question, it soon showed itself reasonable and open-minded about fair compromise. And India, when once she had recovered from the shock of seeing Pakistan under an Army-controlled régime, and satisfied herself that the last thing which this régime contemplated was indulgence in rash military adventure, soon came to realize that her neighbour was now governed by men who could be relied upon to keep their word, and who were genuinely anxious to reach agreement with her. The Bank took the fullest possible advantage of this new and promising situation, redoubling its patient endeavours in a final effort to persuade both countries to accept the solution worked out by the engineers.

In less than a year after President Ayub Khan came to power in Pakistan, it was found possible to begin drafting a formal international treaty covering the division of the water resources of the Indus system. The formal treaty was chosen as the vehicle of agreement for two reasons. First, it provides a safeguard for both parties that its terms would be honoured because it is capable of being registered by the United Nations as part of the current structure of internationally-recognized inter-Statal obligations: and next, it provides the most appropriate basis for the operation of the financial provisions upon which the practical execution of the division depended. For the magnitude of the expenditure involved in the plan which the engineers had worked out is something far outside even the combined resources of India and Pakistan: only an international financial consortium would be able to cope with it.

The drafting of the treaty was a long and complicated business, because care had to be taken to respect the susceptibilities of both countries. India's position over the Mangla Project had to be secured while the Project itself had to figure among Pakistan's replacement works. India had to be given the right to draw off a limited quantity from the upper waters of the western rivers, for certain carefully-defined uses in the State of Jammu and Kashmir, without committing Pakistan to any admission of India's right to control territory in that State. But all difficulties were at length overcome; and on 19th September 1960, the treaty was signed by Mr. Nehru for India, by President Ayub Khan for Pakistan, and by Mr. Iliff for the International Bank. At the same time an international financial agreement, pledging definite contributions to the expense of the new construction works, was signed by representatives of the Governments of Australia, Canada, Western Germany, India, New Zealand, Pakistan, United Kingdom, United States, and also of the International Bank.

The detailed provisions of the treaty repay study by anyone who has followed the course of the long and dangerous dispute which it brought to an end: but in essence they can be summarized into a few simple undertakings. First, and perhaps most important for the future, is the recognition by both countries of their community of interest in the optimum utilization of the resources of the Indus River system, and their pledge to set up machinery—a standing Indus Commission: a network of hydrological and meteorological stations and a pooling of the information derived from them—for effective co-operation. It is an earnest of this future co-operation that India undertakes to give water to Pakistan over a ten-year period, according to a fixed schedule: that she undertakes for ever not to interfere with the flow of the western rivers into Pakistan: while Pakistan undertakes, within the ten-year period, to construct works to replace the water which India will afterwards be entitled to retain for her own use. Second, there is a detailed exposition of the development projects to be undertaken by each country, costing more than £380,000,000, of which £310,000,000 is to be spent in Pakistan. This sum will cover 400 miles of link canals: two storage dams, each of more than 4,000,000 acre-feet; inter-river links to integrate the present river and canal system: tubewells and drainage to restore cultivation to 2,500,000 acres: and power stations of 300,000-kilowatt capacity. The details of the programme have been settled by an advisory board of Pakistani, British and American engineers in consultation with the Bank: the work is to be executed under the direction of the Water and Power Development Authority of West Pakistan. In India there is to be a new dam on the Beas river of 5,500,000 acre-feet and extensive hydro-electric potential.

All this is made possible by an Indus Basin Development Fund, administered by the Bank and financed from a number of sources. Beside the £62,000,000, to be spread over ten years, which represents India's contribution, Australia, Canada, West Germany, New Zealand, the United Kingdom and the United States all contribute their quota, as does the Bank; Pakistan's own contribution to the Fund is just under half a million sterling. In addition, further loans from the Bank and the United States are taking care of particular projects.

The settlement of the Indus waters dispute is an excellent example of the enlightened co-operation of a group of industrially-advanced nations—not only Commonwealth countries but 'outsiders' as well—in a project to assist the less-fortunately situated peoples of Pakistan and India. It is perhaps significant that the good offices of an international authority were originally involved by the need to calm an explosive situation which threatened to involve India and Pakistan in open hostilities: only later did the entire enterprise take on its present aspect of a planned contribution by a group of the 'have' nations to the development of two economically under-developed countries.

Since patient mediation by a disinterested but sympathetic outside authority has achieved such success in the case of a dispute so dangerous to peace as that which concerned the Indus waters, many observers have wondered why a similar process cannot be applied with equally happy results to other sources of friction between India and Pakistan, and in particular, to the Kashmir quarrel. Undoubtedly it ought to be so applied; indeed the Security Council has from time to time devoted quite as much pains and care to the problem of Kashmir as the World Bank has applied to the Indus waters question. Why, then, it may be asked, has the same process yielded success in one case, and only baffling, dangerous deadlock in the other? The answer lies in the fact that the obstacles to agreement over the Indus waters, although formidable, were essentially practical in their nature, needing for their resolution no sacrifice of national prestige, no compromise of national ideology, nothing, indeed, but business-like give-and-take. Each side, it is true, has had to surrender something fairly substantial. India has had to submit to certain limitations on her use of her own waters for a specific period: she has also had to undertake a heavy financial burden. Pakistan, in addition to waiving the rights which international lawyers are now increasingly agreed in assigning to lower riparian owners, has had to incur some grave risks in pinning the fate of her irrigation

system to schemes, still untested, for using storage dams to supplement water-shortages during critical periods. Storage dams are wasting assets: they silt up, and then new sites must be found. No engineer
will substitute static for live water if he can help it: but Pakistan has
undertaken to do just this for the sake of agreement with India. Further the link canals which she has undertaken to provide will undoubtedly complicate the measures needed to deal with flooding and
salinization. Finally, the replacement-works which the Treaty necessitates are likely to tie up the engineering skill and resources of Pakistan
for a decade, at the expense of new development work which the
country requires urgently. Even so, broadly speaking, both countries
are likely to reap great and increasing advantages from a sensible
compromise, made practically fruitful through the financial and
moral guarantees provided by an international consortium.

The issues involved in the Kashmir quarrel are of another order
altogether, because they are bound up with ideological differences
which directly affect national prestige on both sides. These ideological
differences stem primarily from the divergent outlooks of the Congress
and the Muslim League prior to partition. As has already been
pointed out, the Congress, under the inspiration of Mr. Gandhi and
Mr. Nehru, envisaged the future India as a multi-racial Union of
peoples, each possessing an individual heritage of its own, which
could contribute to the economic and cultural wealth of the whole
Union without losing its identity. Over this Union there would pre-
side a strong central Government, pledged to religious neutralism, to
the safeguarding of human rights, and to the advancement, social,
economic and cultural, of the country as a whole. In such a polity, the
Congress conceived, the Muslim minority would be as free as the
Hindu majority to enjoy its rights and to make its contribution.
Religion, in fact, was to be a private matter, with which the State was
not concerned except to ensure that discrimination on religious
grounds between citizen and citizen was not permitted. But, as we
have already seen, the majority of the Muslim community had no
confidence in the efficacy of this plan as a means of protecting their
interests: it was not so much religious persecution that they feared, as
social and economic handicaps, and a nebulous but formidable discouragement of the Islamic way of life by the pressure of the Hindu
majority. Accordingly, under the lead of Mr. Jinnah, they demanded,
and obtained, a homeland of their own in which the main link between citizens was to be a common religion—although religious

minorities were to be assured of full civic equality and complete toleration.

The fundamental assumptions of the Congress and of the League were thus so different that the new countries which each came to control were bound to follow divergent paths. It was a misfortune both for India and for Pakistan, and a double misfortune for the Kashmir people, that the State of Jammu and Kashmir provided the first example of an active clash between these two ideologies. To India, the fact that most Kashmiris are Muslim, linked by religion to Pakistan, appears irrelevant in face of the fact that the Maharaja formally acceded to India, as in constitutional law he was entitled to do. For to admit that religion can override political and constitutional ties would be to undermine the entire basis on which the Indian polity has been founded, and to cast doubts upon the loyalty to India of the 30,000,000 Muslims who remain her citizens. To Mr. Nehru, himself of Kashmiri origin, the mere idea that religion might prove the decisive factor in determining the political destiny and future allegiance of the Kashmiri people appears an intolerable reversion to atavistic ways of thinking, a deliberate denial of every modern and progressive outlook. Cynics remark that this is why he has never permitted a plebiscite to take place.

The Pakistani outlook as we have noticed, is very different. To Pakistan, the Kashmiris are brother-Muslims, and, on that score alone, are entitled to sympathy and support. But quite apart from this, the Kashmiris, in Pakistan's eyes, are entitled to determine their own political future: if religion is a factor which sways their decision, that is all the more commendable; it certainly does not render the decision itself less valid, or prejudice their right to take it. The denial of this right appears to Pakistan a definite wrong, inflicted not only on Kashmiris as human beings, but on Kashmiris as fellow Muslims, just as the measures taken by the Maharaja to restore his authority appeared an intolerable persecution of Muslims by Hindus.

The clash of ideas which found early expression in the bitterness of the Kashmir quarrel has been reflected in the pattern of external relations which each country has constructed for itself. As might be expected, the foreign policies both of India and of Pakistan have undergone certain changes and modifications, with the lapse of time and with the varying characteristics of the international horizon; but each has continued to follow its own broad general pattern.

The foreign policy of New Delhi has been mainly shaped by the convictions of Mr. Nehru himself. Long before his country achieved independence, he had become the acknowledged expert on international affairs in the inner circles of the Congress Party: and it seemed only natural to his colleagues that when he took office as Prime Minister, he should keep the portfolio of External Affairs in his own hands. It has been a wonderful piece of good fortune for India, and one that Pakistan may well envy, that he has already continued in unbroken control of his country's destinies for fifteen years. The convictions which shape his policy are based upon the Hindu ideal that influence, persuasion and example, not physical force, should govern the dealings of nation with nation. It was on this basis, in the early Middle Ages, that Hindu Powers had established contacts with the countries which are now known as Ceylon, Burma, Thailand, Cambodia, Southern and Northern Viet Nam, and the Indonesian Republic. The relationship was peaceful: these lands, at varying periods and for different lengths of time, became accustomed to respect India not as an Imperial Power, but as the metropolis of culture and civilization. But in 1947 it was a very long time since any Hindu statesman had been in a position to grapple with the complexities of foreign affairs, so that it fell to Mr. Nehru to bring to the ancient Hindu tradition certain new elements, derived partly from his own turn of thought, and partly from his conception of present-day requirements.

The ancient Hindu tradition of eschewing the use of physical force as far as possible in international affairs has been fortified in Mr. Nehru's mind by a number of factors. First, and by no means the least potent, has been his respect for the Gandhian philosophy of non-violence, with its accompanying tenets of respect for human rights, and insistence upon goodwill towards all men. Only less influential, perhaps, as a factor in shaping his outlook, has been the broad internationalism which he has acquired through travel, through contacts with men of many races, and through deep historical study. This basis of Hindu tradition, of Gandhian ideas, and of a cosmopolitan outlook has been consolidated by Mr. Nehru's perception that since India cannot hope to compete in physical strength with giant industrialized Powers like the United States and Soviet Russia, her own present and future influence in international affairs is necessarily bound up with the hope of substituting moral for physical force as the decisive factor in shaping the fate of nations.

This philosophy underlies the respect in which Mr. Nehru has always held the United Nations Organization—a respect which was certainly not weakened by the leading part which India found herself called upon to play in its counsels almost from the moment of her entry upon independent nationhood. For in 1947, with Communist China and Japan alike absent, with Indonesia in confusion, and with Pakistan still striving to find herself, India stood out at Lake Success not only as the largest and wealthiest of the Asian countries, but also as the natural expounder, in the counsels of the West, of the ideals and the aspirations of the entire continent. Her representatives excelled in their mastery of English, in their experience of Secretariat practice, in their marked ability, in their expert knowledge of committee procedure, and in their debating-powers. It must be recorded that Mr. Nehru used with great discretion the position of prominence into which India so naturally stepped, and used it, moreover, to ensure that the voice of Asia, and not only the voice of his own country, was heard with due attention. His sensitivity to any suggestion that Asian opinion is being accorded less than its due weight in the handling of international affairs by the Great Powers on the Security Council has been occasionally misunderstood in the West. It is not a claim to Indian leadership in Asia—a claim which he has constantly repudiated: it is rather a determination to ensure that great world issues are not settled merely with reference to the interests and convenience of the Soviet Union, the United States and Western Europe. But his critics have noted that Mr. Nehru's general support for the United Nations Organization has not prevented him from vigorously opposing the efforts of the Security Council to settle the Kashmir quarrel by the use of expedients of which he does not approve.

Apart altogether from the undoubted fact that India's national interests, to say nothing of her prospects of exercising a measurable influence in international affairs, incline her to a policy of neutralism as between the great power blocks of the Communist and non-Communist worlds, Mr. Nehru's own political philosophy would forbid him from identifying his country with one side or the other, and thus committing her, if not to possible future hostilities, at least to a restricted range of international friendships. India's policy of neutralism has not only enabled her to act as the nucleus for an informal grouping of a number of like-minded countries, first in Asia and later also in Africa; it has further placed her in a position to render valuable services to the cause of international peace both by the exercise of her good offices to reconcile competing interests, and by the supply of civil and military personnel for the use of the United Nations in such trouble-spots as Korea, the Gaza Strip, and the Congo. But, along with the great increase in the number of newly independent countries brought about by the progress of freedom in the former colonial territories of Africa, there has come a certain change in the nature, rather than in the extent, of Indian influence on the 'uncommitted' group. Not all the new political leaders have Mr. Nehru's great experience: some of them have their own, more narrowly racial, points of view. Mr. Nehru's ideas are still always heard with respect, but are not now always adopted, although his general policy of non-alignment finds ample support. But at moments of crisis, as during the Belgrade Conference of uncommitted nations in September 1961, there is still a general tendency to look to him for a lead. Will this tendency survive the blurring of the Gandhian image of India, as a Power championing lofty moral principles, by the sudden surprise annexation, in December 1961, of the helpless but valuable pockets of Portuguese Indian territory?

It has not always been easy for Mr. Nehru to follow his chosen policy, for he, like any other statesman, is subject to human emotions, and among these emotions is his passionate anti-colonialism. He has been led by his own experience to associate colonialism mainly with the Western Powers—with Britain, France, the Netherlands and Portugal: his critics accuse him of forgetting that the Soviet Union not only inherits the long Tsarist tradition of colonial domination over the peoples of Central Asia, but is even today running true to that tradition by her colonial domination, enforced through her Red Army, over Czechoslovakia, Hungary, the East German Republic, and Poland. It has further been remarked that he tends to attack the Western Powers for looking over the stable door, while at the same time he allows the Communist *bloc* to steal the horse without comment. But his unhappy experience of Chinese genocide in Tibet and of Chinese recalcitrance in border disputes seems to have convinced him that the Communist Powers are no more disinterested in their conduct of international affairs than are their rivals. Nor does Mr. Nehru's neutralism prevent him from being very tough indeed with the Indian Communists—who are tolerated as a recognized political party—when their activities threaten law and order, or when, as happened during the border dispute with China, they set Indian interests at defiance.

The influence on Indian foreign policy of the nexus of ideas and convictions held by Mr. Nehru is illustrated by India's tireless support of peoples struggling to free themselves from foreign domination: and by the importance she attaches to the substitution of national independence for the colonial system all over the world. It is this which lends so strange an appearance of contradiction to Mr. Nehru's opposition to the exercise by the Kashmiri people of their right to self-determination: an opposition which stands out as an exception to the general run of his policy. Another feature of Indian foreign policy is Mr. Nehru's dislike of territorial alliances for mutual security: although here again his critics have pointed out that he often speaks more kindly of the Warsaw Pact than of the North Atlantic Treaty Organization, of the South East Asia Treaty Organization, and of the former Baghdad Pact, now represented by the Central Treaty Organization. He believes that such alliances, by further emphasizing the division of interest between the Communist and the non-Communist worlds, serve to increase, rather than to diminish, the risk of a physical conflict: and he particularly dislikes the supply of arms and munitions by industrially-advanced members of these groupings to their Asian fellow-members. To round off this outline of the principles which govern Indian foreign policy, it must be recorded that Mr. Nehru has from the first been a stalwart supporter of the Commonwealth, which he regards as a most valuable organization for the pooling of information: for the promotion of informal personal contacts: for the frank exchange, off the record, of opinions between the representatives of the sister nations: and for the cementing of good understanding among countries with the differing Anglo-Saxon, Asian, and African traditions.

With the exception of this last feature—support of the Commonwealth—there are very few points where the foreign policy of Pakistan coincides with that of India. There, it is true, the two countries genuinely see eye to eye. From the very beginning Quaid-i-Azam strongly supported the Commonwealth: Liaquat Ali Khan and others who have directed the policy of Pakistan right down to the Revolution have been equally convinced of its value. There has, from time to time, been criticism of the obvious reluctance of the Commonwealth countries to intervene in the Kashmir quarrel officially: but there is a general conviction that Pakistan's position has never lacked either sympathy or support in these quarters. President Ayub Khan remains firm in his support of the Commonwealth connection. India and Pakistan, also, have made common cause against

South Africa's *Apartheid* and in favour of the Algerian independence movement. They are alike in their pursuit of world peace—although even there their approaches to the problem are quite different. And for the rest, Pakistan's foreign policy proceeds from assumptions which differ from those of India, and, accordingly, results in completely contrasting actions.

It must be remembered that Pakistan is the largest and most important of all the States which accept Islam as their official creed: and, in common with them she has inherited the political and cultural traditions for which Islam stands. These traditions include the equality of all human souls before God: the conception of world-wide brotherhood between Muslims, regardless of race and colour: the duty of defending the weak against the oppressor: and of succouring the needy: the obligation to sacrifice life itself in a righteous cause. Pakistan, though herself a new country, has stepped naturally into international life with the confidence derived from the enjoyment of the great Islamic heritage of practical experience. Accordingly, in her dealings with other countries, she has never felt the need to be stridently self-assertive, dogmatic, or apologetic: she treats them, great and small, as equals, and expects from them in return acceptance of her own equality of status. She has confidence in her own standpoint, but makes allowance for the standpoint of others without considering herself the sole repository of infallible judgement or of a higher morality.

It is a remarkable tribute to the strength of these Islamic principles that Pakistan has never departed from them. The original pattern of her external relations, which Quaid-i-Azam first outlined and which Liaquat Ali Khan filled in, continues valid today. Unlike India, Pakistan's foreign policy has not been shaped and executed by a single individual statesman: it proceeds from the very core of her being. Her attitude to Communism is clear: she holds it to be a godless philosophy which she cannot tolerate: and she regards Communism in its militant international form as an enemy. Towards Communist countries as such, she bears no ill will: their creed—or lack of it—is a matter for their own judgement, in which she does not claim to interfere: and she is ready to adopt towards them an attitude of 'peaceful co-existence' which is compatible with normal diplomatic relations and with the exchange of goods and services. But she remains suspicious of their probable aspirations to world-domination, which she is determined to resist, whether these aspirations are confined to cultural penetration or include the employment of physical force.

Because Pakistan's outlook is shaped by these clear-cut convictions, she has found no difficulty in aligning herself politically with the Western democracies, whom she regards as entitled to the support of all men who prize freedom to worship God in their own way and to live under the political system which best suits their own needs.

As the principal Islamic Power, Pakistan has always taken a lively interest in the efforts of the Arab States and of the Muslim peoples of the North African seaboard to achieve full independence from any surviving relics of Western colonization. This interest continues to-day, and it is an important factor in shaping her policy. But it has never led her to aspire to leadership among them, or to think of creating a special political *bloc* from among the Muslim countries. The most that she has ever tried to do is to encourage the growth of economic and cultural co-operation between them, while at the same time throwing her international influence into the scales in support of their aspirations to freedom. Thus, while her sympathies are largely in harmony with the ideas of the 'anti-colonial' group of nations, her support of these ideas is discriminating. Her restraint proceeds in part from a characteristically practical appreciation of the difficulty of creating a united front from among countries deeply divided by dynastic and national jealousies, and in part from her perception that Communism is a far greater danger to national freedom and national aspirations in the world today than is the almost defunct 'imperialism' of the Western Powers, which the Arab States of the Middle East and North Africa have selected as their main target of attack. But Pakistan's conviction that in the conflict between the Communist and the non-Communist world, it is the Western Powers which merit her support, does not prevent her from criticizing strongly certain policies which these Powers adopt from time to time in their dealings with the Muslim countries. British, French and American backing of Israel has been attacked by Pakistan on several occasions; the Anglo-French swoop on the Suez Canal stirred Pakistan deeply, in spite of her disapproval of certain features which then characterized President Nasser's policy towards the Western Powers. More lately, President Ayub Khan has been untiring in his efforts to secure recognition from President de Gaulle of the Algerian claim to self-determination and independence, and has accorded recognition to the Algerian Provisional Government,

To Pakistan, a policy of neutralism, such as India has adopted, appears neither practical nor possible for herself. For one thing, the traditions of Islam harmonize pretty well with the old Puritan maxim: 'Fear God: back your friends: keep your powder dry!'—which expresses accurately Pakistan's general outlook. For another, a country which, from the time of her emergence into nationhood, has found herself confronted with the formidable problem of defending the North-West Frontier and the marches of Baltistan and Bajaur against an ever-present risk of armed aggression, has experienced small temptation to undervalue the defensive power of the sword as a deterrent to rash enterprises. Finally, the conviction that Communism, apart altogether from its merits or demerits as an economic pattern, has been magnified by certain groups of those who practise it into a new world-religion, with aspirations to the forced domination of all mankind, has set Pakistan squarely in the anti-Communist camp. There are no Gandhian traditions, there is no pacifist Hindu philosophy, in Pakistan to blunt the edge of her determination to identify herself with the causes which she regards as morally right and politically justifiable, and to defend them, if need be, with all her available resources.

Taking up, as she does, this position, Pakistan finds it logical to make use of territorial alliances of the kind which Mr. Nehru, as we have seen, deprecates so strongly. She first found in the Turkish Republic a natural ally: and following negotiations for commercial and cultural exchanges, a Treaty, embodying the possibility of military co-operation in defence of common interests in the Middle East, was concluded in 1954. Turkey had her own defence arrangements with Iraq: Pakistan concluded a Treaty with Iran: so that the four countries were linked into what, with British participation and American goodwill, became known as the Baghdad Pact, embodying a network of defensive arrangements for the Middle East. When Iraq dropped out after the revolution of 1958, the organization continued in being as the Central Treaty Organization. In 1955 Pakistan joined in the eight-Power South-East Asia Treaty Organization, of which Britain, Australia, New Zealand and the United States are also members. Pakistan's relations with Turkey and Iran are particularly close—the conclusion of the Treaty with Iran, as Mr. Ghulam Mohammad told me with pride and satisfaction in the autumn of 1955, just after ill-health had caused his resignation from the post of Governor-General, establishes her land-link with Turkey, and through Turkey, with the North Atlantic Treaty Organization. It was a natural consequence of these territorial groupings for defensive purposes that in 1954 the Eisenhower administration should have given Pakistan military assistance in the form of arms and equipment under the American Military Security Act. The use of this assistance is specifically limited by the terms of the agreement to purely defensive purposes—a limitation entirely in accordance with the wishes of Pakistan, who has no desire at all to embark upon militaristic adventure.

It is obvious that the foreign policy of Pakistan does not run parallel to the foreign policy of India. Mr. Nehru's object is to keep his country out of the Communist versus non-Communist world grouping, and to pursue, and to encourage others to pursue, a policy of neutralism. Pakistan has thrown in her lot with the Western Powers. If Pakistan had been a distant country, Mr. Nehru, although disagreeing with her policy, could not have made a grievance of it: but Pakistan is both a close neighbour to India, and a co-occupier of the same sub-continent. Even if Indo-Pakistani relations had been of the friendliest possible character, the conflict between the external policies of New Delhi and of Karachi would have embarrassed Mr. Nehru, because Pakistan's policy seems to him to involve one part at least of the sub-continent in military undertakings and alliances which may prove incompatible with his own aim of keeping war away from India at almost any cost. But Indo-Pakistani relations, as we have seen, have from the very beginning been the reverse of friendly: hostilities have broken out in Kashmir and might easily have broken out over the Indus waters dispute, or over any one of half a dozen other controversies which inflame public opinion in both countries.

It is therefore perhaps not unnatural for Mr. Nehru to consider that Pakistan's foreign policy is directed largely against his country, since he regards it as being aimed at gaining outside support for Pakistan in her differences with India, and, in particular, in the quarrel over Kashmir. India views with great suspicion any action by Pakistan which is calculated to improve her relations with other Muslim countries: and has devoted much pains and care to fostering the creation of the Afro-Asian *bloc*, with anti-colonialism as a common platform, to offset any possible grouping of Muslim countries around Pakistan on the basis of religion. Because Pakistan appears as an obstacle to certain Indian plans, particularly in Kashmir, and possibly also on the North-West Frontier, it would appear that Mr. Nehru, with the support of many of his countrymen, has come to regard her as a potential aggressor, and has concentrated the bulk of his available forces, and, more especially, the main weight of his armoured regiments, within striking distance of the Pakistan border. As might have been expected, the Indian Prime Minister took the gravest possible exception to the Eisenhower policy of strengthening Pakistan with American munitions, even though similar supplies would readily have been placed at India's disposal, had she been willing to accept them, as part and parcel of the American aid which has been given so generously to both countries in the economic and technical fields, with the object of enabling them to stand their ground against any outside aggression.

From the analysis which I have already set out of the principles which govern Pakistan's foreign policy, as well as from my personal study and observation, I feel certain that the image which India has built up of Pakistan as an ambitious, restless Power perpetually poised to attack her neighbour, is misconceived. How far this misconception can go was illustrated in December 1961, when India seized Portuguese territory. I was in Western India at the time, and was astonished to encounter a widespread alarm lest Pakistan should intervene to protect Goa by invading India. Strong armoured reinforcements were rushed by India to within striking distance of Lahore; it was rumoured that the border State of Kutch was to be abandoned. There seemed to be no basis whatever for this scare, except that some Pakistani Army manœuvres, planned, as I later discovered, six months previously, were taking place in Sind according to programme. Pakistan had, I soon discovered, no such aggressive intentions. Indeed she made no change in the disposition of her own forces; and behaved with strict propriety in refusing permission for Portuguese troop-carrying planes to refuel in her territory. She even interned in Karachi waters an ammunition-ship and a small war vessel which were bound for Portuguese India when they entered her jurisdiction. As might have been expected, the Pakistani Press commented acidly, with pointed reference to Kashmir, on India's readiness to use force against a weaker neighbour. In the eyes of many people in Pakistan, I found, India's alarm seemed like an attack of bad conscience; but I also found a disposition to wonder if they can rely on India's peaceful intentions when they have the examples of Kashmir and Goa in front of them.

Pakistan's foreign policy has been shaped, not by hostility to India, but in accordance with fundamental principles derived from the Islamic heritage. The pattern of this policy would have been the same even if India had not been unfriendly, because it is governed by Pakistan's outlook on world affairs. She freely acknowledges New Delhi's right to frame Indian foreign policy in accordance with Mr. Nehru's view of India's needs and interests: why, Pakistanis ask, cannot India admit Pakistan's right to act in corresponding fashion? The adoption of a different foreign policy, Pakistan feels, implies no hostility to India: why then should India resent it? Added to which, as Pakistan has frequently pointed out, no country in possession of its senses would even dream of attacking a neighbour whose resources, military, economic and industrial, exhibit the margin of superiority which India enjoys over Pakistan in all three respects.

Pakistan is no more attracted to neutralism than India is attracted to alignment; first because, in her view, both moral and practical considerations impel her to support the Western democracies; and secondly because she does not believe that neutralism really works in face of fanatical conviction, boundless ambition, and tireless energy which inspire the policies of the Communist world. It is unlikely that Pakistan ever cherished the illusion that Communist countries look on the 'uncommitted' nations as anything more than a fruitful field for activities designed eventually to secure their incorporation in the Communist *bloc*: but if she did so, the illusion must have been destroyed in 1955.

Following on the Bandung Conference, when the nations of Asia, under the lead of China, by whom India was momentarily overshadowed, drew up a charter of peaceful co-existence amidst scenes of wild enthusiasm and speeches of brotherly amity, Karachi received— as I have been assured on unimpeachable authority—a private message from Peking. The Chinese People's Government assured the Government of Pakistan that there was no conceivable clash of interests between the two countries which could imperil their friendly relations: but that this position did not apply to Indo-Chinese relations, in which a definite conflict of interests could be expected in the near future. No more cynical expression of *realpolitik* can be imagined: for India and China were closely linked by a treaty of friendship which actually embodied the *panchshila*—the five principles of good neighbourliness—to which Mr. Nehru attaches so much importance as the panacea for all international problems. Moreover, Mr. Chou En-lai and Mr. Nehru had recently exchanged the

most cordial sentiments at Bandung. Whether this message was intended to constitute a *démarche* for the enlistment of Pakistan's sympathies on the side of China in the event of a Sino-Indian clash, I do
not know: if so, it failed. When, some three years later, the clash
came between Delhi and Peking over Chinese oppression in Tibet,
over Chinese incursions beyond the MacMahon Line, and over
Chinese occupation of hundreds of square miles of territory in Indian
possession round Aksai Chin in Ladakh, President Ayub Khan immediately offered Mr. Nehru any support and assistance which Pakistan
could provide, and suggested the formulation of joint plans for the
defence of the sub-continent as a whole against any external aggressor.

The offer was not accepted and thus came to nothing. But it illustrates Pakistan's outlook very clearly. In this outlook, hostility to
India plays no part: President Ayub Khan was influenced only by his
perception of the danger which Communist aggression holds for both
countries. Pakistan herself keeps a most careful guard, as might be
expected, upon her own frontier with Sinkiang: no Chinese encroachment is permitted—and, doubtless for this reason, no encroachment
has ever seriously been attempted. Recently Peking has suggested
negotiations for a boundary delimitation in certain areas of Baltistan
which have not been completely mapped. India has lodged a protest,
on the ground that Pakistan ought not to be in Baltistan at all. But the
Chinese are realists, and are unlikely to pay great attention to the
latest of the numerous protests which New Delhi has entered against
Chinese frontier policy.

The foreign policy of Pakistan, like that of India, runs true to a
carefully-considered outlook on the world; but, again, like that of
India, undergoes from time to time occasional reorientations to meet
changing needs. The Revolutionary Government which came to
power in 1958, while firmly holding to the main principles which have
shaped Pakistan's foreign policy from the beginning, has made certain
adaptations in it which deserve to be noticed. In the first place, President Ayub Khan, who is convinced of the fundamental identity of
interests between Pakistan and India over a wide range of subjects,
has made persistent efforts to improve his relations with Delhi. He
has imparted new energy and purpose to proposals, originally set on
foot from the Pakistan side under a preceding régime, for settling the
recurrent boundary disputes which have been an irritant to both
countries. In East as well in West Pakistan, the frontier has been
rectified by the removal of anomalies and by certain small exchanges

121

of territory; joint parties of Indian and Pakistani surveyors have worked amicably together in aligning the border, assisted by the formulation of sensible 'ground rules' designed to avoid incidents and to remove friction. Good progress has been made in the conclusion of useful commercial agreements: in negotiations over refugee property, and in the initiation of better understanding in a number of other fields. The successful conclusion of the Indus Waters Treaty, which has been described in detail, represents a further, most notable, landmark along the road to more cordial relations: and President Ayub Khan's *démarche* about joint defensive arrangements, although it evoked no response from India, is an earnest of the spirit which shapes Pakistan's attitude. Only over Kashmir has there been no progress to record; and this, unfortunately, is a quarrel so serious in its implications that it could, if not wisely handled, bring to nothing the sincere efforts which Pakistan has been making since 1958 to improve her relations with her neighbour.

The second modification which Pakistan's foreign policy has undergone since 1958 has been an enlargement in the circle of her friends, accompanied by the establishment of more cordial relations with certain countries, such as Egypt, with whom, in the past, misunderstandings had arisen. President Ayub Khan, as Head of State, has greatly extended the range of countries which had been visited by his predecessors; and the value of the personal contacts thus established has already been shown by an increased appreciation of Pakistan's importance among nations who had previously known too little about her. Relations with Japan and with West Germany, to take only two examples, have become markedly cordial. Although President Ayub Khan is deeply suspicious of international Communism, both as an economic creed and as a driving force to inspire aggression, he has been at pains to ensure that Pakistan's relations with Communist countries are entirely correct; he has encouraged them to learn more about his own land, and has accepted from some of them offers of technical assistance in particular fields, such as oil-exploration. The President's frank, genial disposition, and his unstudied directness of speech, inspire confidence wherever he goes; it has been remarked, indeed, that he himself is his country's best ambassador. But the enlargement of the circle of Pakistan's friends, and the growth of a wider understanding of her position and her policy, has not carried with it any weakening of Pakistan's close ties with her allies. Ties of this kind are, however, essentially two-way affairs; and the Revolutionary Government, while showing that Pakistan values them highly, has made it clear that her opinions are entitled to the respect of her friends, and are not to be taken for granted.

With the advent of the Kennedy administration in the United States, certain reorientations took place in American foreign policy which resulted in a substantial increase of the assistance guaranteed to India for her third Five Year Plan, amounting to $2,280 million, together with a tendency in Washington to look with much greater favour on Mr. Nehru's neutralist standpoint as a buttress of democratic Government, based upon Western Parliamentary institutions, in Asia. Pakistan began to feel that her loyal adherence to the Western alliance, which had remained unshaken against all the threats of Soviet Russia at the time of the U.2 incident in 1960, was, by comparison, underestimated; and this feeling was strengthened when the foreign aid which she needed for the fulfilment of her own Second Five Year Plan was forthcoming in measure less generous than she expected, and, in her view, deserved, to the amount only of $320 million. Pakistani opinion was further alienated by a somewhat ill-judged American inquiry about the use of American arms by Pakistan's defence forces in repelling attacks from Afghanistan across the Bajaur border; for the restriction imposed on the use of these arms for purely defensive purposes had in fact been strictly observed. Pakistan felt that if the United States Government insisted upon prior sanction being obtained before such arms are employed at all, an undeserved slight would be cast upon her own good faith, and the Mutual Security Alliance would lose all meaning for her. President Ayub Khan expressed a resentment general among his countrymen when he reminded the United States that if Pakistan's territory is violated, she will deal promptly with the aggressor, and will not waste time putting American arms in cotton-wool first. Fortunately, a great many of these misunderstandings were cleared up in the course of a visit which President Ayub Khan paid to President Kennedy in July 1961. President Ayub Khan's forthright statement of his country's policy and his country's needs made a most favourable impression upon influential sections of American public opinion: it was even remarked that his plain speaking had helped forward the American foreign aid programme. At the end of the visit, a joint communiqué issued by the two Presidents revealed a marked clearing of the atmosphere between their two countries. The United States Government reiterated the pledge given in 1959 that it regards the independence and integrity of

Pakistan as vital to American national interests, and reaffirmed its view of the importance of the existing Mutual Security arrangements. The continuation of American military assistance to Pakistan was guaranteed, and American interest in finding sufficient funds to enable Pakistan to carry out her development programme was specifically affirmed.

Satisfactory as the upshot of President Ayub Khan's American visit was from the point of view of Pakistani-American relations, it had the effect, no doubt completely unintended, of again exacerbating Indian feelings. The President's soldierly bluntness of phrase, particularly about Kashmir, gave considerable offence to Mr. Nehru, who expressed himself with unusual bitterness about what he regarded as an attack upon the whole Indian position. Indian resentment was sharpened by the approval accorded by large sections of the American Press to President Ayub Khan's assertion that because Kashmir belonged to the Kashmiris, they ought to be free to decide their own future; and by the hope which President Kennedy himself expressed that the Kashmir question will be satisfactorily settled. Since, in Indian eyes, the Kashmir question has already been determined finally in India's favour, so that the only point which remains to argue about is when Pakistan will withdraw, American admission that the question is still alive, and American sympathy for President Ayub Khan's espousal of the cause of the Kashmiris, proved somewhat disconcerting to New Delhi, whose wrath, however, was directed not so much against the United States as against Pakistan.

The impression which President Ayub Khan's presentation of the Kashmir case made upon American opinion was by no means effaced by Mr. Nehru's subsequent visit. It was, if anything, deepened by the widespread disapproval evoked in the United States by India's cynical use of armed force to seize Portuguese territory in the subcontinents in December 1961. Many Americans began to feel that if India could override in this way international rights of long standing, her policy in Kashmir perhaps merited more critical examination than that hitherto devoted to it. Could it be, they asked, that India's championship of self-determination and freedom for smaller nations applied only to questions where her own rights and interests were not involved? Although there are many people in the United States who like, and indeed admire, India, a certain uneasiness about her attitude over Kashmir became noticeable when she strained every nerve to obstruct a discussion of Kashmiri affairs in the Security Council early in 1962, and when she refused President Kennedy's suggestion —a suggestion which Pakistan promptly approved in principle—that Mr. Eugene Black, of the World Bank, should be asked to employ as mediator those same 'good offices' which had brought the Indus Waters dispute to a happy solution.

The result has been to confirm the Pakistan Government in its conviction that Indo-Pakistani relations can never be satisfactory, in spite of President Ayub Khan's best endeavours to settle outstanding disputes, until the Kashmiris are given the opportunity of freely deciding for themselves what their political future is to be. Then, and only then, will it be possible for both India and Pakistan to abandon postures of mutual defiance; to group their forces where these are really needed—on the frontiers of the sub-continent—instead of keeping powerful contingents facing each other across the Indo-Pakistani boundary line; and, while agreeing to differ on the pattern of their external understandings, to co-operate effectively, to the great advantage of both, over a wide range of domestic policies.

Chapter 6

INFIRMITY OF PURPOSE

Pakistan has taken shape so recently as an independent State that it is easy today to find men, still active in official, professional, and industrial life, who vividly remember the sense of amazed gratitude to Providence which shaped their thinking when Quaid-i-Azam's campaign was crowned with success. This sense of gratitude was, if anything, strengthened by the survival of Pakistan in face of the pressing dangers and difficulties which fell to be surmounted during the first few months of her existence; but by itself it could not inspire the continued unity of purpose which Quaid-i-Azam's leadership had imposed upon the diverse interests and personalities which came together to make up the new nation. When Quaid-i-Azam died, many Pakistanis have told me, everyone felt that, for the first time, the future had become uncertain. 'Here is the country to which Quaid-i-Azam led us. Now what are we going to do with it? There is no Quaid-i-Azam to guide us!' This uncertainty was all the more serious because of the complex nature of the movement which brought Pakistan into existence.

From earlier chapters, it will have become clear to the reader that there were two principal bodies of opinion among the Muslims of the sub-continent which combined, under Mr. Jinnah's leadership, to create the immense upsurge of political emotion which made Pakistan inevitable. The first, characteristic of the Muslim *élite*, was the determination to achieve a Muslim homeland, a country of their own in which Muslims were to find the opportunities which had so often escaped them in the past because of the superior intellectual agility and traditional social exclusiveness of the Hindu majority. This *élite* was itself made up of a number of elements—landowners, public servants, men of business, politicians, religious leaders—each with particular interests of its own. But, broadly speaking, they shared one common characteristic. They sought no radical changes in the political and social organization to which they had become accustomed under British rule, and, while they realized that the institutions which must be created would have to face some new problems, and might even wear an unfamiliar aspect, they expected the final shape to be neither novel nor startling.

The second body of opinion behind the Pakistan conception was quite otherwise. The masses had rallied to Mr. Jinnah because they were hoping for the creation of an Islamic State. What exactly this would imply in the shape of formal institutions, the masses did not know, and perhaps, did not greatly care: they looked for a polity in which the Islamic ideals of social justice, of benevolent rule, of responsiveness to popular needs, and of the protection of the poor from exploitation, would provide the governing principles of political life and of economic progress. Their hopes were strengthened by Quaid-i-Azam's repeated pronouncements that the future of Pakistan depended upon the ordinary men and women, whose interests must at all times be the main concern of any Government which would be set up. Thus, while it is true to say that the appeal which the idea of Pakistan made to the Muslim masses was largely religious in form, its content was much more social than doctrinal. It was the improvement of their lot that the masses really wanted; although the fact that they hoped to find it through the application of the eternal principles of Islam to their daily life was important politically, as will be seen.

In the campaign for Pakistan, the masses had been roused to an appreciation of the issues at stake by the efforts of political leaders, students, and voluntary workers, all adherents of the Muslim League. But they had also to some extent been rallied by the religious leaders —the *ulema*, the *pirs*, the *maulvis* and the *mullahs*—whose opinions as 'official guides' to Islamic doctrine carried great weight. But this influence, though very powerful at particular times and places—for example, it was the widely-respected Pir of Manki Sharif who helped to secure the defeat of Congress influence in the North-West Frontier Province when the referendum was held in 1947—was collectively less significant than might have been expected because the *ulema* themselves were not unanimous in support of Mr. Jinnah's Pakistan campaign. Some of them held that it was wrong to associate the universalist message of Islam with any projected new State: others believed that, because of the pledges which Mr. Gandhi and Mr. Nehru had given, the interests of the Faith would not suffer in an undivided India. Even so, a considerable number lent their influence in support of the demand for Pakistan.

Mr. Jinnah, himself a modernist in outlook, was very much on his guard against the possibility that in a Muslim State, such as Pakistan would inevitably become, religious fanaticism might prove a dangerous hindrance to political and social reform. He was a convinced opponent of anything resembling what he termed '*mullah* Raj'—that is, a condition of affairs in which the professional exponents of Islamic doctrine are in a position to exploit popular prejudices to obstruct healthy evolution and change. Not long before he died, he went so far as to say that in the Pakistan which was being built up, there ought to be no Muslims and no Hindus, only Pakistani citizens. In proclaiming this enlightened ideal, Quaid-i-Azam displayed a prescience which was characteristic of him: for, as many modern students of Islam will agree, the Muslim divines of the undivided sub-continent had for some time enjoyed throughout the rest of the Islamic world a reputation for ultra-orthodoxy, for a hard-bitten conservatism of outlook, which sometimes resisted, in the name of religion, the operation of that dynamic spirit and continual capacity for fulfilling developing human needs, which are some of the noblest gifts of Islam. True, there were also to be found great and liberally-minded men, who combined profound scholarship with a conviction that Islam is a force for progress and enlightenment; but there were others whose outlook was once picturesquely described to me by no less an authority than a distinguished Rector of Al Azhar—the world-famous Islamic University of Cairo—as being something like that of 'frogs in a well'.

So long as Quaid-i-Azam lived, his immense prestige and the force of his personality kept in control, and even in harmony, these different trends of opinion. To the *élite*, he was not only a national hero, whose will was law: he was also Head of the State, Governor-General, President of the Constituent Assembly, President of the Federal Legislature. To the masses, he was the Great Leader, whose name, like that of Islamic sovereigns of former times, was recited in Khutba after the Friday prayers in the mosques. He commanded their fullest allegiance, he embodied their brightest hopes, his influence surpassed that of any religious leader. But when Quaid-i-Azam died, there was no successor to wield the unquestioned supremacy which he had exercised over the whole nation; and the main elements which had created Pakistan began to draw apart.

In the course of the stringent process of self-examination and 'balancing of accounts' which marked the national mood following the Revolution of 1958, when the effective leadership of President Ayub Khan restored to Pakistan the unity of purpose which she had lacked for a decade, there was a natural tendency to lay at the doors of the *élite* the major share of responsibility for the misfortunes into which the country had fallen. The accusation is broadly true; indeed it can only be wholly denied by those who are interested in defending their conduct of public affairs or in palliating their own mistakes. The hard fact remains that Pakistan was brought to the brink of ruin primarily because the *élite* who were in authority had lost touch with the masses, whose interests were sacrificed because of the prevalence of incompetence, self-seeking, and corruption in governing circles. Yet there are good grounds for believing that the men who controlled Pakistan during the period of her decline were certainly no worse than their 'opposite numbers' who came to power in other newly-liberated countries in South-East Asia; indeed, in many respects they were superior. Under their rule, for all its deficiencies, Pakistan continued to make progress in a wide variety of fields. It was partly their misfortune, as well as their fault, that they forfeited the confidence of their countrymen, and that their shortcomings were publicly exposed with pitiless clarity in a surge of nation-wide indignation.

For it must be remembered that between the death of Quaid-i-Azam in September 1948 and the advent of the Revolutionary Government in 1958, Pakistan lacked a leader of unquestioned national stature. A leader of this kind, since he enjoys the confidence both of the *élite* and of the masses, can make an outstanding contribution both to political stability and to economic progress in any new country. His shoulders are broad enough to sustain, even when circumstances do not permit him to rectify, such blunders as may be made by the men around him without any loss of credit to the régime as a whole. He can commit errors himself with virtual impunity, because the confidence which he enjoys from the nation at large convinces his people that his mistakes are honest ones, and proceed from his single-minded desire to serve his country even at the price of zeal outrunning discretion. It would be difficult, in this connection, to set too high a value on the services which Mr. Nehru, in India, President Nasser, in Egypt, and President Soekarno in Indonesia, have rendered to their respective nations. Apart altogether from the personal contributions which each has made to the progress of his country at home and to the growth of its reputation abroad, all have supplied an element of continuity in government, and of purposeful guidance in policy, which have proved assets of priceless worth, not only in themselves, but because they have dwarfed into insignificance the mistakes which every new régime inevitably commits from time to time.

Pakistan, unfortunately for herself, enjoyed no such advantages. Quaid-i-Azam survived only a year after she came into existence. Liaquat Ali Khan, who continued as Prime Minister, was a man of unquestionable patriotism and great ability, diligent in business, experienced in the management of affairs. During the years when he worked with Quaid-i-Azam, which was the period when I knew him best, the quality in him which most impressed me was his capacity to rise to the ever-increasing responsibilities which Mr. Jinnah allotted to him. But he was essentially Quaid-i-Azam's 'man', accustomed to receive clear guidance, and then to execute with great thoroughness the details of the broad policies which his Leader laid down. In a mature State, his gifts would have enabled him to achieve much greater things; but after September 1948, when he found himself alone, confronted with problems of a complexity which only Quaid-i-Azam could have handled, he seemed to lose something of his former certainty of touch.

The materials available to him in his task of continuing to build up Pakistan at home and abroad were too awkward for a man of his modest, frank and straightforward personality to handle with any hope of success. In the undivided India, comparatively few Muslims had taken any part in public life outside the purlieus of their own Provinces; and the political leaders who now found themselves in Pakistan owed such reputation as they enjoyed to their skill in manipulating local factions and placating local interests. In West Pakistan, a mixture of Punjabis, Pathans, Sindhis and Baluchis, divided into a number of separate Provinces and States, there was hardly a political leader of experience on whom the Prime Minister could depend to take anything wider than a purely local view: the majority were precocupied by the aggrandizement of their local interests. The fact that the great majority were large landowners, highly conservative in outlook, and with axes of their own to grind, added to Liaquat Ali Khan's difficulties in finding supporters of the right kind. In East Pakistan, conditions were different: the population was almost entirely homogeneous, the Hindu element being racially indistinguishable from the Muslim majority. East Pakistan contained some shrewd and experienced politicians who had held office in the old undivided Bengal: the educated classes were politically more sophisticated, and more keenly alive to the realities of public life, than their counterparts in

West Pakistan. But East Pakistan, even while Quaid-i-Azam lived, was becoming resentful of the preoccupation of the Central Government with such typically West Pakistani problems as Kashmir, the North-West Frontier, canal waters, and refugee property. After Quaid-i-Azam died, the East Pakistanis fell into a defensive mood, and firmly directed their main endeavours to the promotion of their claim to rank equally in all respects with West Pakistanis in the distribution of political power and economic privilege.

There was yet another complicating factor in the emerging political life of Pakistan. The outlook of the leaders both in East and West had been mainly conditioned by their experiences in opposition under the British Raj. Their training had been almost entirely in destructive criticism, their relative prominence in public life being determined by the vigour and ingenuity which they could display in attacking the Government of the day. Accordingly, when Pakistan came into being, and there was neither a British Raj to indict as the present, nor a Hindu majority to pillory as the future, enemy, the task of reorientating their outlook into one of constructive co-operation with the government of their new country proved beyond the capacity of many of them. Moreover, although they had been brought up in the tradition of Parliamentary institutions introduced by the British—so much so, indeed, that they could hardly envisage any other system as suitable for Pakistan—this tradition embraced only the negative functions of opposition. They did not possess the sense of public spirit, the habit of disinterested service to their constituents, and the nation-wide breadth of vision, without which the successful operation of Parliamentary democracy as a governmental system is extremely difficult. Nor did they realize that, in the absence of an instructed electorate, this system requires expert, unselfish guidance of the kind they were incompetent to furnish. Inevitably, their instinct was to range themselves in support of personalities rather than of programmes, to split into factional groups, and to change their political allegiances in accordance with the shifting vagaries of their own personal interests.

The various influences which began to shape political life in Pakistan reacted on and were in their turn affected by the position of the new public services. Under the British Raj, Muslim politicians who had held office, or had been in opposition, at the Centre or in the Provinces, had become accustomed to rely upon the public services for a particular type of help. They knew that these services would carry out the policies of the Government of the day with complete fidelity and great diligence: but they also knew that the services could put up a most effective resistance to any attempt at interference with their duties by political pressure. The effectiveness of this resistance lay in the strong *esprit de corps* which the services had developed. It operated to protect individual public servants from corrupt influence, and to instil into each individual a sense of self-respect and an independence of judgement based upon high standards of official integrity. It was not easy to create these standards quickly in a new administrative cadre. Although a Public Services Commission was set up in Pakistan, it worked at first under considerable difficulties. As has been noted in an earlier chapter, the shortage of trained staff inevitably led both to the promotion of some individual officers to positions of responsibility which they were unfitted to occupy, and to the rapid improvisation of new cadres out of the rather poor material which was all that was immediately available. In such circumstances, personal recommendations and political influence played an unduly large part in many of the early appointments.

By degrees, these defects have been remedied: entry into the services became properly regulated, training institutions were set up, and the standards of the 'young entry' into the all-Pakistan cadres, as I saw for myself, became within half a dozen years impressively high. Pakistan was in no hurry to part with such British officials as opted to serve her: she made extensive use of them to train her own young men. Moreover, she took full advantage of the opportunities for overseas training open to her under the Colombo plan: and this type of training has greatly improved the standards, and broadened the outlook, of her public servants of the administrative generation which is now rising to positions of responsibility. But it naturally took time before these excellent young officers were in a position to raise the morale of the services which they were entering by their own competence and keenness. Meanwhile, during the years which immediately followed the death of Quaid-i-Azam, the services as a whole were, by and large, only just beginning to develop the qualities of integrity, devotion to duty, and independence of judgement which the handful of senior men, carrying on the traditions developed under the British Raj, were doing their best to inculcate by influence and example. The result was that during the period of Pakistan's decline, the reputation of the services tended to decline also. They proved over-malleable to political pressure and incapable of holding their own against corrupt influences. The effect upon their own morale was serious: they became slack in the discharge of their duties—for they soon came to find that subservience to authority, rather than conscientious work, opened the door to promotion—and high-handed in their dealings with the public. Moreover, while they were eager to carry out the orders they received from their political superiors, they were often too timid or too incompetent to furnish those superiors with the respectful but firm guidance which it is the duty of the well-trained public servant to supply; and they lacked the skill, so essential in any bureaucratic system, to rectify initial errors and mistakes in the execution of policy before much harm can be done. Thus, while the political leaders were partly responsible for the shortcomings of the public services, these shortcomings in turn constituted a grave handicap to the successful execution of such useful schemes as the political leaders were able to set on foot for the benefit of the country. For while, on the one hand, the politicians obstructed the work of the public services for the sake of vested interests and party advantage, the public services often failed to give the politicians the kind of advice which every Minister has the right to expect—even if he does not follow it. To some extent, therefore, the services came to share the disrepute which the political leaders incurred in public estimation during the years immediately preceding the Revolution of 1958: and one of the first efforts of the Revolutionary Government was directed towards the removal of incompetent and corrupt occupants of official positions, and towards a firm insistence upon the observance of high standards of hard work and integrity as a condition for retaining any post in the public services.

Three or four months after the Revolutionary Government took over control, I remember asking a senior member of the Civil Service of Pakistan how well he thought the rapid and drastic 'purges' of Governmental officials which were being put on hand were operating from the Service point of view. He told me that a Government officer expects his political superior to do three things: to listen carefully: to give due weight to expert advice: to give a clear order at the end. All these three he himself was getting from the new Government, and he was entirely happy working with it. I further questioned him about the dismissals which had taken place—some of them affecting officers in quite high positions. What was the effect upon the morale of the services of the searching inquiries, then being instituted throughout every department by special tribunals, sometimes presided over by a military officer, into the conduct, financial position, past record, and present duties of every 'gazetted' (i.e. formally appointed to a permanent service) officer? These inquiries had already resulted in a short space in the dismissal or demotion of several hundred officials. My informant assured me (and his assurance was later confirmed from a number of other well-informed sources) that there had been no 'witch-hunting': the dismissals, without any exception which he knew of, had been enforced on three grounds only: corruption: lack of proper attention to duties: or failure to observe the long-standing tradition that a civil servant ought to set out his own point of view, and, if overruled by his political superior, should obey: *but*, if he finds that he cannot conscientiously execute the orders given to him, he *must* take one of two courses—either he resigns or requests a transfer to another branch of the service. It was the men who had not possessed the moral courage to act in this way who had been sternly dealt with. His own conclusion was that the feeling throughout the services was one of profound relief that so much 'dead wood' had been cut away: and that they were at last free to get on with their proper work unhindered by the political pressure of vested interests. Yet the very scale of the 'purge' which the Revolutionary Government carried through testifies to the decline which the services themselves had undergone in the general atmosphere of political wire-pulling and corruption which had spread like a miasma through Pakistan between 1951 and 1958.

Chapter 7

CHASING A CONSTITUTION

During the period which immediately followed Quaid-i-Azam's death, there developed a fierce competition for influence, wealth, power and prestige between the various interests and personalities which made up political life. The arena in which this competition first manifested itself was the procedure for framing the constitution which was to give formal expression to Pakistan's polity. It was in this sphere of activity that Quaid-i-Azam's guiding hand was especially missed, because he would have been able, as he had already demonstrated during the twelve months when he directed the destinies of the nation, to enforce upon all the interested parties a due sense of proportion; to moderate excessive demands and selfish aspirations; and, above all, to convince the *élite* that the drawing up of a constitution, important as it was, represented only one of a number of tasks which the nation must quickly undertake. As a foreign visitor to Pakistan, I was often startled by what seemed to me the obsessive preoccupation of many of my Pakistani friends with quite small details involved in the process of constitution-making, which engrossed their interest, as it seemed to me, to the exclusion of matters at least equally, and probably more, important for the welfare of the country. Whenever I came to Pakistan in the years prior to 1958, I felt that a wholly disproportionate share of the national brains and energy were being devoted to the job of working out a constitution, while other problems were being relegated to a secondary position.

Few of my Pakistani friends seemed to realize that no constitution can be of much use unless it suits the needs of the people of the country; and this, it appeared to me, was among the least regarded of the criteria which were being applied. What counted for far more with my friends was how power was to be divided between the Centre and the Provinces and between East and West Pakistan: how far the shape of a modern State could be squared with the principles of Islam: and how the different competing interests—landlords, reli-

135

gious leaders, business men, industrialists—could receive recognition of their claim to power and influence. I myself was constantly struck by the sobering thought that no constitution, however perfect on paper, is better than the men who work it: I did not think that many of the then political leaders really measured up to the responsibilities which faced them. What was perhaps the worst consequence of this single-minded concentration upon constitution-making was that it quickly opened a gulf between the *élite* and the masses. While the political and religious leaders wrangled, and struck bargains with each other, the masses remained largely uninterested: so that the circle in which political life was lived grew more and more specialized and self-contained, less and less representative of the interests of the country as a whole. And since this political circle was, in the main, highly urbanized, public attention, as reflected in the Press and from the platform, paid small heed to the problems of the countryside, in which nine out of every ten Pakistani men and women actually lived. Thus, the political leaders, of West and of East Pakistan alike, came to live in a kind of artificial gold-fish bowl of their own creating, which distorted their sense of values, and fixed their attention, not upon the needs of the country, but on competition for power, influence and the spoils of office.

The details marking the various phases of this political free-for-all were represented by those who participated in it as matters of epoch-making national importance: but when the definitive story of the rise and progress of Pakistan comes to be written they will, I think, provide very little that is of permanent interest. There are excellent books of reference in which the main phases of this process, and, in particular, the battle-royal which raged for some time between the religious-minded divines and the secularly-minded politicians, can be followed. It was noticeable that most of the domestic news about Pakistan which reached the outside world after the assassination of Liaquat Ali Khan in 1951 dealt with the successive failures to frame a constitution which would please everybody, and with the game of political 'ins' and 'outs' which was played within a narrow circle of participants. Since I am not writing a formal history of Pakistan, but only setting down my personal impressions of the course of events, I shall deal summarily with these constitutional developments during the decade which elapsed between the death of Quaid-i-Azam and the emergence of the Revolutionary Government.

When Quaid-i-Azam died, he could, in the nature of things, leave no real successor; but Liaquat Ali Khan who, as we have seen, continued as Prime Minister, inherited some share of his Leader's prestige, and remained in office until his assassination in 1951. But the nation-wide authority which Quaid-i-Azam had exercised disappeared just at the moment when it was most needed to sublimate regional and personal jealousies into a sustained effort for the common good. Before he died, Quaid-i-Azam had delivered a series of stern warnings against the dangers which 'provincialism'—partisanship for West or East Pakistan regardless of the merits of the issues at stake—held for the future of the nation; and it was this spirit of partisanship which haunted and frustrated Liaquat Ali Khan throughout his term of office. His power depended upon the support of the Muslim League, and upon his ability to retain a working majority in the Constituent Assembly which also functioned as a legislature. In the Assembly, East Pakistan, because of its numerical preponderance, held a majority of seats: and almost the first thing that Liaquat Ali Khan had to do was to placate East Pakistani opinion by securing the appointment of Khwaja Nazimuddin, Chief Minister of East Pakistan, as Governor-General. This appointment marked the beginning of a convention, which was broadly observed until the Revolution of 1958, that when the Prime Minister comes from West Pakistan, the Head of the State should be an East Pakistani, and vice versa. But it also marked the inception of a period when the jealousies between East and West Pakistan had to be recognized, often at the cost of the national interest, by any Prime Minister who wanted to retain his office.

Liaquat Ali Khan enjoyed one advantage which none of his successors were to possess; his personal position, as the man upon whom a portion at least of Quaid-i-Azam's mantle had fallen, was too strong to be challenged. But this position was no longer decisive in the execution of policy. The new Governor General, a man universally loved and respected for his gentle character and unaffected piety, confined himself to the discharge of the honorific functions which fall to a Head of State: he accepted, in entirely constitutional fashion, the recommendations of the Prime Minister, but he could give him no real help. Liaquat Ali Khan remained very much alone, thrown upon his own resources. This was the more unfortunate because he had inherited from Quaid-i-Azam a Cabinet containing some personalities potentially more forceful than his own. Quaid-i-Azam, who had picked these men for their ability, could control them. He presided over

Cabinet meetings, as I have been told by men who were present, with the unchallenged authority of a benevolent dictator: no one dared to question his decisions. But Liaquat Ali Khan could not do this; some of his colleagues were too forceful and too ambitious to accept his sensible, self-effacing advice. He fell back upon the plan of settling issues by majority voting—a thing unheard of in Quaid-i-Azam's time—and not infrequently failed to convert his colleagues to his own way of thinking. Some of his Ministers began to form their own groups of supporters in the Assembly; and even to communicate their own views to the Press, when these differed from majority opinion in the Cabinet, upon such controversial matters as whether Pakistan should follow India's example in devaluing the rupee in 1950-1.

All this considerably hampered the Prime Minister in his task of consolidating the work which Quaid-i-Azam had begun, and weakened the prestige of the Central Government throughout the country at large. This was serious, because, in the absence of a strong Centre, the efficiency of the administration was bound to suffer. East Pakistan, though in a jealous and resentful mood towards Karachi, was at least a single homogeneous unit, badly handicapped, it is true, by the gaps in many branches of political, administrative, professional and commercial life resulting from the Hindu exodus, but with possibilities of rapid recovery. East Pakistan was already demanding full regional autonomy, drastic limitations upon the powers of the Central Government, and complete recognition of the claims of Bengali to rank as a national language alongside Urdu. The real root of the trouble was largely economic: under the British Raj, East Bengal had been relatively undeveloped, and there was so much leeway to be made up that the East Pakistanis did not trust a Central Government located in Karachi to do all that was needed. West Pakistan, a mixture of races, was broken up into a number of units—three Governor's Provinces, one Chief Commissioner's Province, a number of States, and certain tribal areas—each controlled by local leaders determined to maintain their own authority by any means they could devise, regardless of the real interests of the country as a whole. In order to achieve their ends, they lobbied in the Central Assembly, combined into temporary alliances, intrigued against their rivals, and sought to obtain protection for their interests by pressing for particular constitutional safeguards. Cutting across many of these territorial, regional and personal jealousies were the controversies based upon doctrinal grounds, centring upon the problem of reconciling the basic principles of Islam with the requirements of a modern State.

The task of framing a constitution which would hold the balance even between these various interests, and would at the same time meet the real needs of the population as a whole, proved almost impossible to accomplish; and such progress as the First Constituent Assembly was able to achieve in seven years was largely due to concentration upon the first rather than upon the second, objective. The truth, as plainly appears when the activities of this Assembly are considered retrospectively, is that its constitution-making functions were incompatible with its functions as a provisional legislature whose majority support was essential to the survival of the Government of the day. The debates, the proceedings of the various committees, sub-committees, and boards of experts were treated at the time as matters of supreme public interest. They still fascinate foreign and indigenous students of constitutional theory. But, in the event, all this labour came to little, because in 1954, just when the Assembly, after infinite trouble, intrigue, compromise, and bargaining, had produced a draft constitution, which placated many interests and made substantial concessions to the demands of the religious groups, the political functions which represented the other side of its dual role brought it into conflict with the Governor-General of the day, Mr. Ghulam Mohammad, who dissolved it on the grounds that it had lost the confidence of the people. Since it had for a long time represented nothing but the interests of those who happened to compose it, Mr. Ghulam Mohammad was probably correct in his estimate.

From the protracted, and not uninteresting, legal controversy over the Governor-General's powers and functions which followed, the finding emerged that only a new Constituent Assembly could frame a constitution; and that it must also, for the period of its life, function as a Legislature. The one solid conclusion which survived from all the labours of the First Constituent Assembly was that there should be parity in representation between East and West Pakistan in the new body. The assent of the Bengali leaders to this arrangement, which ignored weightage of population in the interests of practicability, was gained by the promise of the restoration of Parliamentary government—which had been suspended by the Governor-General in 1954 on grounds of public safety—to East Pakistan. The new Assembly, like the first, was indirectly elected by members of the provincial legislatures. It differed from its predecessor in two important respects: it consisted mainly of 'professional' politicians: and its members were sharply divided into more than half a dozen separate groups, of which the Muslim League was still the largest, but without an absolute majority.

As a constitution-making body, the new Assembly did better than the old one, from whose immense legacy of reports, memoranda and conclusions it profited. It began work in July 1955 and presented a draft constitution in January of the following year. This was finally passed in February 1956, but was never, in fact, put into complete operation. As a scheme to be judged *in vacuo*, this 1956 Constitution possesses distinct merit. It is an able compromise between the various interests which make up the nation: and it builds upon the positive provisions of Islamic doctrine instead of dwelling upon the negative probabilities of conflict between the secular and the religious spheres. The real difficulty is that it assumes a higher level of political sophistication than the people of Pakistan at present possess: and had it been put into effect, it would almost certainly have enabled the then existing defects in political life to perpetuate themselves indefinitely. The Second Constituent Assembly did, however, make two important contributions to the final shaping of Pakistan. Acting on the principle that the Head of an Islamic State must be a Muslim, and probably influenced in some degree by the decision to adopt republican institutions which had been taken by India in 1949–50, the Assembly declared in favour of Pakistan being constituted an Islamic Republic inside the Commonwealth—a decision duly carried into effect in March 1956 with the cordial good will of Pakistan's fellow-members.

The second important change affected by the new Assembly was the passing in September 1955 of a measure designed to merge the various territorial units which made up West Pakistan into a single Province, with an executive and a legislature exercising authority over the whole area. Many people had for some time been pressing for this kind of arrangement, which would simplify the make-up of Pakistan by creating a unified Western wing as the counterpart of an already homogeneous Eastern wing. I learned from Liaquat Ali Khan that Quaid-i-Azam had thought of this, but had died before he could do anything about it. Liaquat Ali Khan himself favoured it, but, daunted by the formidable vested interests which opposed it, put the idea aside for the time. He too died before he could tackle the problem. It had now become a logical consequence of the principle, already recognized, of parity of representation between the two parts of the country. But there were many people, whose personal position would be affected, to put up strenuous opposition. Mr. Ghulam Mohammad, as Governor-General, was so convinced that unification was essential to the best interests of the country as a whole, that at the end of 1954 and the beginning of 1955, he tried to achieve it by purely executive action. He was defeated, because of legal obstacles pointed out by the Federal Court. The decision of the Assembly in favour of unification, which was the result of a good deal of wire-pulling and political bargaining, strengthened his hand, and the plan was eventually put into execution in the teeth of a good deal of opposition. When I toured West Pakistan in 1955, I found that most of the officials were heartily in favour of unification, partly on administrative grounds, and partly because they thought that it would reduce the numbers of self-seeking politicians with whom they would have to reckon. Pathan opinion was, on the whole, doubtful, but felt Lahore, the seat of the new unified Government, would be nearer than Karachi for people who wanted to get into touch with higher authorities. Bitter feeling however survived; those whose personal interests had suffered in the process of rationalizing and abolishing redundant posts and institutions remained still unreconciled when the Revolutionary Government came into power; they thickened the prevailing atmosphere of axe-grinding and political intrigue.

Unfortunately, the new arrangement, logical as it undoubtedly was, did little to curb the self-seeking of the local political leaders. Unification concentrated power and influence in Lahore. Since the stakes were higher, and the prizes larger, competition for power became fiercer than ever. Adult suffrage, which increased the influence of quasi-feudal interests because of the power of a landlord to dragoon his tenants into voting for his nominee, soon made the new West Pakistan Legislature a byword for political intrigue. Nor were things any better in East Pakistan, where in 1958 partisan fury between rival factions reached such heights that the Speaker of the Legislative Assembly was attacked, and his Deputy so badly beaten up that he afterwards died. The General Officer then commanding in East Pakistan told me himself, a year or two afterwards, that the Deputy Speaker actually rang him up from the Assembly building and begged for military protection. When the General said that he could not send troops unless the Government of East Pakistan asked for them, the unfortunate man replied: 'But it is the Government's men who are trying to kill me—*they* will never send for you!' A few moments later, the Deputy Speaker received the terrible injuries from which he later died in hospital. It is hardly to be wondered at that by 1958, the masses in East and West Pakistan had become thoroughly disgusted by the behaviour of the politicians who controlled their destinies: indeed, on the North-West Frontier, to call a man a 'politician' had become an insult only to be wiped out in blood.

So far as the framing of the constitution went, the first and second Constituent Assemblies were able to show some results; further, as we have seen, they made definite contributions to the shape of present-day Pakistan. But in their capacity as legislative bodies, their record cannot be considered a worthy one. The members were, broadly speaking, incapable of making sacrifices of personal ambition and factional advantage: they lived a narrow life, cut off from the needs and aspirations of the common people, and paying inadequate attention to the interests of the country at large. They were elected by constituencies consisting of the local legislatures, themselves a prey to faction, intrigue and vested interests. A sidelight upon how these local legislatures were themselves elected can be obtained by talking to the Heads of Universities and other educational institutions in East and West Pakistan. The student community were assiduously wooed by politicians of all persuasions, who found them invaluable for canvassing, distributing bribes, and intimidating electors by organized hooliganism. Import licences worth thousands of rupees in the market were given to students who could influence their fellows: in every College and University, student political organizations, headed by self-styled 'Cabinets', controlled the activities of the student community, and mobilized them in favour of the party which bribed most heavily. The effect of practices such as these upon the students themselves can be imagined; discipline disappeared: the teaching staff lost all authority: even the conduct of examinations was interfered with by political leaders wishing to curry favour with students: the whole functioning of the system of higher education was disrupted by rottenness and corruption.

In the countryside, things were no better: the electors were terrorized by their landlords' agents or by bands of hooligans recruited and paid by some ambitious local notable: the secrecy of the ballot was continually violated by corrupt supervision: a candidate who saw that he was losing would hire ruffians to burn the ballot-boxes or wreck the polling-booth, To recruit its adherents, and to swell Party funds, the Governments of the day, in West as well as in East Pakistan, in the Centre as well as in the provinces, would create monopolies as a reward for political services, and unblushingly accept bribes from interested parties.

Smuggling grew to the proportions of an industry, carried on by highly organized rings with influential protection. In East Pakistan, the illicit exchange of food for manufactured articles flourished. When offenders were caught, they were freed by 'influence', and the police were so discouraged that they became apathetic. In West Pakistan, the illicit import of gold took place on a colossal scale. The Preventive Services knew all about it, but were helpless—the smugglers were too well protected by politicians who shared their profits. Tax evasion was practised almost as a matter of course: wealthy men knew that judicious bribery could postpone prosecution indefinitely.

It took some time for these practices to develop fully, but when they began to flourish, there was nothing and nobody to stop them. The permanent officials, especially those with traditions inherited from the British Raj, were reduced to impotence: they were hampered at every turn by political interference. Some of the men I had known in the old days could not tolerate this state of affairs: they resigned. Others sought transfers to posts where they could do an honest administrative job because no financial stakes, such as alone interested the politicians, were involved. Yet others bowed to the storm, and tried to console themselves with the reflection, that if they departed, their places would be filled by men with no standards of honesty at all. Such things were openly talked about: an atmosphere of complete cynicism prevailed. To their everlasting credit, some of the most respected figures in public life, including more than one leading industrialist, withdrew altogether from politics because they found the atmosphere of intrigue and corruption too stifling to be endured. In name, it should be noticed, provision for remedial action did, in fact, exist. Legislative penalties for corruption, including fine, imprisonment, and disqualification from holding public office for varying periods were solemnly inscribed upon the statute book; but it lay with the Government of the day to invoke them; and since it was generally the Government of the day which stood to profit most from corrupt practices, retributive action was very rare. Plainly, legislative bodies whose members were swayed so largely by their private interests, and were so susceptible to corrupt manipulation, were of very little use to the country, and, indeed, to anyone at all except to those who found political life an exceedingly lucrative pursuit under the conditions prevailing in the years immediately prior to the Revolution of 1958. The public knowledge—for the thing was no secret—that leading figures in the Second Constituent Assembly had made adequate arrangements, by bribing, bargain-fixing, and promise of future favour, to ensure their success in the General Election to be held early in 1959; and the resulting conviction that under the new constitution the corrupt cabals in political circles would be in a position to perpetuate their power, was an influential factor in rallying public opinion in support of the drastic action by which the Revolutionary Government achieved the purification of political life from some of its worst elements.

A view of the weaving section of the Adamjee Jute Mill at Narayanganj

The spillway of the Kaptai Dam

A bathing *Ghat*, East Pakistan

On the Karnafuli River

Chapter 8

POLITICAL RECORD

I t is now time to look at some of the personalities who influenced the destinies of the country between the death of Quaid-i-Azam and the vesting of supreme authority in President Ayub Khan.

Liaquat Ali Khan's wisdom and patience, though they could not impose harmony upon the divergent interests which confronted him, had at least kept political life reasonably reputable so long as he lived. But his very moderation, and his refusal to be stampeded into rash courses, offended some extreme sections of opinion. His determination to seek a peaceful solution of the Kashmir dispute; his negotiations with Mr. Nehru over the protection of religious minorities and the resettlement of the refugees; his eagerness to rationalize Indo-Pakistani relations in the interests of both countries—all these things offended hotheads and religious fanatics. In 1951 a small group of Army officers, following the example of what had happened in Egypt, plotted to overthrow the civil Power, and, with help from a Communist country, to set up a military dictatorship. The plot was discovered, the conspirators were arrested and put on trial: public security was at no time endangered. But the Rawalpindi Conspiracy Case, as it was called, showed once again how greatly the guiding hand of Quaid-i-Azam was missed. In a young country, it is not sufficient to appeal to reason; the emotions too must be engaged if there is to be national unity. This, Liaquat Ali Khan, in spite of all his many admirable qualities, was unable to achieve: it was private enmity based upon religious fanaticism which seems to have caused his assassination in October 1951. There were ugly rumours at the time that political rivals might have plotted to remove him; but the most searching inquiries, culminating in a protracted investigation conducted by an expert loaned by Scotland Yard, failed to connect the individual assassin with any group or interest in political circles.

Liaquat Ali Khan's death was an enormous misfortune for Pakistan, not only because he was the last real link with Quaid-i-Azam, and, as a 'landless' refugee, stood in an impartial position between

Punjabi and East Pakistani interests, but because his great political wisdom and long experience could not be bequeathed to any successor. The choice of the Cabinet fell upon Khwaja Nazimuddin, the Governor-General, as Prime Minister. Ghulam Mohammad, who had been Finance Minister from the earliest days of Pakistan, was selected as Governor-General. He had undergone a long training in financial affairs, and had come to enjoy a considerable reputation among experts from the skill which he had displayed in balancing successive budgets, in finding money for important long-term projects, and in obtaining financial support for the economic development of Pakistan from the United States as well as from Commonwealth countries. He was a man of great force of character, impulsive, and with flashes of brilliance, fighting with enormous courage against enfeebled health. He had ideas on what Government policy ought to be in almost every branch of the administration—I have listened for hours, fascinated, while he expounded his ideas at length, in his husky voice, pathetically impaired by illness; and I never left his presence without a renewed respect for his foresight and 'drive'. If he could, he would have liked to exercise throughout East and West Pakistan the kind of power, overriding local authority, which had characterized Quaid-i-Azam's tenure of the office which he now held; but during Liaquat Ali Khan's term as Prime Minister and Khwaja Nazimuddin's term as Governor-General, the relative importance of the two positions had been altered: it was now the Prime Minister who counted most.

Ghulam Mohammad thought that this was a mistake: he believed that Pakistan needed strong leadership from the top by a Head of State who, because he was independent of all party ties and affiliations, could afford to ignore everything but the interests of the nation at large. He determined to take as active a part as possible in shaping policy, and to secure, so far as he could, Prime Ministers and Cabinets who would fall in with his ideas. Himself a fervent patriot, he suspected the loyalty of a good many East Pakistani leaders, believing them to be more concerned with the interests of their own part of the country than with the well-being of Pakistan as a whole. He was for this reason disliked in East Pakistan; and among his own Punjabi people he was respected and feared rather than loved. He therefore stood a good deal alone: and preferred to act on his own judgement. Many scholars who have written about constitutional developments in Pakistan have been, I think, a little unfair to him because he overrode incipient Parliamentary conventions and had little patience with institutions and persons who opposed him: but he was no self-seeker, and he did his best to serve his country well.

Khwaja Nazimuddin did not make a good Prime Minister, because he proved too modest to trust his own judgement and to impose his will on other people. Official business fell badly in arrears: he could not make up his mind to pass definite orders. He permitted interested persons to take advantage of his unsuspecting nature; for example he allowed import licences to be granted more freely than was consistent with the need for conserving, and turning to good purpose, the foreign exchange accumulated during the Korean War by the high Pakistani rupee. In purely political affairs he was fairly active, and exerted himself to see that East Pakistan did not feel neglected. In so doing, he offended Punjabi interests; and some leading personalities in the Punjab, hoping to exploit his piety and well-known deference to religious opinion, began to raise an agitation early in 1953 against Sir Zafrullah Khan, his very able Foreign Minister, who adhered to the Ahmadiya sect, which is abhorent to the orthodox. The Punjab Government stood aside while certain religious leaders aroused the fanaticism of the mob against the Ahmadiyas, demanding their condemnation as heretics. Serious rioting broke out.

Khwaja Nazimuddin first tried to use his influence with the *ulema* to secure pronouncements disclaiming the agitation. He hesitated to take more drastic action, even when the Chief Minister of the Punjab telephoned to say that Lahore was in the hands of the mob and would soon be in flames. Fortunately, the Central Government's Defence Secretary, Iskander Mirza, whose name and earlier exploits have been mentioned on preceding pages, made up the Prime Minister's mind for him by telling him that the Army could clear up the trouble in a few hours. Khwaja Nazimuddin agreed to let the Army try, and order was restored almost immediately. The local military commander, General Azam Khan, whom we shall meet again later in this narrative as Minister of Reconstruction in the Revolutionary Government, and later as Governor in East Pakistan, made a great name for himself, even outside professional military circles, for the tact, humanity and firmness with which he had handled an ugly situation. The contrast between the fumbling uncertainty displayed by the civil authorities and the calm, good-tempered efficiency of the military, made a deep impression on public opinion both inside and outside the Punjab— and, indeed, on Mr. Ghulam Mohammad himself. Furthermore, the danger of fomenting religious intolerance became very clear to everyone, so that the influence of some of the more extreme *ulema* was lessened.

The Governor-General, who had long been dissatisfied with the capacity of the Prime Minister to cope with his duties, took the opportunity to dismiss him. Khwaja Nazimuddin had strong Bengali support, and still commanded a majority in the Legislature. But in face of Ghulam Mohammad's determination, opposition collapsed, and his nomination of another East Pakistani, Mohammad Ali of Bogra, as Prime Minister went through in April 1953. The new Prime Minister, an experienced diplomatist, with great social gifts, was perhaps as surprised as anyone by his own appointment. He had been Ambassador in Burma, and High Commissioner in Ottawa; he was actually on leave from the Pakistan Embassy in Washington when the Governor-General called him to his new position. He was determined on securing a good position for East Pakistan out of the constitutional wrangles in the Constituent Assembly but did not remedy the plight into which the country was falling; and although he was successful in cementing very cordial relations between Pakistan and the United States—a land for which he had a sincere affection—he achieved little of note in other directions. He possesses a lively mind: for example, he proposed to bring Pakistan into line with many other countries by following the American rule of the road. I could not find out whether the new rule was ever put into force on any scale; but I was assured that it was quickly defeated by the passive opposition of the camels and bullocks—still a mainstay of Pakistan's local transport—who caused chaos by refusing to do other than take their accustomed left-hand track when meeting oncoming traffic. He resigned in 1955 and before long resumed his useful diplomatic career. In 1962 he was elected to the National Assembly and re-entered the Cabinet as Foreign Minister.

It was during the Prime Ministership of Mohammad Ali of Bogra that Governor-General Ghulam Mohammad, learning that the first Constituent Assembly was trying to limit his powers, and was proposing to perpetuate in the new constitution the division of West Pakistan into a number of units, dismissed it, as we have already seen, in October 1954. There followed the legal quarrel mentioned on a previous page, and the reappointment by the Governor-General of the Prime Minister with a hand-picked Cabinet which included Major General Iskander Mirza and General Ayub Khan. Major-General Iskander Mirza had been sent as Governor to East Pakistan by the Governor General: he was now recalled to be Minister of the Interior.

General Ayub Khan, then Commander-in-Chief—the first Pakistani to attain that rank—was not interested in politics, but agreed, on Mr. Ghulam Mohammad's insistence, to join the Cabinet as Minister of Defence. He found the political atmosphere which surrounded him uncongenial, and soon returned to military duty. Mr. Ghulam Mohammad was in very poor health, and had begun to despair of the possibility of putting things right in the country while political life remained as it was. In a moment of depression, remembering how effectively the Army had intervened to restore order in Lahore at the time of the anti-Ahmadiya riots, he suggested to General Ayub Khan that the Army should take control over the whole of Pakistan. True to the principles which he has later maintained as President, General Ayub Khan refused: he felt that there was no such national emergency at that time as could justify the supersession of the civil power. If Mr. Ghulam Mohammad's illness had not sapped his vigour, he might have done a good deal for the country, for he took a serious view of the situation, and was prepared to impose drastic measures of reform. But in August 1955 he became so enfeebled that he had to give up all official duties, and Major-General Iskander Mirza became Acting-Governor-General, in which office he was subsequently confirmed in October 1955. Ghulam Mohammad lingered on for some months. A broken man physically, his intellect was clear to the end, and he retained all his old interest in public affairs. Only a short time before his death in August 1956, I had a long talk with him, and found him delighted with the newly-established cordial relations between his country and Iran, but deeply unhappy about the persistence of corruption in public life at home. It will be a long time before his work is forgotten.

Major-General Iskander Mirza too, is certain of an important place in the history of his country, although there will be differences of opinion about precisely what that place should be. His early career had marked him out for great things: he was among the very first batch of young Indian officers to be commissioned from Sandhurst. Seconded from military duties into the Political Service under the British Raj, he built up a steadily-growing reputation for resourcefulness and ability in that most testing of all fields, the North-West Frontier. His adroitness in confusing opponents by playing one off against the other, and getting his own way in the end, became proverbial. When Pakistan came into being, he was already one of the most experienced political officers at the disposal of the new Government, and was quickly selected for positions of greater and greater responsibility. For many years he had done no regimental duty, and his outlook had become more that of the permanent official than of the soldier. It was his advice, as Defence Secretary, which had persuaded Prime Minister Nazimuddin to sanction effective action against the Lahore rioters: and Mr. Ghulam Mohammad, who had a high opinion of him, had no hesitation in sending him to East Pakistan to rule as Governor when constitutional government was suspended because of political chaos and threatened administrative collapse. Iskander Mirza, unhampered by a local Cabinet and Assembly, exercised full powers over all branches of the administration. He did a magnificent job, restoring public confidence, reforming the administration, and bringing order out of chaos. He coped energetically with floods, epidemics and famine; and was the first high official to travel by helicopter over flooded country, to see the situation for himself, and to land in isolated areas in order to supervise personally the mass-inoculation of the people against cholera and other water-borne diseases.

A warm-hearted man of great social gifts, an excellent sportsman, and a generous host, Iskander Mirza lived every moment of life with zest, and won many warm friendships. He showed himself to be an administrator rather than a statesman, dealing efficiently with difficulties as they arose, but making few long-range plans. The exercise of administrative power appealed to him: he preferred doing things to talking about them. In East Pakistan, the muddle which he found reinforced the very poor opinion which he had formed in West Pakistan about the suitability of existing Parliamentary institutions to serve the real needs of the country; and when he was recalled from Dacca to become Minister of the Interior in 1954, he began publicly to voice his conviction that religion and politics ought to be kept quite separate, and that some sort of 'controlled' democracy—that is, presumably, an executive appointed for a fixed term and not dependent for its existence on a shifting and uncertain Parliamentary majority—was the best form of polity to aim at. These ideas did not, of course, please the members of the Constituent Assembly: and Iskander Mirza found that if he wanted to put them into operation, he would have to do things for himself. Soon after he became acting Governor-General, the Prime Minister, Mohammad Ali Bogra, lost the support of the Muslim League Parliamentary Party, and resigned. The League elected as leader Chaudhri Mohammad Ali, a permanent Civil Servant, who, after some hesitation, had lately taken the great plunge of entering political life. Mr. H. S. Suhrawardy, a most experienced politician, considered that he had received an undertaking that he would be invited to form a Government pledged to carry through the final stages of the unification of West Pakistan; but the Governor-General preferred Chaudhri Mohammad Ali, who became Prime Minister in August 1955.

Chaudhri Mohammad Ali, a very fine type of Civil Servant, had done admirable work as Cabinet Secretary and as Finance Minister. His patriotism, integrity and ability were alike unchallengeable. I had a long talk with him quite soon after he became Prime Minister, and I found the clarity of his ideas impressive. He was convinced, he said, that his most urgent task was to unify West Pakistan. It would then be possible to found a federal constitution upon an equitable division of power between the East and West wings. This was the next thing to be done. When once that had been settled, it would be possible to go ahead with other urgent matters—the raising of living standards, the adjustment of relations with India, the settlement of the Kashmir problem.

On this last question, he spoke with great but controlled emotion: India, he said, was doing a dreadful thing in trying to prevent, partly by force and partly by bribery, a nation of three or four million souls from determining their own political destiny. I could see that he was not only moved by the plight of the Kashmiri people; he was also alarmed lest desperation should drive them to throw in their lot with the Communist countries. More than once, in our talks, he mentioned his hopes of building up Pakistan's social services on a sound economic foundation, and of transforming village life by the steady encouragement of enlightened self-help. He thought that by entering political life, he would be better able to achieve all these things than if he had remained a Civil Servant, however highly placed. His plan, he said, was to deal openly with everyone, to put all his cards on the table, and to base his policy on stark facts. No one, I think, could help liking as well as respecting him: but I left him with some uneasy queries in my mind. Was he not naïve in assuming that a constitution, however perfect on paper, would really help the country forward so long as it would be worked by the kind of men already in political life? It seemed to me, too, that his own political ideas had been so profoundly influenced by his experience of Parliamentary institutions of the type introduced during the British Raj that he was quite unable to conceive of any other system, or to judge impartially whether such institutions were really suited to Pakistani conditions. Further, I doubted if he possessed the toughness, resilience, and imperiousness to hold his own in the cut-throat game of Pakistani politics. He had always borne the reputation of working himself almost to death: he looked frail. How would he sustain the physical strain of his duties as Prime Minister?

When I compared him with Major-General Iskander Mirza, Chaudhri Mohammad Ali, for all his great ability, appeared inexperienced in the handling of men. The ideas of the Governor-General and the Prime Minister, as has been shown, were quite different: Chaudhri Mohammad Ali was a convinced constitutionalist: Major-General Iskander Mirza was very dubious about the prospects for Parliamentary institutions of any kind in Pakistan. Even so, the country expected great things from this combination of two trained administrators in the highest positions: it was hoped that the influence of the professional politicians would be lessened and that more attention would be paid to the real needs of the people by suppressing corruption, undertaking agrarian reform, and promoting economic development. In effect, not much was done in these directions. The Governor-General proved expert at dividing his opponents, and thus obtaining a free hand to deal with the administrative problems—such as that of maintaining law and order in restless East Pakistan—which mainly interested him. The Prime Minister, preoccupied in steering his plans through the opposition which he encountered, found himself obliged to meet the intrigues which confronted him with combinations of his own.

The two men worked together not too badly from August 1955 to September 1956, during which period Chaudhri Mohammad Ali's Government successfully unified West Pakistan and induced the Assembly, as we have already noticed, to accept and ratify the draft of the constitution of the Islamic Republic of Pakistan. Neither result was easily achieved: the bargaining and the 'deals' necessary to reconcile the various interests really wore the Prime Minister out. A new Republican Party came into existence to support Dr. Khan Sahib, who was selected as Chief Minister of the unified province of West Pakistan, against a section of the Muslim League which opposed the appointment of a Pathan. Chaudhri Mohammad Ali resigned because he was uncertain about the support he could command, in spite of the efforts of General Iskander Mirza, who had become President of the Islamic Republic in March 1956, to persuade him to continue in office.

Then followed a Ministry which seemed at one time to promise well—that of H. S. Suhrawardy. He had long experience of political life, and knew how to direct Party affairs. More important, he was quite prepared to work with the President; and the two made an exceedingly strong combination. General Iskander Mirza helped Mr. Suhrawardy to carry through the principle of voting by joint electorates (this is, Muslims, Hindus and other minorities on a common electoral roll) upon which the new Prime Minister's political strength in East Pakistan depended. In turn, Suhrawardy helped the President to calm public agitation against the West during the Suez crisis, and to keep Pakistan aligned with her allies in spite of all the efforts of would-be trouble makers. But the President and the Prime Minister parted company over the best way of dealing with a political coalition which was attempting to reverse the decision to unify West Pakistan. General Iskander Mirza insisted upon exercising his power to dismiss and create Ministries, and the Suhrawardy Cabinet fell in October 1957.

Between October 1957 and October 1958, when the entire unsatisfactory fabric of political life in Pakistan was swept away by the Revolution, there were two short-lived ministries. One, headed by Mr. I. I. Chandigar, a well-known jurist, fell because of political intrigue after a couple of months: the other, headed by Firoz Khan Noon, a very respected senior statesman with a considerable knowledge of foreign affairs, lasted from December 1957 to the outbreak of the Revolution. During the early months of 1958 there occurred an unseemly scramble for influence over the elections which were shortly due to take place: everyone was manœuvring for position. In East and West Pakistan alike, political life touched the lowest depths to which it had ever sunk. Fortunately, neither the politicians themselves nor the principles—or lack of principles—for which they stood were representative of the real spirit of Pakistan. The country and the people were still sound at heart. This was shown, first, by the wave of indignation which in October 1958 swept away, in one mighty burst, the current regiment of politicians and all their works: and secondly, by the very real social and economic progress achieved throughout Pakistan within eleven years, in spite of the selfish preoccupations which had diverted political leaders from discharging their proper duties to the nation. The first of the two healthy manifestations of public spirit merits a chapter to itself: it will be dealt with later. But in order that the reader may not be tempted to condemn the people of Pakistan because of the confusion into which a handful of political leaders had plunged public life since 1951, another side of the picture must now be shown. The combined efforts of enthusiastic public servants and patriotic private citizens, often carried on, far from Headquarters, in face of the indifference and even discouragement which they encountered, had laid, within a decade, the foundations upon which a better life for the common man could be erected by any Government deserving of public confidence.

Chapter 9

SOME ECONOMIC FOUNDATIONS

Mention has been made in an earlier chapter of the impressive effort which Pakistan put out in the early years of her existence to shape a new economic pattern for herself; and of the stimulus imparted to this effort by India's reluctance to ease in any way the difficulties which confronted her new neighbour. To write a balanced survey of all that Pakistan accomplished during the first decade of her nationhood would need a separate book: all that I can attempt to do here is to outline certain of the developments which I had the opportunity of seeing for myself, in the course of my successive visits to the country. The favourable impression made upon me by this achievement, mainly to be observed in the countryside, contrasted so strongly with the growing dejection which overtook me when I saw the decline of political life in the great cities, that it deserves, perhaps, to be set down, even if it relates merely to a fractional part of the whole development field.

Something of the economic difficulties which beset Pakistan at the time of her birth have been outlined in an earlier chapter. Although she produced 70 per cent of the world's jute, partition found her with no jute mill, and only a few baling-presses, in her territory. Although cotton is the largest cash crop in West Pakistan, and is extremely important in East Pakistan also, there were only a few cotton mills—quite inadequate to handle it. In the whole country, less than 77,000 kilowatts of generating capacity existed: Pakistan's two ports, Karachi and Chittagong, were poorly equipped to deal with incoming and outgoing cargo. Such natural resources as existed had hardly been developed: rail and road communications were poor. Agriculture, by which 80 per cent of the population lived, was still carried on by antiquated and inefficient methods in which mechanization played no part at all.

Almost immediately after partition, a Development Board was set up to co-ordinate the many schemes which had to be put into execution before the economy of the country could take shape. Three years later, the Board was replaced by a Planning Commission and an Economic Council; a six-year plan was formulated for the years 1951–7 as part of the Colombo Plan. Priorities were given, in that order, to agriculture, transport and communications, industry and mining, fuel and power, and social uplift schemes. Soon afterwards, a two-year priority plan was superimposed; and in 1953 the Planning Commission was directed to work out a new Five Year Plan (the first to cover the years 1955–60.

From the very beginning, Pakistan's aim has been to encourage industrialization, not only because this process offers the best hope of raising the living standards of the people, but because it also lessens her dependence—initially, almost complete—upon the outside world for everything that she needs. In early years, Pakistan exported only jute, cotton, wool, hides and tea. Great efforts have been made to extend the foreign markets for all these commodities by improving their quality under Government encouragement. The group of jute mills at Narayangunj in East Pakistan is now the largest in the world, employing 25,000 workers. Cotton mills have multiplied throughout West and East Pakistan, so fast that it has now become quite a problem to balance the needs of the export market for raw cotton, cotton yarns, and cotton goods against the steadily rising demands of the home market. An interesting and encouraging development has been the broadening of the basis of the export trade to include processed goods, such as ready-made garments, serges, knitting yarns, cotton goods, domestic hardware, furniture, sports goods, and many other commodities. This has been the result of an amazing growth of light industry in the towns. In the neighbourhood of Lahore, for example, there is now an industrial suburb which extends for miles along the road to Rawalpindi: the same kind of development can be seen round Rawalpindi itself, and also round Peshawar. It is even more striking in the case of Karachi, where an enormous range of goods, from plastics to pharmaceutics, of the kind which, only a short time ago, could be obtained only from the West, are now locally manufactured. The pace of expansion in Karachi has been very remarkable, and has been accompanied by a complete change in the character of that city. Since Pakistan came into existence, Karachi has increased its population eightfold. In 1947, it was quite a business to drive at night from the centre of the city to the international airport at Drigh—a real danger from 'hold-up men' and other bad characters made many chauffeurs reluctant to risk the journey. Now the entire area has taken on the aspect of a well-planned modern city where complete order prevails. The road to the international airport—which has been expanded and improved until it has become one of the most convenient, as well as one of the most impressive, nodal points for world air communications to be found in any country—is wide and well-planned, with buildings and modern housing estates on each side of it for the entire journey. Karachi, in fact, has expanded in almost every direction: to the east is the new township of Landhi: to the north is the Sind Industrial Trading Estate. I shall be mentioning the still newer city of Korangi on a later page.

In planning her development, Pakistan has adopted from the beginning a policy which is based rather upon practical needs than upon any theoretical choice between capitalism and socialism. She has welcomed foreign capital investment and foreign technical experts, who work side by side with her own citizens in easy friendliness. The liberal help which she has received from the United States and from American agencies like the Ford Foundation, as well as from the United Kingdom, Canada, Australia, New Zealand, West Germany, and other countries has aroused no inferiority complex in her: she welcomes her helpers as equal partners with her in promoting the interests of her 94 million people. There is no rigid theoretical demarcation line between the public and the private sectors of national development, such as has been drawn in India; in Pakistan the two sides work in well together without rivalry. Apart from the large-scale irrigation, reclamation, settlement, and hydel projects, and the exploitation and distribution of the natural gas found at the great field at Sui, which are the direct responsibility of the authorities, the Government also takes the lead in starting the kind of industrial undertakings that do not, for one reason or another, attract private enterprise—either because the initial capital investment does not promise a quick return, or because no immediate market exists for the end-product. The agency employed for this purpose is the Pakistan Industrial Development Corporation, which is authorized to operate in the fields of jute, paper, heavy engineering, shipbuilding, heavy chemicals, fertilizers, sugar, cement, natural gas, and sources of power like coal and peat. The PIDC has now completed more than fifty industrial projects in East and West Pakistan, and as soon as each has been established on a firm basis—a good example is the great Chandragona Paper Mill in East Pakistan which exploits the natural forest wealth of the Chittagong Hill Tracts—it is made over to private enterprise, and the PIDC moves on to something else. In various places in West and East Pakistan I have seen something of the work which has been done: a dozen jute mills, three woollen mills, four sugar mills, six cotton ginning mills, two cement factories, two shipyards, a newsprint factory, and several chemical and fertilizer plants, including the largest factory in the world—at Fenchuganj in East Pakistan—for the manufacture of urea fertilizers from natural gas. The PIDC is now divided into two separate establishments, one for West Pakistan and one for East Pakistan, each with its own Board and Chairman.

Great attention has also been paid to the encouragement of medium and small-scale undertakings, which, in a country like Pakistan, have more immediate impact upon the mass of the people than the large-scale, impressive projects which will eventually become pillars of the national economy. Touring the rural areas, as I have been able to do, I have seen growing up, in a multitude of large villages and small towns, little factories, little ginning plants, little workshops—all focal points for local and regional industries which, with the improvement of communications, are beginning to find ready markets at home and abroad. The products of these small industries are too numerous to list: they include carpets, printing ink, leather goods, home handi-crafts, soap, boot polish, paints and varnish, rubber boots and shoes, cycle tyres and tubes. Much of this healthy development, all the result of private enterprise, has been made possible by the Pakistan Indus-trial Finance Corporation, which makes loans on easy terms and on more flexible conditions than are ordinarily obtainable in the money-market. There is no doubt, looking at the country as a whole, that this policy of spreading industry, as well as of setting up concentrations of industry where circumstances justify such a course, is the right one. It is putting more money into the pockets of an increasing number of people, and these little centres of industry are also little centres of prosperity. I was not surprised to learn from Pakistani statisticians that if the level of industrial production in 1950—only three years after Pakistan's creation—is taken as 100, the figure for 1958 was more than 400.

The problem of increasing productivity in agriculture—the pursuit by which eight out of every ten Pakistanis still live—is enormously complicated, as, indeed, it is in all Asian countries. From the earliest days of partition, its importance was accentuated for Pakistan by the heavy influx of refugees, who had to be received, clothed, looked after, nursed, provided with food, and eventually re-settled. During the first hideous period of the inter-communal massacres, some five million refugees arrived in West Pakistan from India, while simultaneously Pakistan lost the services of Hindu administrators, Hindu technicians, Hindu doctors, Hindu nurses, Hindu bankers, many of whom held key positions in those very sections of the national economy which underwent the heaviest strain from the refugee influx. An example of what happened came under my own notice. The Lyallpur Agricultural College, a key institution for experiment, research and training in the whole rural economy of West Pakistan, lost nine-tenths of its Professors and four-fifths of its lecturers—all Hindus. It had to be built up again almost from nothing—a task brilliantly achieved in a year or two. Meanwhile, it could contribute little to the problems of refugee resettlement.

Now that the refugee problem can be surveyed, from first to last, in some kind of perspective, its solution, though it took time, seems almost miraculous. The truth is that the people of Pakistan determined to preserve their new country at the cost of any sacrifices, achieved prodigies of extemporization with very limited resources. Quaid-i-Azam took a keen personal interest in the problem: his prestige was so great that disturbances and dislocations were reduced to a minimum. The Central Government intervened vigorously to stimulate and co-ordinate the efforts of the hard-pressed local authorities, and to mobilize the efforts of private individuals.

In the latter field, a development of outstanding potential importance took place: the women of Pakistan in large numbers threw off the veil and flocked to the refugee camps to render aid to the suffering and distressed. They organized the distribution of food and clothing: they nursed the sick: they set up dispensaries, hospitals and crèches. Their work was beyond all praise, and, in addition to giving valuable help in the immediate emergency, they established once and for all their claim to a place in every branch of organized social welfare. The nation, seeing what they could do, came to realize that their services were indispensable to healthy development in many fields of progress. That great lady, Begum Liaquat Ali Khan, took the lead in setting up, a few months after partition, the All Pakistan Women's Association. Affectionately known as APWA, this organization now has branches all over West and East Pakistan, and mobilizes the women of the country to initiate, and to run, schools, colleges, crèches, adult education and infant welfare centres. It encourages girls to enter the medical, nursing, teaching and social service professions: and helps to bring to the women of the masses the advantages which their sisters of the upper and middle income-groups already enjoy. The success of Pakistani women in claiming their share in nation-building activities is shown by their prominence, and the importance of their position in the Basic Democracy, Community Development and Village Aid organizations which are transforming the countryside. They are entering the medical and nursing professions in increasing numbers. The success of the Fatima Jinnah Medical College for Women in Lahore has led to the establishment of similar institutions in other parts of the country. Pakistani girls are now entering Domestic Science Colleges and other technical institutions as well as the Universities: they are even becoming Air Hostesses! There are now more trained women social workers per thousand of the population in Pakistan than in other countries which are undertaking large-scale village development: and all this beneficent activity took its rise from what, to begin with, looked like an unmitigated calamity—the influx of refugees.

Most of the first massive wave of refugees were agriculturalists, and, enormous efforts were called for to settle them on the land. This process necessitated expanding the area of cultivation: hence Pakistan's emphasis upon large projects of irrigation and land reclamation, often with the generation of electric power as a by-product. I visited a number of these projects from time to time, and saw them in process of completion. Among the most impressive of them in West Pakistan is the development of the Thal, a dreary, barren, desert of 5 million acres, bounded by the Salt Range on the north, the River Indus on the west, and the rivers Jhelum and Chinab on the east. The British had done a good deal of preliminary work in preparing irrigation schemes for the area; and by 1947 the headworks at Kalabagh were almost ready. The new Pakistan Government completed them, named them the Jinnah Barrage, and extended a network of canals designed to cover nearly two million acres. Side by side with the extension of irrigation went the resettlement of refugees on land which, for the first time, had been reclaimed for cultivation. A Thal Development Authority was set up in 1949 to co-ordinate the two processes.

Six years later, my wife and I toured the area to see what had been done. We went in August, in order to experience conditions at a thoroughly unfavourable period of the year. Temperatures were certainly high—the mercury in the clinical thermometer which we carry

A country craft near Chittagong

Fishing near Cox's Bazaar

Harvesting jute in East Pakistan

Tea-picking in a tea-garden near Sylhet

with us rose right off the scale above 109 degrees and firmly stuck there until we reached a cooler climate. After a journey in the sun, even the clothing in our suitcases was almost too hot to touch. Travelling was very strenuous—our days began before dawn and ended only after dark. On occasion, our car became immobilized by loose sand in a wholly shadeless area under the full noonday sun until help could be brought from the nearest village to dig us out. On one black day, our thermos flask of ice—a cherished companion on these long hot journeys—leaped out of the car and shattered itself on the ground. But never, I think, have we enjoyed a more interesting experience, or seen more dramatic examples of the conquest of natural obstacles by human energy.

The whole area has been physically transformed. Five considerable market towns—Jauharabad, Quaidabad, Liaquatabad, Bhakkar and Leiah were flourishing as the commerical, cultural, and educational foci of an entirely new population. We saw a couple of cotton mills, two sugar mills, and a woollen mill, all modern, well laid out and flourishing, providing between them both an outlet for local raw materials and steady employment for local labour. The desert was being reclaimed, section by section, by heavy agricultural machinery most effectively employed: we saw sand-dunes being moved bodily by bulldozers: shifting soil being pegged down by the use of quick-growing plants with binding properties; and good tarmac roads being laid to link new village with new village. The individual units of the Agricultural Machinery Organization were kept in constant touch with the Base Workshop and with the Divisional Engineer by a radio-communications system given by the New Zealand Government; the operations were conducted according to a master-plan with almost military precision. Forests were being planted to stabilize the soil, to act as windbreaks, and to increase humidity. Wheat, sugarcane, maize, barley and other crops were growing well: fruit cultivation was flourishing, as was proved by the groves of oranges, sweet limes, pomegranates, citrus and other varieties which we visited.

As in the case everywhere in West Pakistan, animal husbandry plays a vital part in the process of reclaiming the land. With the help of New Zealand, Canada and Australia, a splendid livestock farm has been set up at Rakh Ghulaman, where buffaloes, cattle, sheep and other livestock are raised. Poultry of improved breeds are being acclimatized—we spent a day with an Australian poultry expert, whose keenness was in no way diminished by the climatic problems which faced him. There are laboratories, a dairy factory, and a veterinary hospital: the farm raises all the food needed for staff, animals and poultry.

One of our main objects in making the tour was to see the newly-established villages, in the allocation of which the Government had made generous provision for Christians and other minorities. We found that all the villages which we visited were arranged in a uniform plan. The settlers had been brought over in neighbourhood or kinship groups: and about twenty-two family units occupied each *chak* or 'lot' of about 1,000 acres. The houses are everywhere of good design and solid construction. Outside the residential area lie the village compound: the common grazing ground: and the cultivable land, of which each family receives approximately twenty-two acres. Most of the villages are occupied by refugees; but there is a fair sprinkling of outsiders, like Mahsuds and other tribesmen from the North-West Frontier, who have been attracted there by the good land to be had on very easy terms. The tribesmen work hard and intelligently; they prosper, and are well liked. But there is also a good leavening of villages settled by retired Service men from the Army, Navy and Air Force. They are model colonists: their villages are perfect pictures of neatness, order, and prosperity. Their pride in their homes, in their crops, and in the new life which they have built for themselves was heart-warming to see. By and large, at the time when we visited the Thal area, over a thousand new villages, accommodating something like 100,000 souls, had been established; and were flourishing so satisfactorily that many settlers had bought their land outright by paying down lump sums, instead of taking advantage of payment by easy instalments over a term of years. Since then, I believe, the number of colonists has considerably increased, and, all told, the cultivated area now extends to one and a half million acres. The whole enterprise has succeeded so well that newly-reclaimed land can now be auctioned in lots of twenty-five acres for about Rs. 800. an acre, as compared with the price of Rs. 150. an acre at which the original settlers were allowed to purchase it. But in order to preserve the character of the locality, and to keep out moneyed people who do not want to work the land themselves, no one is allowed to purchase more than two lots. Health is well looked after by five hospitals, four health centres, twenty-three rural dispensaries, and some mobile medical units. There are two High Schools, one for boys and one for girls:

SOME ECONOMIC FOUNDATIONS

four Middle Schools for boys and one for girls: and more than seventy Primary Schools.

Nor is it only the outward appearance of the Thal that has been changed by this remarkable reclamation effort. Irrigation canals, cultivated lands, forests, and the pegging down of the shifting dunes are gradually altering the climate. Heat and cold are less severe: humidity has increased: the average rainfall is higher. The work achieved by the Development Authority is one of which any Government in the world might well be proud. The Thal project, like many other large-scale schemes, has now been taken over by the Agricultural Development Corporation, and forms part of a nation-wide programme of reclamation and resettlement.

The reclamation of the Thal is only one of several major irrigation and settlement projects in West Pakistan which have been carried through remarkably quickly. They were inspired partly by the need to find more land on which the refugees could be resettled, and partly by the requirements of the overall development plan of which they were an integral portion. Among them may be mentioned the great Ghulam Mohammad Barrage at Kotri, which enables a network of existing inundation canals to function at seasons when the river is not in flood, and also extends new irrigation facilities over a wide area. There are also a number of promising projects, such as the Taunsa Barrage, designed to provide perennial irrigation for more than half a million acres now served by inundation canals, and to bring water to an additional three quarters of a million acres in the Muzaffagarh and Dera Ghazi Khan districts. Mention has been made on an earlier page of the Mangla Dam project. This impressive multi-purpose irrigation and hydel scheme, which will necessitate moving the existing town of Mirpur in Azad Kashmir, and will bring under cultivation some three million acres, is among the works sanctioned by the International Consortium to replace the water which Pakistan will surrender under the Indus Waters Treaty with India. The Taunsa Barrage and the Mangla Dam schemes have been sanctioned for some time; but until the Revolutionary Government came to power, they have existed mainly on paper. Now they are being tackled in right earnest.

Among the projects in which the whole of Pakistan—East and West alike—takes pride is the Warsak Dam near Peshawar, constructed at a point where the Kabul River emerges from the hills into the plain. This project is one of the triumphs of the Colombo Plan: it shows how much can be achieved by successful international co-operation.

Not only have Canadian and Pakistani engineers worked together from the commencement of the project to its completion, but the Canadian contractors, by employing local labour from the Khyber and Mohmand areas, have contributed substantially to the rapid success of Pakistan's frontier policy, the outlines of which have been described in an earlier chapter. More than seven thousand tribesmen have been engaged upon the work, which has converted many of them from 'frontier raiders' into skilled craftsmen, who, after the completion of the project, are finding lucrative employment in many parts of Pakistan. Great care was needed in the initial stages to secure co-operation between the various tribes: to respect tribal jealousies: to arrange a truce to blood-feuds. The heights above the project-site had to be picketed: permanent watch-towers, adequately garrisoned, were erected. When my wife and I visited the site in 1955, these watch-towers were still strongly manned, and sniping was not uncommon. But as the work progressed, and the initially delicate relations between Pakistani political officers and Canadian engineers on one side, and tribal leaders on the other, passed into the stage of friendly comradeship and mutual respect, 'incidents' became rarer and rarer. On the later occasions when we visited the place, the watch-towers were almost all untenanted. It was an inspiring sight to see typical Mohmand and Afridi tribesmen handling with skill the latest type of earth-moving machinery and power-drills. Obviously they were taking great pride in their work; and there was a spirit of purposeful 'drive' about the whole labour-force which argues well for the value of the contribution which Pushtu-speaking peoples can make to the industrial progress of Pakistan.

Part of the attraction of Warsak lies in the sheer beauty of the situation, which has been in no way spoiled by the impressive dam, powerhouse, and irrigation headworks, all of which seem to blend naturally into the background of an amphitheatre of towering hills. A great new lake, twenty-six miles long, and running right to the Afghan border, forms a magnificent adjunct to the surrounding scenery; and from it great tunnels bored through the living rock carry water to the Khyber and Mohmand tribal areas as well as to the land round Peshawar, where the existing irrigated area will be almost doubled. The cheap electricity generated by the newly-harnessed water power is already encouraging the growth of industry throughout the neighbouring areas; and the Peshawar district is now plainly entering upon an era of expanding commercial and industrial prosperity.

It would be difficult to imagine a greater contrast in natural scenery and living conditions than that which exists between these big irrigation and power projects in West Pakistan and their counterparts in the eastern wing of the country. Throughout West Pakistan, the country is, as a whole, brown and barren, except where irrigation-schemes have brought the life-giving water. Water is the universal need. But in East Pakistan, the country is green and lush. Water, indeed, is in such ample supply that the main problem is how best to control it and to turn it to productive purposes. Devastating floods and destructive cyclones are of almost annual occurrence: even without them, water seems everywhere. In such conditions, the rivers are the main highways: roads and railways, though being steadily extended, and now coming to play an increasing part in the local system of communications, are still less important for a quasi-amphibious population than the network of navigable waterways. To fly over East Pakistan from Dacca to, say, Sylhet, in one of the East Pakistan Government's handy little amphibian planes, or in the new admirable air-bus service which Pakistan International Airlines has recently introduced, is to gain the impression of crossing a single enormous water-meadow of flooded rice and jute fields, out of which the individual villages, each surrounded by its fleet of boats, emerge on mounds of higher ground. The country is remarkably fertile, with enormous forest wealth, and with almost a monopoly of large-scale jute growing. But when Pakistan began, East Pakistanis felt that they lived in a thoroughly neglected area—virtually nothing had been done for them since Lord Curzon's viceroyalty, they told me—and they had inherited from the British Raj little more than the public buildings and modest amenities created for the short-lived Province of Eastern Bengal and Assam.

Some of the difficulties which beset East Pakistan in its early days because of the sudden withdrawal, after partition, of Hindu administrative 'know-how', Hindu professional skill and Hindu business experience, have been outlined on a previous page: but it was not until I toured East Pakistan some half a dozen years later that I came to appreciate certain additional handicaps which have served to slow down progress. I found, for example, that practically all the plant of the railway workshops at Chittagong, and much of the port equipment, had never been brought back after its removal westward to escape the expected Japanese invasion. At the time of partition, this equipment was in India, where it has remained. To keep the railways operating and the port open, required one of those triumphs of courageous extemporization in which Pakistanis seem to excel. In some respects, also, East Pakistan was unlucky in the aid which it received from international sources. Badly-needed rolling-stock came—but it came from a country ignorant of the requirements of tropical construction, and soon proved useless. On the occasion of one of my visits, I saw a big quay at Chittagong Port piled high with drums of salad oil—which East Pakistanis do not like and cannot be persuaded to use—each stencilled: 'A Gift from the People of America.'

But along with these failures have gone very real successes. Foreign help and Pakistani determination have turned Chittagong into the kind of major port which East Pakistan needs. It is a virtually new creation, with new quays, new cranes and cargo-handling equipment, as well as with workers' houses, offices, hospitals, dispensaries, schools, clubs and other amenities. Enormous new warehouses—all within an easy reach of three modern fire stations (for 'jute burns if you look hard at it!'), cope adequately with the jute export trade, with tea a long way second; but with other commodities, such as paper and sugar, beginning to play their part. The port can now handle twenty-four ships at a time; it earns a surplus every year which is ploughed back into improved facilities; since 1960 it has been given a Port Trust in the Karachi model.

Chittagong stands to benefit considerably, both directly and indirectly, from the biggest hydel-cum-water control-cum-irrigation project in East Pakistan, the Kaptai Dam, located in the Chittagong Hill Tracts half a day's journey by launch up the Karnafuli River. This river is one of the main highways of East Pakistan, and is crowded with barges, lighters, water buses, and country craft of every description, including vast rafts of bamboos and logs coming down from the forests. These rafts, often hundreds of yards square, are in charge of crews who live on them, and build huts for shelter, during the leisurely journey down river. I remember seeing one such raft, crewed by about a dozen men, clad only in loin cloths, passing close to the bank near Chandragona. Suddenly a thunder-shower broke: as if by magic, twelve black umbrellas appeared, and remained erected until the shower was over. To travel along the Karnafuli River from Chittagong to the dam site is a never failing entertainment. As soon as one leaves the flat plain, the river winds through hills clothed with orchid-decked tropical forest, which comes right down to the water's edge, and is heavily populated with monkeys, green parrots, and some of the large fauna, such as elephants. In occasional clearings on each side of the river there are the villages of the hill-tribes, mainly Buddhist by persuasion; hospitable, cheerful people, greatly reverencing the gentle saffron-robed monks of the village temple, who are so courteous to strangers.

Some of the bluffs underneath which the river winds are impressive: one of these is known locally as 'The Cliff of the Father-in-law'. Legend has it that a local chieftain promised the hand of his beautiful daughter to any young man who would jump from the top of the bluff into the river. But alas! at that spot it is virtually impossible to dive safely into the water because of the rocky spit which lies at the foot of the bluff. It is said that every suitor crashed to his death on the cruel rocks until there came the turn of one candidate whom the princess herself favoured. As the young man approached the chief to make his reverence before undertaking the leap, the princess snatched from her father's hand his gilded umbrella of state, and thrust it into her lover's grasp. He leaped: the support of the umbrella just gave him those few precious additional yards which carried him safely into the water: and he won the princess's hand. Strange to say, this same bluff claimed more victims during the last war. Two British aviators, flying a plane riddled by bullets from Japanese fighter aircraft, escaped across the border from Burma. They reached the Karnafuli River safely, only to crash in flames against the Cliff of the Father-in-law. Their grave is close by.

Between Chittagong and Kaptai, either by road or by river, stands the great paper mill at Chandragona, an enterprise started by the Pakistan Industrial Development Corporation, as earlier mentioned, and since transferred to private management. It finds its raw material from the forests of the Chittagong Hill Tracts, and has given much employment to the local hill tribes. To begin with, they were suspicious, and would have nothing to do with it. The Pakistan Government thereupon re-engaged the services of Lt.-Col. Niblett, a retired British Deputy Commissioner long familiar with the whole area, who was widely liked and trusted by the tribes. Under his persuasions, the supplies for the paper mills were assured. He also did invaluable work, up to the time of his greatly-lamented death under the trampling feet of a rogue elephant, in reconciling the Chakmas and other hill tribes to the necessity of moving to new locations provided by the Government, in anticipation of the time when the sites of their

167

original villages would become submerged by the enormous reservoir, more than 250 square miles in extent, which is a major feature of the Kaptai project.

This project, which I have been fortunate enough to visit at frequent intervals from its early beginnings to its virtual completion after ten years, in 1962, is of great technical interest. Its main feature is one of the largest earth-fill dams in the world, more than 2,000 feet long, and towering 150 feet above the foundation level. This is designed to store up the water from a catchment area of more than 4,000 square miles: and the resulting reservoir, the level of which will rise above the highest point of the present District Headquarters—Rangamati—will provide access for heavy craft to the innermost depths of the Chittagong Hill Tracts. In addition to improving navigation along the entire Karnafuli River, and protecting the river and the surrounding area from floods, the Kaptai project will enable a deep-water channel, free of silting, to be maintained at the port of Chittagong and from Chittagong to the sea. The electrical generating capacity of the powerhouse is 120,000 kilowatts, which will provide cheap current to a considerable area of East Pakistan.

I recall, in particular, four visits which I paid to the Kaptai dam site, because of the contrast between the conditions which I found. I shall never forget arriving there by launch one dark and rainy night in September 1955, and seeing the electric lights of a small new settlement on the left bank twinkling through the murky, steamy atmosphere. A scramble up the steep muddy bank, and a short drive by jeep, ended in a hospitable welcome at the brightly-furnished Engineer's Rest House. Next morning, the sun broke through, and it was possible to look round the site. Close at hand elephants were working alongside bulldozers in shifting soil! The Pakistani engineers, labouring under great difficulties caused by shortage of spares for heavy earth-moving equipment, shortage of money, and the general remoteness, of the site, had made an excellent start. A soil laboratory was busy testing the features of the soil at every working depth for weight, permeability, compressibility, and texture; and was thus collecting the essential data for what was to be a dam with many novel characteristics. The layout of the settlement was well-planned: the labour force was excellently housed: there was a hospital with six doctors: there were recreation grounds, clubs, workshops, a mosque, and an admirable school—one feature of which was a notice board on which the schoolmaster wrote up the latest world-news received by wireless from Radio Pakistan. Day and night work was the rule; for the effective operational period between the heavy rainy seasons was only five months in every twelve. The engineers begged me to impress upon the Central Government how disastrous was any delay in the arrival of spare parts: and when I returned to Karachi I was able to speak to the Prime Minister about their needs.

Four years later, I found the Kaptai scene transformed. Large-scale American help, financial and technical, had begun to make a notable impact. Operations were now concentrated almost entirely on the right bank, where a model town with every amenity, including piped water, a super-market, and well-laid all-weather roads, served a population of 300 Americans—engineers and their families in the service of the Utah Construction Company. Together, American and Pakistani engineers had overcome all initial difficulties: the great dam had taken shape: the installation of the three generators in their individual tunnels was almost finished: and it was possible to forecast the time when the dam, with the spillway closed, would impound the vast volume of water which the upper reaches of the Karnafuli River draw from its extensive catchment area. Plans for the resettlement of the tribes who were to be displaced by the reservoir had been completed: the villagers affected had seen the new land allotted to them: had judged the worth of the compensation which was to be given to them: and were well satisfied. The progress made towards the completion of the entire project was impressive. The up-to-date earth-moving equipment brought by the Americans was admirable in its efficiency; the shortness of the working season seemed only to act as encouragement to greater efforts on the part of everyone concerned. The impetus given to the work on every front appeared to me only less astonishing than the completeness of the domestic comfort with which the American families had surrounded themselves in this remote jungle area. Their entire colony was a 'little America' in the heart of the forest: even the teacher who presided over the American school drew a salary, I was told a little enviously, in excess of that allotted to a Pakistani Cabinet Minister!

Only twelve months later when I came again, the Americans had gone, leaving behind them their excellent buildings, their modern township, and a memory of warm friendliness and good fellowship born of strenuous work well shared. A new population had flocked in hard on their heels: light industries were springing up, and the final stages of the project were now in Pakistani hands. Arrangements were in train for the transfer of all the inhabitants of Rangamati to the site of the New Town three miles away. The resettlement work was going on fast; the chiefs and tribal leaders had left their ancestral homes and were occupying their new houses: along with them had gone the great mass of the population, 60,000 of them, all told. In a word, the great project was ready: it only waited for the last few final adjustments which would bring it into effective activity. The sheer determination, skill, and perseverance which had achieved the completion, not only of the engineering operation itself, but of the administrative task connected with the re-settlement, aroused my warmest admiration: I felt that a country which could work this jungle-miracle could surely do anything which it had made up its mind to accomplish. My fourth visit, made in March 1962, saw the whole project completed. Power was already being transmitted to Dacca; a lake of 250 square miles was in being; the scientific extraction of timber from the hitherto inaccessible portions of the Chittagong Hill Tracts forests was already proceeding; plans were on foot for establishing at Kaptai a centre of tourism, a model township, a technical school for the training of Chakma craftsmen, and a rest camp for men on leave from the armed forces. Full advantage is being taken of the natural beauty of the surroundings to make Kaptai a source of delight, as well as of great and lasting profit, to the people of East Pakistan.

It would be a mistake to conclude that these impressive projects in East and West Pakistan which I have described are in the nature of show pieces, deliberately created. They are all, in fact, part of the general scheme of planning for higher living standards: they take their place in the general record of industrial and commercial development which must in fairness be set on the credit side of the national ledger as against the debit raised by the deplorable nature of the contemporary political life. But for them, and for the spirit of enterprise which they exemplify, many of the achievements of the present Revolutionary Government would have been much more difficult. They have provided the foundation for the Pakistan of today.

Hardly less important for the nation as a whole than this process of material growth has been the steady transformation of village life over great areas of the country by the Village Agricultural and Industrial Development movement. This, too, has proved an indispensible foundation for the new and dynamic policies which the Revolutionary Government is pursuing with such marked success.

Village AID started from modest beginnings in 1953, and its steady progress until 1961, when its functions were divided between the new Agriculture Development Corporation, the Basic Democracies, and the Agriculture Departments of East and West Pakistan represents a triumph of perseverance and enthusiasm in an extremely difficult field. So useful did the Village AID prove that it is still retained for the present in its original form in areas like Azad Kashmir and Baltistan, where the people are not yet quite ready for the split-up of its duties which has taken place elsewhere. The idea behind it is not, of course, peculiar to Pakistan: the Government of almost every Asian country with a predominantly rural population has striven to discover how village life can be transformed for the better by encouraging local leadership, co-operative effort, and self-help. In the days of the British Raj, the 'Gurgaon Experiment', initiated by Brayne, showed what could be achieved by drive and enthusiasm in the direction of increasing village income, improving village amenities, and raising hygienic and sanitary standards. The work in Gurgaon inspired many emulators, and some progress was made: but the fact that the leadership came from outside was a serious weakness: when this leadership was removed, the growth withered from lack of roots.

After the war, most of the newly-independent countries of South-East Asia adopted with enthusiasm what came to be known as the Community Development movement, with programmes for raising the low standards of village life by introducing improved farming methods: setting up cottage industries: establishing schools, dispensaries, health, maternity and child-welfare clinics, adult literacy centres, reading rooms and libraries: and by providing clean water and good drainage. In the execution of these programmes, much help was given by the technical branches of the United Nations Organization, as well as by such bodies as the Ford Foundation. Several countries, notably, perhaps, India and the Philippines, took up this movement with enormous enthusiasm, placed it high on the priority list in their programmes of national development, and spent very large sums of money, partly from their own funds and partly from the funds placed at their disposal by international foundations, on the task of promoting, organizing, and extending it. By and large, a great deal of progress has been achieved: but it is also clear that the overall results have not always shown good value for the large sums which have been spent. Critics have noticed that the Community Project Movement in India, for example, has become just one more elaborately organized Government Department of the Public Works type; and that in the process of building schools, dispensaries, community centres and libraries, the all-important aims of encouraging local initiative, stimulating self-help, and converting the traditionally conservative outlook of the villager into creative energy, and readiness to accept new ideas, have somehow slipped into the background.

The Village AID movement in Pakistan has successfully avoided this pitfall, partly because, in the early days, the country could not afford to spend spadefuls of money upon it. Since it had to operate, as it were, upon the proverbial shoestring so far as finance was concerned, it was obliged to rely upon devoted enthusiasm and a kind of missionary spirit. From the very beginning, it had the women of Pakistan behind it, and, due partly no doubt to their influence and their instinctive flair for what is really essential in a movement of this kind, it has always given the utmost possible value for every rupee spent upon it. Its first aim was to devote all its available resources to the job of training village-level workers, both men and women, who can carry to the villager the techniques recommended by the various expert nation-building departments of Government, and promote the adoption of new crop-varieties, better seed, improved tools and methods: who can actually live as villagers, win the confidence of the people, and persuade them to make efforts to help themselves in such ways as improving their surroundings, increasing their income, and interesting themselves in village problems of health, sanitation, literacy, child welfare, and the like. With the help of men and women specially trained in the United States, three centres of instruction for village-level workers were set up in East Pakistan and six in West Pakistan, all of which turned out, year by year, their quota of village-level workers properly equipped for their jobs. In East Pakistan, where the population is dense and villages often lie close together, a worker generally had about seven villages in his or her charge: in West Pakistan, where distances are greater, and the population more scattered, five villages were as much as one individual can manage. Wherever possible, married couples were encouraged to undertake training together and afterwards to look after a group of villages as a team. Their united efforts often solve problems which would baffle a single worker, whether man or woman.

A year or two after the movement had started, my wife and I had the opportunity both of visiting some of the training centres, and of seeing the kind of work which village-level workers do after they have been trained and sent into the field. The training of the women workers in home economics, in cooking on improved smokeless stoves of a design which can be made in every village, in nutrition and diets, in fly-control, in child care, in sanitation, in raising vegetables, in house decoration, in garment-making and in many other useful crafts, was at once highly practical and very thorough. The men were trained in improved agricultural methods, in soil-testing, in cottage industries, in road alignment, in elementary sanitary engineering, in seed-testing, and in other serviceable skills. Both men and women were most carefully instructed in the art of gaining the confidence of those among whom they will work: they are taught how to avoid arousing antagonism by over-much haste or zeal: how to enlist the co-operation of the leaders of village opinion: how to make sure of every step, with infinite patience, before they embark upon their enterprises: how to rely upon example rather than upon precept in the introduction of new ideas. Great care was taken, we found, to ensure that the village-level worker did not feel isolated. He was supplied with a perpetual flow of useful information; he was kept up to date with technical improvements in agricultural methods; he was brought back at regular intervals for refresher courses in his training centre.

We had the opportunity also, of visiting a number of villages in both East and West Pakistan, and of seeing for ourselves the kind of field-work that is being done. We found that while the village-level workers were keeping themselves carefully in the background, and were assigning the credit for everything that had been achieved to the villagers themselves, their influence was very great. Under their tactful encouragement, village streets were being paved and drained, waste land was being reclaimed and cultivated, link-roads were being built, improved seeds and new methods of cultivation were being tried out; trees were being planted in large numbers for firewood and humus: the cultivation of new vegetables was spreading: poultry farming was becoming popular with the introduction of improved breeds of fowls: schools, dispensaries, clinics and adult literacy centres were being started and maintained, cottage industries were being organized. Village councils were being set up by the villagers themselves to look after this development work, and to enlist the support of the whole community in carrying it out. The village-level workers were regarded, not as intruders into village life, but as the natural counsellors and friends of everyone. Real progress was to be seen wherever Village AID had penetrated; it was solidly based because it proceeded from the initiative of the villagers themselves: it had become a source of pride to them. The traditional isolation of the villages was yielding to wider horizons and better communications: the co-operative movement was linking village to village: a new and healthy spirit of emulation between individual villages and groups of villages was a marked spur to progress.

About 150 villages are grouped into a Development Area, with an advisory committee of village representatives and Government technical officers to co-ordinate schemes, and a Development Officer to be responsible for their progress. The Development Areas are grouped in turn into larger units with a Development Director—some of whom are women—at the head: and in these larger units the links with administrative officers and with the more senior representatives of the nation-building departments grow closer and more intimate. Before long, it was found necessary to establish two Village AID Academies, one at Peshawar for West Pakistan and one at Comilla for East Pakistan, to undertake research in the techniques, psychological as well as material, of village development, and to provide advanced instruction for senior Government officers, both administrative and technical, in the scope, importance, and methods of village development work in its bearings upon every branch of their own special responsibilities.

Everything that we have seen of the progress of the movement in the course of our visits to Pakistan from about 1955 onwards has convinced us that Village AID, even prior to the Revolution of 1958, was becoming a real force for good. It spread steadily and solidly: the people themselves both wanted it and worked it. Within five years of its birth, it was covering nearly 50 per cent of the entire country. It was putting all its resources into the training of its workers, and wasting no money on showmanship. It was affording an increasing scope for women's activities: the number of women workers in each Development Area had been increased from five to ten. It was now very firmly keyed into the structure of district administration by equating the boundaries of Development Areas with those of administrative sub-divisions. The soundness of its methods was shown by its remarkable success in such remote areas as Gilgit and Baltistan, where it was acclaimed with enthusiastic and real gratitude. It was penetrating into Azad Kashmir, and even influencing the tribal territory of the North-West Frontier. Noticeably good work was being done in Zhob and Loralai, in the Kurram and Malakand areas, as well as in Swat. The closely-knit tribal organization favours the spread of the movement: when once the leading men are converted, everyone follows them. Almost as important for the country as a whole as the development and 'uplift' work of Village AID was its remarkable potentialities as a link between the masses and the Government— potentialities which it took a Revolutionary Government to exploit, but which were there, none the less, ready to its hand. By the time that the Village AID organization was taken over by the Basic Demo- cracies, the Agricultural Departments, and the Agriculture Develop- ment Corporation in 1961, it had laid firm foundations for a new and better rural economy. The Basic Democracies now select their own workers, and send them for training in their duties; the Agricultural Departments are responsible for improved seed, for the supply of literature and for instruction in advanced methods; the Agriculture Development Corporation co-ordinates schemes, supplies expert advice, and encourages higher standards of scientific practice through- out the country.

One of the most significant things about the Village AID move- ment between 1953 and 1958 was its freedom from all connections with political life. It dealt with matters which did not interest the men who spent their time intriguing for place and power. At the same time, it was confronted by difficulties which it could not vanquish by its own resources, and which, before long, would inevitably have limited its usefulness. Chief among these was the crying need in West Pakistan for agrarian reform: for the abolition of the quasi-feudal system of land ownership: for the institution of tenant rights and of peasant proprietorship. Small yeoman and middle-class proprietors, owning modest estates, and cultivating their land themselves with the help of tenant farmers, welcomed Village AID, and co-operated heartily in the extension of activities which benefited owner and tenant alike. But much of the land was in the hands of really big land- lords. A number of these obstructed the advance of Village AID into their estates: they did not want their tenants to be educated or to be raised from their position of helpless dependence. Others, more pru- dent in their tactics, did not openly oppose the movement, but con- trived in a number of ways to discourage and cramp the village-level workers, many of whom came from outside. On the whole, the large landed interests in West Pakistan were unfriendly towards Village AID; besides which the village-level workers found themselves handicapped in their work because many of the villagers, being only tenants-at-will or share-croppers, were unwilling to devote their energies to the improvement of holdings which they might lose at the mere whim of the landlord. In East Pakistan, the problem was different. Even before the Revolution, agrarian reform had made considerable progress—so much so, indeed, that holdings were limited to thirty acres and the large estates were broken up. This change, though initiated with the best intentions, had driven away the yeoman class, who no longer found agriculture an attractive profession when practised on such a modest scale; and the villages, thereafter, were deprived of the presence of the sort of man who welcomed Village AID and who would take the lead in working it. The absence of the yeoman class was the more serious because the East Pakistani peasants are, as a whole, very poor indeed; and it proved much harder than in West Pakistan to give the Village AID movement real impetus. In some cases, it was helped forward by the Union Boards, bodies which had been in existence for about two decades before Pakistan was created. These Boards represented grouped areas of revenue-collection. Their purpose was to interest local people in local improvements: they were empowered to levy modest cesses and to expend them on village development. Originally, the franchise on which the members were elected entailed a property qualification; but just before the Revolution, adult suffrage was introduced. On the whole, the experiment was not a great success; all real authority tended to be exercised by the official administering the area—the Circle officer; and the elected members, like the general public, remained uninterested. But some Boards, under energetic chairmen who made a hobby of their duties, did excellent work, and co-operated enthusiastically with the Village AID movement: gradually it spread until it covered about one-third of East Pakistan.

Thus, by 1958, Village AID had made real progress in spite of the difficulties to be overcome. It was among the most promising of the achievements which must be set to the credit of pre-Revolutionary Pakistan, deserving to rank alongside the advance of industrialization and the progress of the great development projects.

Finally, in estimating the condition of Pakistan before the Revolution, some mention must be made of two further nation-building departments—health, and education. Both of these came in for unfavourable public comment in the pre-Revolutionary period: both have been radically reformed since 1958 to bring them into broader harmony with national requirements. Nevertheless, in both, foundations were laid upon which satisfactory edifices could be erected by a Government prepared to recognize their real importance and to deal with them without regard to political intrigue and vested interests.

The public health system of Pakistan had to be constructed, like so many other nation-building departments, almost from nothing. The central research institutes, like the Pasteur Institute of Kasauli, the institutes of Hygiene and Malaria at Calcutta, the College of Nursing in Delhi, all went to India. The bulk of the medical and technical staff in the territory which became Pakistan were non-Muslims, and departed. Everything had to be planned afresh, at the very moment when the burden of looking after the medical and sanitary requirements of millions of refugees was superimposed on the other difficulties and shortcomings which had to be faced.

The new Government of Pakistan took as its model the admirably comprehensive survey of the requirements of a national health service which had been drawn up for India in 1943 by the committee presided over by Sir Joseph Bhore. There were some advantages in planning a new service from scratch, as it were: but the problems were enormous. Only one medical college—Lahore—was producing medical graduates: the colleges at Dacca and Karachi were still being developed. These institutes had to be enlarged and supplemented immediately: the Fatima Jinnah Medical College in Lahore was founded to educate lady doctors: additional medical colleges were started at Hyderabad, Multan and Peshawar, and another college for women planned at Chittagong. A Medical Council for Pakistan was set up in 1948 to maintain medical standards. Nurses were in short supply: every Provincial Government was encouraged to start training-centres, and a College of Nursing was founded for the post-graduate training of qualified nurses. A Central Malaria Institute was set up in 1947, first in Karachi: it was afterwards transferred to Dacca while maintaining the Karachi institute as a branch. Social Hygiene centres were started at Karachi and Chittagong. Tuberculosis control programmes and B.C.G. vaccination campaigns were set on foot. In all this activity, substantial help was received from the World Health Organization, UNICEF, and the United States authorities. But while much good work was done, and the foundations of a national health organization were being laid, the public remained dissatisfied. It was not merely that medical facilities were too thinly spread; even where they existed, the complaint was that bribery played too large a part in securing medical attention at the hospitals: that rare drugs were sold in the market; and that poor people in urgent need of treatment were turned away, while those who could afford to give presents and to pay fees were admitted.

The educational structure, also, had to be entirely re-created. Much attention was paid to higher education—the introduction of politics into colleges has already been noticed—while middle and primary education, although not neglected, was not 'pushed' with the determination which its importance merited. On the whole, however, the record was creditable: by 1957 Pakistan possessed 6 Universities, 158 general Colleges, ten Teachers' Training Institutes, 30 professional Colleges, 2 Polytechnics, nearly 6,000 Secondary Schools, and about 45,000 Primary Schools. But there were complaints that the whole educational structure bore too little relation to the real needs of the country: that it was insufficiently practical: and that not enough stress was laid upon producing the technicians in agriculture, forestry, engineering, and applied science, whom Pakistan badly needed.

Chapter 10

REVOLUTION AND RENAISSANCE

Thus, in spite of somewhat sensational political confusion and corruption, which naturally attracted more attention in the world's Press than the country's solid achievements, Pakistan, during the first decade of her existence, was very far from stagnating: real progress was recorded, as we have seen in the last chapter, in a number of important directions. But to an observer like myself, who had been visiting the country at fairly regular intervals, the pace of this progress seemed to be slowing down as I watched it. The initial impetus imparted to the task of nation-building by Quaid-i-Azam was gradually declining; every time I left Pakistan to return to England, I felt more apprehensive about what I should find when I came back.

I shall not easily forget the impression which I carried away with me in 1957 and early 1958. Things were obviously going very wrong indeed, especially in the great cities, Karachi, Dacca, Chittagong, Peshawar and Lahore, where political life seemed to have fallen into the depths. As we have noticed in Chapter 7, many of the leaders, from the highest downwards, were considering how best they could manipulate the forthcoming elections, planned under the 1956 Constitution, but several times postponed, in order to secure their own return to power. An instance which came to my personal notice may be worth recording. A barrister friend of mine told me that he had been consulted by a prominent personage who inquired whether there was any provision in the Penal Code which would get him into trouble if he promised export licences to wealthy industrialists in return for subventions to the funds of his Party. To my friend's horrified protests, the politician merely retorted: 'I don't want to hear any ethical lectures: I only want to know if I can be prosecuted!' Learning that the proposed course of action could incur prosecution under PRODA (Public and Representative Officers Disqualification Act), the political leader remarked: 'That's all right, then: that Act can't be invoked except by Government, and *we* shall be the Government.'

Ironically enough, the election for which the sums were raised did not take place and the funds remained with the political leader. They eventually fell into the hands of the Revolutionary Government, which returned them—along with a sharp warning—to the donors.

In East Pakistan, fierce internal rivalries, which later in the year led (as we have noted) to the beating up of the Speaker, and the murder of his Deputy, were raging. There was serious labour unrest, accompanied by rioting. Feeling against West Pakistan ran higher than I had ever known it: there was open talk of the possibility of leaving Pakistan altogether, and of trying to set up a separate independent Bengal with the help of some of the Bengalis living in India. Smuggling had attained dimensions which set it wholly beyond the control of the police: and when the Army, whose help was enlisted, proceeded to check it by effective measures, these were quickly nullified because political pressure promptly secured the release of all the offenders from custody, and an alteration of the rules was rushed through to make Army intervention impossible in future.

In West Pakistan, things were no better. Lahore was rent by intrigue: a formidable drive by interested parties was in progress to rescind unification and to split West Pakistan once more into separate States. Karachi had become notorious for graft and corruption. Conscientious officials found themselves helpless: their weaker fellows unashamedly identified themselves with the interests of their political superiors. Subordinates with the 'right influence' found themselves Heads of Departments, regardless of qualifications, experience, and even character. Revenue receipts had fallen heavily into arrears. Smuggling, particularly of gold, provided enormous profits to those engaged in it. Leaders of the Karachi gangs boasted openly of the political 'protection' which enabled them to carry on their lucrative pursuit with impunity. No secret at all was made of such things: honesty in public life was at a discount: all that mattered was 'influence'. One among many instances which came under my notice will illustrate this.

On earlier pages I have mentioned the formidable problem of refugee resettlement, and how it was being tackled. By the beginning of 1958, the great majority of the agriculturalist refugees who had arrived in the early mass-movements had been resettled on the land. But the 'urban' refugees, people accustomed to town life, who naturally flocked to the great cities, were mostly still living in miserable conditions. Moreover Muslim discontent with conditions in

India continued to inspire small but steady and unceasing movements of infiltration from India into West Pakistan. Most of these later migrants gravitated to Karachi. Praiseworthy and continuous efforts were made to house them and to encourage them to find a livelihood. APWA was particularly active in this field. Yet, whenever I returned to Karachi, I noticed the same depressing collections of miserable refugee huts, dotted in insanitary clumps round the perimeter of the city. This puzzled me, because I knew that quite a lot of suitable houses had been built by the civic authorities to accommodate these unfortunate people. Inquiries showed that many refugees had indeed been given new quarters; but had promptly let them to tenants at a good rent, and contentedly remained in their old insanitary surroundings. As soon as efforts were made by responsible officials to check this practice, political interests stepped in. 'Don't interfere with these people—let them do as they like, or you will lose me their votes!' And so the eyesore of the refugee hutments remained, to the scandal of everyone concerned, in spite of the large sums of public money expended in building new quarters.

If conditions in the cities were depressing early in 1958, those in the countryside were downright alarming. The rural population was seething with discontent against the Government because of high prices, shortages of basic commodities, rising cost of living, and disappointed hopes of agrarian reform. The politicians, provincial and central, were being openly cursed by name for selfishness, corruption, and neglect of everyone's interests but their own. Men of solid standing were refusing to pay their taxes, saying that the country in which they lived was not the Pakistan for which they had hoped, prayed and worked. The structure of administration was crumbling: good officers found that they could achieve nothing and were profoundly discouraged; bad officers drew their salaries and neglected their duties. It was difficult for an observer to avoid the conclusion that an explosion was imminent. The only question was just what would set it off.

The underlying cause of the high cost of living and of the shortages of essential commodities which caused increasing anger in every Pakistani, except the politicians and grafters who profited from them, was financial mismanagement. There were experts available to put things right, but they were not allowed to do so because there were too many competing claims, all with powerful political backing, to permit the institution of the economies which would be necessary if the country was to live within its means. Some figures may help to fill in the picture. Out of a total expenditure of £112 million on the country's development, only about £15 million came from taxation and foreign loans: the balance had been met by borrowing and by printing more paper money. Between 1955 and 1958 Pakistan, which formerly fed herself and could even export food grains, had to spend £129 millions on imported food. Between the same years, the foreign exchange reserves fell from £71 million to a nominal £30 million (but really to a minus figure) and were vanishing even more rapidly as the months of 1958 drew on. Wealthy men were concealing their assets: arrears of taxation leviable on undeclared income had grown to some Rs. 300 million. Actual income-tax arrears mounted to about the same figure. It is hardly a matter for surprise that inflation assumed alarming proportions, that food and other commodities were unscrupulously hoarded, that only the black-market flourished, and that prices soared. Food riots in the large towns grew so serious that the resources of the civil authorities were hardly equal to the task of preserving law and order.

It was from the Army that salvation came. For a long time, the High Command had been seriously uneasy at the situation in the country. Through its recruiting officers, it was closely in touch with feelings in the villages: it knew that a formidable agrarian revolt against landlord tyranny and economic oppression would soon break out. It realized that the entire political life of Pakistan was riddled with graft and corruption—a conclusion reinforced by the Army's own experience in trying to stop smuggling in East Pakistan—and that the administrative machine, thanks to continued political interference, and the resulting discouragement and apathy, was on the verge of a breakdown. Even so, the tradition, inherited from British days, that the armed forces do not intervene in politics, remained sufficiently strong in the High Command to inhibit action, although those whose profession it was to defend the country were uneasily conscious that if drastic remedies were not soon applied, they might well discover one day, that there was no country left for them to defend. The time has not yet come to set down the complete story of the chain of events which finally precipitated the Army's action. All that can be stated here is that General Ayub Khan found himself unexpectedly confronted with conclusive proof that a *coup d'état*, of the kind which had brought General Kassim into control of Iraq, was being prepared. Such a move, if it had been permitted to mature, would have involved the entire country in bloodshed, and profited no one but the Communists. Armed with this information, and the proofs of its accuracy, General Ayub Khan flew to Karachi to confer urgently with President Iskander Mirza.

Until, with the passage of time, more material becomes available for study, the reasons for President Iskander Mirza's failure to remedy the lamentable condition into which Pakistan had fallen by the autumn of 1958 cannot be determined. That he had for some time been gravely disturbed, I know from my talks with him; but he seemed to retain to the last a conviction, in the face of what appeared to me formidable evidence to the contrary, that he could put things right by a series of careful manoeuvres designed to reduce the political leaders to impotence and to leave himself, as President, with a free hand to remedy the situation. There are grounds for thinking that he rather welcomed General Ayub Khan's news, for it gave him the opportunity to take the kind of forceful action of which he was a master. The Constitution of 1956 had severely limited his powers: further, it contained no provision, such as the Indian Constitution prudently includes, for enabling the Head of State to assume control of the country in a national emergency. President Iskander Mirza therefore suspended the Constitution altogether, thus abolishing the central and provincial legislatures. He dissolved all political parties and assumed supreme power himself: he declared martial law: he appointed General Ayub Khan as Chief Martial Law Administrator.

'Operation Overlord', the assumption of control over Pakistan by the Army, was carried through swiftly and efficiently. There was no bloodshed, no use of force: 'not even an ant was killed' as Pakistanis told me afterwards. In Karachi, some members of the Cabinet were dining one evening at a hotel, entirely unaware of what was happening, at the very moment when the troops were engaged in occupying all strategic points and taking over Government offices. Next morning, when these Ministers listened at breakfast to Radio Pakistan, they learned for the first time that they were out of a job. In Lahore, Dacca, and other great cities too, the change-over was entirely peaceful. Radio Pakistan's announcement about the Revolution spread like wildfire throughout the country, and official measures were taken to ensure that the Press gave the 'straight story'. The relief of the whole nation was so profound, and their acclamation of the Revolution so enthusiastic, that political leaders everywhere could only throw in their hand, retire into obscurity, and hope for the best.

Some were, in fact, prosecuted for peculation; but in most cases they were given the choice, either of standing their trial, or of retiring from public life for a period of years. Many chose the latter option, and have remained unmolested.

In spite of the fact that President Iskander Mirza and General Ayub Khan were old friends, they did not long continue to see eye to eye regarding the emergency which had brought them together. The President looked on martial law as a means of reducing to impotence the political leaders whom he disliked and despised, and of securing to himself the supreme executive power. General Ayub Khan, on the other hand, saw in martial law a true opportunity for—in his own phrase—leading the country back to sanity, and setting on foot a complete moral, economic and administrative rehabilitation of the nation. In planning for this task, the Chief Martial Law Administrator soon decided that President Iskander Mirza was likely to be something of a liability—not because of any failure on his part in ability, drive, or patriotism, but because he was so closely associated in popular estimation with the régime which had been displaced that the people of Pakistan refused to believe in the reality of the 'new deal' for which General Ayub Khan was working so long as President Iskander Mirza remained at the head of affairs. In forming this opinion, General Ayub Khan gave early evidence of a characteristic which continues to impress those who work with him, namely, a power of combining rapid decision with an instinctive perception of what the ordinary men and women of Pakistan are thinking. I believe that his diagnosis was correct. A young Pakistani, on a course in England, happened to be staying with us in our Hampshire home when the news came that President Iskander Mirza had 'stepped down' and was leaving the country. Our guest had earlier spoken hopefully about the Revolution, but was uneasy over the obstacles which anyone who planned real reform would have to overcome. When he heard on the radio the announcement about President Iskander Mirza's departure, he jumped from his chair in his excitement, ran across the drawing-room, and embraced me, saying, '*Now*, you will see that things will go right!'

The judgement may seem harsh even if, as I think, many Pakistanis shared it. It overlooks the distinguished contributions which President Iskander Mirza has rendered to his country during a long and remarkable career in her service. Pakistan at least has cause to be grateful to him for his courage in declaring martial law, which made possible the success of the Revolution. Almost his last official act was to hand-pick an admirable Cabinet, consisting of men of outstanding ability and integrity, who had taken no part in political life. This Cabinet, which was to be responsible to the President, included General Ayub Khan as Prime Minister. It seems probable that in setting up a Cabinet form of Government, President Iskander Mirza was preparing the way for a return to more normal conditions. Already, General Ayub Khan had found it possible to relax some of the rigidities of martial law: the Civil courts were again functioning. But the division of authority between the two men, for the reasons already explained, was proving unworkable in view of the plight of Pakistan at the time. General Ayub Khan knew that only thorough-going and drastic reorganization could save the situation: President Iskander Mirza held less radical opinions. Before the end of October 1958, he agreed to resign and to leave the country. General Ayub Khan became Head of State. He at once reappointed the Cabinet— indeed almost all of them remained with him until the summer of 1962, although there were some re-allocations of portfolios—and several were reappointed under the 1962 Constitution.

Perhaps this is the place to record that the new Cabinet quickly developed considerable corporate responsibility, a sense of common purpose, and strong ties of loyalty to the President. There were, to begin with, three military officers—Lieutenant-Generals Azam Khan, K. M. Sheikh, and Burki (the last a medical officer)—in addition to the President. The eight civilians, drawn half from East and half from West Pakistan, specialists in foreign affairs, finance, railways, education, commerce, local administration, industries, and law—were men who had kept out of politics and were widely trusted and respected. Later, the Governors of East and West Pakistan became ex-officio members—an innovation which has proved extremely useful in linking the Provinces to the Centre, and in promoting good understanding between the two wings of the country. From the outset, I was told by a member of the Government, the President encouraged everyone to speak his mind. At first, the tradition of military discipline tended to keep the Generals silent until the President called upon them: but before long they began to follow the example of their civilian colleagues and to express their opinions freely. The President took part in the discussions himself, and put forward his own ideas, which he did not like his Ministers to follow blindly. He expected them, if they disagreed, to say so: and to ask him whether he had considered such-and-such an aspect: or whether his information about so-and-so was quite complete. The plan that was generally followed, when a difficult problem arose, was to appoint a sub-committee to consider it, with orders to report without delay. This sub-committee consulted any expert opinion that it needed and collected the necessary information. Its report then went to the Cabinet for action. An excellent example of the way in which the Revolutionary Government cut Gordian knots was provided by what it did about a new Capital. For many years, successive Pakistani administrations had recognized that Karachi, highly commercialized, and dominated by 'big business', was unsuited to be also the main seat of the Central Government. Yet vested interests and competing claims combined to inhibit effective action. Shortly after he came to power, President Ayub Khan appointed an expert committee to go into the question. After a rapid but thorough survey of all the possibilities, and the hearing of evidence, the committee recommended the construction of a new Capital city on the healthy Potwar plateau, between Rawalpindi and the foothills of the Himalayas. The Cabinet, after full discussion, accepted the committee's recommendation. The new capital, named Islamabad, is already in course of construction: meanwhile Rawalpindi has become the temporary headquarters of the Government of Pakistan. In this way, a problem which had beset previous administrations for years was successfully dealt with in a matter of months.

The President was careful to see that every question was thoroughly explored: he would often carry over an important matter from one meeting to the next to give time for reflection. Usually a joint opinion emerged, which he always accepted: occasionally he would say: 'How many of us are in favour of Course A?' 'How many in favour of Course B?' and the decision of the majority usually prevailed. I myself noticed two things about the Revolutionary Government which distinguished it from all its predecessors. The first was the rapidity and thoroughness with which policy decisions, once formulated, were put into effect. No delay was permitted. The second was a frank willingness to admit any mistakes that may have been made, and to correct them.

My wife and I were in England when the Revolution took place: the English Press had been full of not over-friendly speculations about the aims and character of the Revolutionary régime, and of gloomy prophecies about the future of Pakistan. One newspaper, which should have known better, had described the installation of the

'military dictatorship' as the greatest shock which has been administered of late to the Commonwealth. In India, where we arrived at the
end of 1958, the tone of comment was equally critical. The abolition
of Parliamentary Government in Pakistan and the institution of a
régime headed by a soldier, were thought to herald an era of adventurous aggression against which India must take all precautions. Yet, so
far as I could gather, this kind of comment was based, not on knowledge, but on sheer speculation. There was no solid reason in the
actions of the new Government either for the British or for the Indian
expressions of censure and pessimism. One thing, as it seemed to me,
most foreign commentators had failed to perceive: the Revolution
was born and bred from purely domestic causes. It had in no way cut
across the traditional alignments of the country in international
affairs, or its relations with the rest of the Commonwealth. As we
noticed in an earlier chapter, the Revolutionary Government has
strengthened these relations in certain directions and has enlarged
the circle of Pakistan's friends. But the foreign policy of the country
has never altered: no desire to change it figured among the causes of
the Revolution. The Revolution, indeed, was an internal movement,
with which only Pakistanis were concerned. To find out what they
thought of it, I was more inclined to trust my own observations than
to rely on information at second hand. Accordingly, I wrote to some
of my Pakistani friends and asked if we might visit them.

We reached Karachi in the first few days of February 1959, and we
sensed at once the change which had come over the situation. It
seemed as if a burden had been lifted from the shoulders of everyone:
the former apathy and cynicism which had depressed us so much at
the beginning of 1958 had given place to a new spirit of energy and
hopefulness. The accounts which we had read in the Indian Press had
led us to expect all the outward trappings of a military régime, such as
soldiers everywhere, and machine-guns posted at strategic points. We
saw nothing of the kind: there were no troops about at all—inquiry
revealed that they were all busy with the normal spring manœuvres
prescribed by the standard training programmes. I asked one or two
ordinary people—taxi-drivers and the like—about this. They replied:
'Oh yes, there were a few soldiers here in October, but now they have
all gone away. We were sorry at first when they went, because we
thought that it meant that the old kind of Government was coming
back. But we are quite happy about it now because the people who
made a mess of things have gone for good and all: the new lot are

quite different, and we ordinary folk are better off because prices have begun to come down, food is cheaper, and we know that the Government pays attention when things go wrong and tries hard to put them right.'

Apparently what had happened was this. Drastic measures were taken at first to bring down prices by regulation, to punish hoarding, and to stiffen the backs of the civil authorities by putting military officers alongside them to assure that the new martial law regulations were obeyed. For more serious offences, special martial law tribunals were created. In a few weeks' time, however, things had become normal enough to allow the ordinary civil courts to take care of the new regulations. The Government found the trading community co-operative: the trading community found the Government reasonable in allowing them working margins consistent with the public interest in the restraint of prices. The military withdrew more and more from day-to-day control: the civil administration resumed its functions; and the only remaining traces of martial law lay in the regulations which the ordinary courts were required to enforce. We talked to merchants, big and small, and found them appreciative of the efforts which the Government was making to restore general business confidence, to allow the laws of supply and demand to function, and to withdraw or modify regulations which had been shown to be unworkable.

As we began to look up old friends, and to widen the circle of our inquiries, one outstanding impression became deepened by everything that we saw and heard. The country had once again got a real Government, a Government that knew what it was doing, was busy doing it, and was strong enough to command obedience. The men at the top seemed to be bringing fresh minds to bear upon old problems, and to be making considerable progress towards solving them. Ordinary people were chuckling over the dramatic smashing of the organized smuggling racket both in East and West Pakistan. Enormous quantities of hidden gold and of contraband cloth had been recovered: the ill-paid men who did the actual smuggling had been let off lightly, while the chiefs of the smuggling-rings had been brought to book and received exemplary punishment. The new Government was displaying a great deal of hard common sense in everything that it was doing: for example, in recovering the heavy arrears of taxation, it gave the defaulters a month's grace to pay up: if they did this, no action was taken against them provided that they undertook to meet their obligation to the State promptly in the future. About £90 million was thus recovered in the space of a few weeks.

What was impressing ordinary people, we found, as much as anything was the change that had come over the public services. The drive against inefficiency and corruption, and the screening process, described in an earlier chapter, resulted in action being taken against 138 first-class civil officers, 221 officers of the second class, and 1,303 third-class employees. Dismissals, compulsory retirements, and reductions in grade totalled 3,000. As we have already seen, this thorough-going shake-up both improved immensely the morale of the good, hard-working officers, who found themselves now empowered to set the tone for the whole of their departments; and also brought home to the subordinate ranks the reality of their responsibilities as public servants. The result was that Government offices were open at proper times: the officers attended to their duties honestly and conscientiously: the clerks were civil to the ordinary citizen and helped him in his difficulties. It was no longer necessary to give a bribe in order to make an appointment far ahead to see the right official: he was on the spot—ready to be seen. There was a notable cutting of red tape: the transaction of official business was thoroughly speeded up. The reaction of the higher officials, of the men who had striven so hard—and often so vainly—to hold the administration together was one of great relief. 'Thank goodness,' one of them remarked to me, 'we can now get on with our job without interference from those wretched politicians!'

The calibre of the new Ministers was notably high: like the President himself, they worked ceaselessly. In the course of our later visits to Pakistan, we came to meet and know them all: the impressions that they made on us may perhaps be of interest. The Minister of Finance, Mr. Mohammad Shuaib, had perhaps the most difficult job at that moment. He is enormously experienced: after having been Controller of Military Finance, he had spent six years in Washington with the World Bank. Incidentally, he is one of the very few qualified Cost Accountants in Asia. For the first time in the history of Pakistan, proper Treasury control was introduced under his guidance. This has been a reform of far-reaching consequences—almost a revolution in itself—but he spoke most warmly of the way in which the system has been accepted, and of the confidence which everyone, from the President downwards, showed in him. He proved himself fully equal to his task. While keeping firmly in his mind the overwhelming importance of conserving resources, arresting inflation, encouraging exports, building up foreign exchange, and improving the balance of payments position, he always contrived to find the means for putting in hand, or for pressing forward with, schemes of improvement which are immediately vital for the well-being of the country. When we met him first, early in 1959, he was struggling against the kind of difficulties which, for many years, had over-whelmed most of his predecessors in office. He obviously knew exactly what he was doing; he was entirely calm, unflurried and cheerful. It was plain to me that he was just the man to help Pakistan to order her financial affairs and to set her on the road to prosperity. This, indeed, he soon began to do: during the years which have elapsed since the Revolution occurred, his wise measures have stabilized the economy, curbed inflation, built up the gold, dollar and sterling reserves, trans-formed the balance of payments position by turning deficits into sur-pluses, produced a succession of balanced budgets free from deficit financing, and laid the economic foundations for Pakistan's Second (1960–5) Five Year Plan. In 1960, he persuaded the Government to adopt decimal currency. Introduced in 1961, it saves time and man-power in accounting: and facilitates the use of calculating machines. It is no wonder that the country has become increasingly attractive to foreign investors, and that experts believe the economy is becoming steadily sounder year by year. So well had Mr. Shuaib performed his task that in 1962 the Government found it possible to release him from his post as Finance Minister and to assign him once more to the International Bank in order to ensure that Pakistan's claims for generous assistance in the execution of her Second Five Year Plan are presented with the maximum force and authority. He has been suc-ceeded by Mr. Abdul Qadir, formerly Head of the National Bank, a financial expert trained in Mr. Shuaib's methods and ideas.

Another Minister who made a great impression on us was General Burki. In his earlier years, he had been the youngest man ever to attain Colonel's rank in the old Indian Medical Service. His parti-cular charges have been Health, Social Welfare, and Labour: by early 1959 he had already galvanized the Health Services into new activity —and had made the hospitals throughout Pakistan the kind of institu-tions to which the public could resort with confidence. Discipline was tightened, bribery strongly put down. The needs of the patient were made the first consideration: no seriously ill person could be turned away on the excuse that there was no room for him; if need be, the medical staff must give up their own quarters. General Burki was able to do magnificent work for the health services. He recently set on foot a scheme, to be completed under the Second Five Year Plan, for establishing a health centre with one male and one female doctor, a laboratory, and three sub-centres, for every 50,000 people throughout the entire country. Under his direction, an enlightened Labour policy has been adopted which has substantially reduced the risk of industrial unrest. Freedom of association and collective bargaining are recognized: sound trade unionism is encouraged: proper amenities are insisted upon: the workers are now convinced that Government cares for their interests and fosters their well-being. Social Welfare, too, has received a new impetus. Organizations like APWA which had sometimes worked, as it were, almost in the wilderness, have found themselves helped, consulted, utilized and encouraged. University students and schoolboys have been enlisted to undertake social surveys: the enthusiasm of youth organizations is mobilized.

Two other Generals then in the Cabinet were outstanding personalities. Lt.-General Azam Khan, in charge of rehabilitation, impressed us as a human dynamo, a dedicated man whose every waking hour was spent in getting things done. His most astonishing achievement was to set on foot, and to complete, in the face of many difficulties, the model community of Korangi, which has finally broken the back of the problem of refugee resettlement in the neighbourhood of Karachi. No question now arises of refugees letting their new houses and returning to their miserable settlements. As soon as the refugees are moved, the hutments are destroyed and the land is put to other uses. Many insanitary eyesores have been healed by Korangi. This enterprise, whose progress my wife and I have been able to watch almost from its inception, has become a scientifically-planned city, with its own light industries, its own opportunities for employment, its own transport system—a city with houses suitable for a wide range of income-groups, with mosques, schools, markets, playgrounds, hospitals and all the other aids to community life. Its aim is not only to house the refugees, but also to integrate them into the community as a whole, and to enable them to build up their life afresh as respected citizens of the new Pakistan. The work has proceeded with great speed—the first 20,000 houses were built in three months—stimulated by General Azam Khan's personal supervision and notable capacity for cutting red tape. The confidence which he inspired was remarkable: we were not surprised to find, on one of our later visits, that he had been sent to East Pakistan as Governor, so that he could help the Eastern Wing to realize its remarkable potentialities. He did a wonderful job there.

His colleague, Lt.-General K. M. Sheikh, an excellent administrator with long experience, held at that time the key-portfolio of Interior Affairs, to which was later added the charge of frontier regions. Later still, he was transferred to the key-position of responsibility for Food and Agriculture. In charge of internal security and police administration, he ensured the smooth working of the partnerships between the local civil offices and the martial law administration. When the Revolutionary Government ended, he became Ambassador to Japan. He impressed us greatly, as did the Foreign Minister, Mr. Manzur Qadir, whose wide reading, long study of international affairs, and complete freedom from all political affiliations qualified him admirably for his post. He had been a lawyer in very leading practice, and son of a famous judge: he told me that it was with great hesitation that he accepted the President's invitation to join the Cabinet. But he thought, he said, that there was no harm in trying the experiment, especially as he felt it his duty to give the new Government all the help he could. He did so well, and he won so much confidence from the President and from all his colleagues as well as from his 'opposite numbers' in other countries, that I am sure he does not regret this short spell of public life.

His civilian colleagues included Khan F. M. Khan, a very experienced East Pakistani who was given charge of railways and communications, in the direction of which he has done extremely well: Mr. Habibur Rahman, whose key-portfolio of education at that time also included the vital services of information and broadcasting—so essential for the task of keeping the people of Pakistan in close touch with all that the Government was planning and doing on their behalf: Mr. Abdul Kasim Khan, a well-known East Pakistani industrialist who held charge of industries, works and power: Mr. Hafizur Rahman, whose task it was to manage food supplies, to stimulate agriculture, and to repair, so far as human ingenuity and hard work could, the ravages of three years of disastrous monsoon shortages. Later, he was given charge of commerce, which to begin with was in the very capable hands of Mr. Zulfiqar A. Bhutto, a young man new to politics, but with a reputation already established among economists. Mr. Bhutto was afterwards in charge of the new and highly important portfolio of Fuel, Power and Natural Resources. Finally, the legal portfolio was held by Mr. Mohammad Ibrahim, a learned, shrewd, and widely-read lawyer.

Presiding over this admirable team was General Ayub Khan himself. He is a man about whom much has been written, and about whom more will be written in the future. It is difficult to convey to those who have not met him his entire lack of affectation and the simple directness of his manner; but perhaps the following anecdote may help explain something of the attraction he exercises over those who know him. At a time when he had been in office for more than two years—years characterized by unchallenged authority at home and an assured reputation abroad—he took the trouble to make arrangements for my wife and myself to visit the village of Rihana, in the lovely Hazara district, set amidst mountains, orchards, and running streams—the village where he was born and brought up. There we were welcomed by his domestics (he himself was away at the time) and entertained to lunch in the modest house which he had built for himself while he was a Major in the Army. A blazer and tennis kit were still hanging up in the small bedroom which he continues to use whenever he can find a moment's leisure. My wife met his sister and her family: her husband is the brother of the President's wife. We were entertained in their home, also, which is in the neighbouring village of Darwesh, from which the Begum Sahiba comes. These were two typical Pathan villages, full of tall, upstanding men, independent and free-spoken, proud that they had given a President to Pakistan. No surroundings could have been simpler, more genuine, more utterly free from ostentation of any kind. When I called upon the President again to thank him for his kindness, he said to me: 'I am so glad that you were able to go. I wanted you to see where we come from—we are just village folk!'

When I first met him as President early in 1959, three months after he had come to power, I was familiar with his reputation as a soldier, but I was unprepared for his broad, statesman-like grasp of civil affairs. I found him modest in his approach to the problems confronting him. 'I am not one of these clever chaps,' he said, with a twinkle in his eye, 'I like to hear what the experts say before we make up our minds what to do.' He does not believe that the solutions which first occur to him are the only ones, or necessarily the right ones: he likes to thrash everything out in his Cabinet. His obvious gifts as an initiator, an administrator, and a man of action are wholly dedicated to the service of his country: and his great strength is his instinctive grasp of the feelings, as well as of the needs, of the ordinary Pakistani man and woman. He knows beforehand what their reactions will be to every step he takes: he allows for this in all he does. He seems to be wholly without personal ambition. In our first talk, he explained to me with the utmost simplicity how shocked he was when he found himself obliged to take over control of the country. All his training, all his instincts, the whole of his outlook, fought against such a conclusion: but he was finally convinced that his duty to Pakistan enforced it upon him. He added one thing that has always stuck in my mind, since it seems to summarize his philosophy of action: 'I want our children and our grandchildren, when they look back on what I and my chaps are doing, to be able to say, honestly and sincerely: "Those fellows may have made mistakes, but they did their best for the country." '

He explained to me the different enterprises which he was immediately putting in hand, starting with the great programme of agrarian reform which has already begun to alter for the better rural conditions in West Pakistan. For years, everyone had known what was wanted: feudalism must be abolished: the great estates must be broken up: in their place peasant proprietorship and full tenant right must be established. But all efforts to achieve these ends had been shattered on the entrenched interests, firmly protected by pressure-groups in the Central and Provincial legislatures, of the landed proprietors: no previous Government had ventured to tackle the problem in the radical manner which its importance necessitated. Almost the whole area of West Pakistan was owned by a few thousand landlords. Some were small men, country squires and peasant proprietors; others were immensely rich landed proprietors, whose estates were measured in square miles rather than in acres, and whose tenants—who could in fact, if not in law, be evicted at will—were numbered in thousands. It was largely these men, with the votes of their tenants at their command, who had dominated and corrupted the political life of the country and had made the working of Parliamentary institutions a curse, not a blessing, to Pakistan. Their political power was henceforth to be broken; and their sectional interests to be subordinated to the wider interests of society at large.

Within a few weeks of taking over charge, President Ayub Khan appointed a Land Reforms Commission to work out a plan to achieve two aims: first to reform land tenure to ensure greater equality of opportunity and social status: and next to increase agricultural production and improve standards of rural living. The commission, headed by Mr. Akhtar Husain, later Governor of West Pakistan, a revenue officer and administrator of great experience, reported at the beginning of 1959. The Government accepted the Commission's recommendations and brought them into operation before the end of January. These recommendations have proved extraordinarily practical; moreover, from the standpoint of the student of agrarian reform in other Asian countries, they are refreshingly free from the doctrinaire assumptions which seem to underlie corresponding schemes elsewhere. They restrict individual holdings to maxima of 1,000 acres of unirrigated land or 500 acres of irrigated land—limitations deliberately chosen to ensure that agriculture continues a worthwhile profession in which middle-class young men will be prepared to invest money, and for which they will be willing to undergo scientific training, so that the general professional competence of those who work the land will gradually improve. All land over and above these ceilings has been resumed by the Government for distribution: compensation to former owners takes the form of interest-bearing bonds spread over twenty-five years. Tenants already cultivating the resumed land have been given security of tenure and may purchase complete ownership by easy instalments over a similar period. A scheme for the compulsory consolidation into workable areas of fragmented holdings is being set on foot, and the future breaking-up of compact holdings into scattered strips is forbidden. All the old semi-feudal dues which formerly burdened many tenants were abolished, as were also ancient claims upon the land-revenue and ancient gifts of land for which the recipients rendered no services. A Provincial Land Commission was set up to put these decisions into immediate effect. With the entire resources of the Government mobilized to prevent delay and obstruction, progress has been astonishingly rapid. Millions of acres have been resumed: nearly 200,000 landless tenants have been settled upon them, with appropriate loans for seeds and implements: while a million and a half existing occupants have received full proprietary rights.

These reforms have already done a great deal of good. By breaking the power of the great landed interests, they have destroyed a sinister influence in public life. They have begun to remove agrarian unrest in West Pakistan once and for all. They have created a class of tenant-proprietors who are showing themselves increasingly eager to co-operate with the Government in raising the level of agricultural production. The difficulties to be faced are formidable: water-logging and salinity must be overcome: waste land must be reclaimed: the use of better seeds, better techniques, and better fertilizers must be extended: the menace of periodic floods and droughts must be lessened: improved credit facilities and more co-operative effort must be organized. Pakistan still has to rely upon foreign sources for some of her food. It will be some time before agricultural output is entirely satisfactory. But in tackling their tasks, Government and the people are standing shoulder to shoulder as never before: everything that is being achieved is solid and real, because it is firmly based upon the support of the masses themselves.

The land-problem in East Pakistan, which, as explained in an earlier chapter, is of a different nature from that of West Pakistan, soon claimed the attention of the Revolutionary Government. The Act of 1952, as we have seen, drastically limited the size of holdings to thirty acres, and prescribed the gradual compensation, over a term of years, of people whose land, or whose rent-receiving interests, were acquired by the State. In the course of the party rivalries which afflicted East Pakistan's politics, doctrinaire sections of opinion succeeded in forcing a decision in 1956 that all these rights and interests should be taken over at a fixed date. Great confusion resulted, especially as the conviction was growing that the thirty-acre limit was driving the progressive, middle-class element in the farming community away from the land. The entire scheme was therefore remitted for examination to an expert committee. Meanwhile, much fallow land was immediately put under cultivation: new drainage schemes to deal with flooding were started: tube wells and pumps were installed to make cultivation possible in the dry season: and coastal embankments, vital for protection against cyclones and tidal waves, were strengthened and extended. The prospects of development for East Pakistan are bright indeed. The Chairman of the East Pakistan Water and Power Development Authority told me, for example, that only a few years ago, his budget was a mere Rs. 5 lakhs. This year his budget is Rs. 25 lakhs; next year he is budgeting for Rs. 40 lakhs; he will soon be up to Rs. 60 lakhs. Among the projects in hand, now that Kaptai has been completed, is an extensive new irrigation plan—the Dacca-Narayanganj-Demra scheme—which will operate on land now subject to inundation south of Dacca. A credit of $1 million has already been received from the International Development Association for this project, which is expected to yield valuable information for similar enterprises elsewhere in East Pakistan.

Among the tasks which the Revolutionary Government has set itself is the strengthening of the ties of cordiality between the East and West wings of the country. The President himself attaches great importance to this: and almost from the moment when he came to power he has made strenuous and indeed successful, efforts to convince the people of East Pakistan that he rates their interests and their feelings just as high as those of the people of West Pakistan. He spends much time in touring the East wing: he gives high priority to the development of the area: he ensures that its needs rank equally with those of West Pakistan in the allotment of the available funds. He has seen to it that the new refugee townships round Dacca are worthy to rank alongside the great achievement of Korangi: and when he made the decision to move the Government from Karachi, and to build a new capital on the Potwar plateau near Rawalpindi, he gave a pledge to the people of East Pakistan that work on Islamabad would not be given priority over the programme of slum-clearance and civic improvement which Dacca so badly needs. He is genuinely anxious that East Pakistanis should learn to look after their own affairs. 'I don't want', he has told them, 'to send outsiders to govern you. I want you to learn to do the job yourselves.'

In the course of our first long talk with President Ayub Khan in February 1959, he made it clear to us that the agrarian reforms in West Pakistan, like the steps taken to convince the East Pakistanis that they and their land are regarded as essential components of the State which Quaid-i-Azam had founded, are all part of a long-term programme of national reconstruction which has been worked out in detail. Among the items in this programme, in addition to the encouragement of industry and the development of natural resources, are educational and legal reform; the improvement of the position of women: the development of regional and national cultures: a progressive labour policy: family planning to check inordinate growth of the population and to speed up the improvement of the living standards of the masses. Special commissions were appointed to look into such matters as the simplification of legal processes: the contribution which applied science can make to the technical problems which Pakistan must solve: the acceleration of agricultural development and of the campaign for growing more food: the selection of the site for a new federal capital, and the like. Work along all these lines has proceeded steadily, ever since: it was co-ordinated by a special committee of the Cabinet, by a Planning Commission, and by a Ministry of National Reconstruction. But the President insisted to us that the aim of all these activities can be simply stated: it was to improve the lot of the ordinary Pakistani man and woman, and, with this end in view, to build up an educated middle class in the countryside as well as in the towns who could sustain the responsibilities of self-government. For this reason, one of the main problems to which he was giving thought at the beginning of 1959 was how to ensure that the people of Pakistan are actively associated in the running of their country's affairs. 'Democracy is vital to us,' he said, 'we cannot do without it: but it must be the kind of democracy which the people as a whole can understand and can work. I have pledged my word that within twelve months of our taking over power, we shall find some arrangement which will do this.'

Chapter *11*

BASES OF DEMOCRACY

In view of the immensity of the tasks which faced the President and his colleagues, I wondered a good deal, when I left Pakistan early in 1959, whether in fact he would find it possible to fulfil his pledge. But in October of that year, when the Revolution was just twelve months old, President Ayub Khan published the Basic Democracies Order, which set up a novel system of local government in Pakistan and laid the foundations for active participation by the people at large in the management of their own affairs. My wife and I had one of the most interesting experiences of our lives when we toured East and West Pakistan towards the end of 1959 after we had received an invitation from the Government to watch the preparations for this remarkable experiment.

The main ideas underlying the scheme of Basic Democracies are a combination of several older conceptions. First, there are the ancient institutions of village self-government, such as the Panchayats (Councils of Five) which have flourished from time immemorial in the Indo-Pakistani sub-continent, and have been studied by sociologists from Sir Henry Maine to Dr. Adrian Mayer. Next, there are the more modern institutions designed to promote self-help, co-operative enterprise in village improvement, and the like, embodied in projects like Community Development. In Pakistan, as we have noticed in an earlier chapter, these latter have found expression in the Village AID movement. In a number of Asian countries, efforts to marry the ancient institutions and the modern welfare schemes have been made: India's Community Development movement is, as we have seen, a large-scale example.

But while the Pakistani conception of Basic Democracies makes use both of the traditions of village self-government and of the impetus which Village AID is imparting to village development, it differs from corresponding schemes in other countries in two important respects. In the first place, it is based upon people, not places. Its foundation is the 'primary constituency' containing 800 to 1,000 men and women.

199

Adult suffrage has been established which enfranchises everybody over twenty-one years of age, so that each 'primary constituency' has an average of about 400 voters. In a group of this size, everyone knows everyone else, at least by reputation: and it is this 'neighbourhood knowledge' which the Revolutionary Government holds to be of the first importance when it comes to a question of choosing representatives. Eight or ten, according to convenience, of these 'primary constituencies' are grouped together to elect what is called in the countryside a Union Council: in the smaller urban centres a Town Committee: and in the larger cities a Union Committee. Each Council or Committee—there are about 4,000 of them in West Pakistan and about 4,200 in East Pakistan—is termed, in the current political shorthand, a Basic Democracy: its members are called Basic Democrats. Each represents about 8,000 people of whom some 4,000 are voters. The second innovation which the scheme of Basic Democracies embodies lies in the fact that every Basic Democracy is the first stage of an ascending hierarchy of Councils—in the sub-division, *tahsil* or *thana*: in the District: in the Division: and finally in the Province. In all these 'higher up' institutions, a proportion of the membership comes directly from the Council next lower down: the result is that representation of the original 'primary constituencies' is carried right through all the grades to the level of the two Provincial Councils each of which deals with affairs of impressive magnitude for the whole of East or of West Pakistan.

The entire scheme was most carefully worked out in detail in the Basic Democracies Order to ensure that it is the ordinary people who will play the dominant part, without any interference or pressure. Very heavy penalties have been prescribed for bribery or undue influence. No Government officer can vote: the Foreign Secretary of the day said to me: 'My chauffeur and my washerman can vote: I can't! But my wife can, and she likes to remind me of it!' To every ten elected members of the Union Committees or Councils, the Government reserved the right to nominate another five persons. The reasons for this provision were explained to me. It was thought that there would be quite a number of 'useful' men and women, particularly, perhaps, retired Government servants and worthy middle-class citizens, who could make a substantial contribution to the working of the new institutions, but who might hesitate to present themselves for election. Further, it was thought that particular classes of the community—minorities, landless labourers, or those who pursued avocations which were not highly esteemed—might fail to secure representation at the polls, but could not be left out. The conditions governing nomination were most rigidly laid down. No defeated candidate could be nominated: every person selected must add demonstrably to the efficiency, or to the representative character of the Council or Committee: every individual nomination, which had to be made by the Head of the whole District—the District Officer—personally, must satisfy the scrutiny of his superiors. Quite frequently, we found later, the ordinary process of election did in fact produce a perfectly satisfactory representation of the primary constituency concerned: and the District Officer was able to report that the nomination of additional members was unnecessary. It is interesting to note, in passing, that this system of nomination was described as 'undemocratic' in several areas of West Pakistan, as we found by talking to voters and candidates: while in East Pakistan, where the people are, on the whole, more sophisticated politically, it was looked on as a good thing. Quite a number of East Pakistani Basic Democrats with whom I discussed the point told me that the power of nomination really strengthened the Basic Democracies because it brought in a number of highly-educated people who helped with their 'know-how' and their grasp of local needs.

Every Union Council and Union Committee has to elect its own Chairman: Government undertakes to provide and pay a trained clerk to keep the minutes and attend to the correspondence. Each Chairman so elected is ex-officio a member of the next higher Council —that of the *thana* or *tahsil*. This Council, of which the Sub-Divisional Officer is Chairman, contains Government officials of various departments directly concerned with village welfare, and persons directly appointed: but the elected membership is in no case less than half the total strength. The next Council in rank, the District Council, of which the Deputy Commissioner or Collector is Chairman, has, as its ex-officio members, the chairman of the *thana* or *tahsil* councils and of the municipal bodies in the area it covers, together with higher departmental officers: to it the Government appoints other members, of whom at least half must be chairmen of Union Councils or Committees. The Divisional Councils—which sometimes deal with an area as big as Wales—are presided over by the Commissioner: chairmen of District Councils and representatives of municipal bodies and of appropriate Government Departments are ex-officio members: and here again chairmen of primary Councils and Committees must form not less than half the total strength of the members directly appointed. It is only at the very top—the Provincial Councils presided over respectively by the Governors of West and East Pakistan —that the proportion of chairmen of Union Councils and of Town and Union Committees falls as low as one-third of the total nominated membership. Each grade of the hierarchy of Councils is given definite executive responsibilities, and the fiscal powers and revenue resources necessary for their proper discharge.

Plainly, even on the most casual study, the Basic Democracies Order embodied a very carefully-thought-out scheme, with obvious potentialities for mobilizing the energy and enthusiasm of the people of Pakistan in support of a great movement of national reconstruction. But two questions presented themselves to my mind: how could the ordinary man or woman of Pakistan be made to understand it? and when they had understood it, how would they receive it? There would be a backlog of apathy, and even of suspicion, to overcome. West Pakistanis would think that the new scheme was just a revival of the old Panchayat system, which meant little to them: East Pakistanis would confuse it with the old Union Boards. Whatever influence the local magnates and the ex-politicians could still command would be used to decry the scheme. Altogether, it would be uphill work to put it across to the people: I wondered how well the job was being tackled.

In the autumn of 1959, as I have related, my wife and I received a cordial invitation from the Revolutionary Government to revisit Pakistan, and to see for ourselves how things were going, so that at the end of that year and the beginning of 1960, we were able to spend six weeks in a rapid tour of West and East Pakistan, covering an extensive area with the aid of aircraft, cars, and the ubiquitous jeep, which can now penetrate to many of the most distant villages. The first thing to impress us was the magnitude of the educational campaign which was in progress to explain what the Basic Democracies scheme could mean to each individual citizen and how people could help both themselves and the country by working it. The administrative resources of Government, assisted by a host of volunteer workers, teachers, students, schoolboys, schoolgirls, members of APWA and of other social-uplift organizations, had been brought to bear on this campaign. The Press, no longer dependent upon the favour of party politicians, free to publish constructive criticism but forbidden to promote purely sectional interests, played an important part in awakening public interest. A very effective film had been prepared, with local variations suited to differences of surroundings, of language, of costume and of customs. We came across this film, in its different versions, everywhere in Pakistan: it was displayed in every cinema in the cities: it toured the countryside in travelling vans which put on open-air shows in the villages. It depicted in clear, vivid terms the change that the Revolution had brought in destroying vested interests and liberating the ordinary citizen: it showed the downfall of oppressive local magnates and the rise of men who had earned the esteem of their fellows for uprightness and benevolence: it urged the electors to choose such men to represent them. Simple plays illustrating the same theme were performed by students and schoolchildren, who toured the countryside. Pamphlets, posters, simple literature, penetrated everywhere, backed up by the speeches and lectures of the Village AID and similar organizations, and of all the District officials.

We had the opportunity first of visiting a large number of urban constituencies: we talked both to candidates and to voters, and we found that they fully understood what Basic Democracies would mean to them, and how, by electing representatives from among themselves, they could choose men whom they knew and trusted: men upon whom they could keep a check: men whom they could harry and pursue if badly-needed local improvements were not put in hand quickly enough. There was one difficulty which we encountered everywhere—that of time. The electoral rolls were out of date, affording an imperfect guide to the new constituencies which were being created: rules had to be framed, forms printed, ballot-boxes made— and all this between October 27th, when the Basic Democracies Order was promulgated, and December 31st when the elections were to be held. But the work was done on time. We watched the careful check that was exercised to preserve the secrecy of the ballot— special cubicles were arranged, which the voters entered alone, containing the voting-boxes with the names and pictorial symbols of the candidates: the organization of the special voting stations for purdah ladies: the ready assistance given by the officers in charge to candidates anxious to ensure that their nomination-papers were correctly filled in. The urban candidates impressed us favourably: they were mainly youngish people from the lower middle-class income groups: solid citizens, who wanted, not to enter politics, but to take a share in the running of local affairs. There was also a fair sprinkling of working-class people, and, at the other end of the scale, of highly-educated men and women with experience of social work. It was only in the larger towns, we found, that women were actually standing for election: but my wife discovered that the women electors in the town constituencies were enormously interested in the personalities of the candidates, and eager to exercise their vote. At a later stage, we watched the actual elections both at the men's and the women's polling-booths. The turn-out of voters was high—in the towns often as much as 70 per cent. The behaviour of the menfolk was orderly in the extreme: voting was not new to them. But the women were so enthusiastic, my wife told me, that it was difficult for the lady polling-officers to persuade them to queue up in line. They treated election-day as a festival, flocking along to their polling-stations with their children and their female relatives. The enthusiasm was tremendous!

But the real test, we thought, would come in the countryside. How would the villagers take the idea, and would it be any more, so far as they were concerned, than just another 'paper-scheme' wished upon them from the top? What we found in rural areas both of West and East Pakistan was reassuring. The campaign of enlightenment had penetrated deeply into the countryside: and we found, on an average, that there were four or five candidates contesting each seat. The arrival in a remote village of foreigners—and particularly of an English-woman—was something of an event: a village meeting was quickly summoned, and we were able to talk to considerable numbers of people. In the countryside hardly any women were standing as candidates, but that did not mean that they were apathetic. My wife discovered that they were, in fact, holding their own meetings in each other's houses, and arranging which of the candidates they would vote for. Most of the candidates were known to them by reputation already—that is the advantage of small constituencies—and they had their own ways of gathering information about what these people were proposing to do if they were elected. The women were insisting, my wife told me, that they would support no candidate who did not pledge himself to work for girls' education, family welfare clinics, sanitary improvements, and better local amenities. Their husbands, my wife found, were taking all this very well: they were not interfering at all in the free choice of the women. The men electors, I found, had a slightly different range of criteria: the candidates whom they were ready to support must work for agricultural improvement—better tools, better seeds, better methods, better animals, more fertilizers—and the extension of schools, hospitals, and dispensaries. Improved roads and more bus services were also asked for.

We found, in a number of places, one or two disgruntled people; unpopular 'know alls' of the kind that many small English villages are familiar with: men who disagree with everyone, are fond of telling other people what ought to be done, but never do a hand's turn themselves: local party-politicians who found that they had no chance of being elected: a handful of persons who were discovering that wealth was no passport to political influence under the Revolutionary régime. These elements counted for little against the solid support which the village as a whole was giving to the Basic Democracies scheme: but the freedom with which they voiced their opinions revealed the complete absence of any intimidation, official or otherwise. There was also a die-hard conservative section among the much older men who thoroughly approved the Basic Democracies scheme, for which they claimed to find Islamic precedents, but who were alarmed by the prospect of increased feminine influence in public affairs which the scheme seemed likely to usher in. One venerably-bearded gentleman of advanced years remarked: 'This introduction of women into men's business is a mistake. I wish that those who believe in it would remember the old Arabic story that my own father used to tell. It seems that a respectable gentleman bought some land and settled down near a village. One day this gentleman came to see the village headman, saying that he wanted advice. The headman asked what the trouble was, and finding it to be a purely family affair, said: "My friend, that is not a question for an outsider: you must consult your household." The gentleman replied: "But my household consists only of women!" After a moment's thought, the headman replied: "I see your difficulty: there is only one way out. Put the matter to the ladies of your household: ask their advice: and, when they have given it, be careful to do just the opposite." '

The point about the Basic Democracies scheme which seemed to make the strongest appeal to the village electors both in East and West Pakistan was the insistence of Government that they were entirely free to choose their representatives, the men or the women whom they trusted as the best people to look after local affairs and to promote village development. Party organizations had been abolished, and, along with them, the 'carpet bag' candidate, a stranger to the constituency, had disappeared. Any man or woman in the constituency aged twenty-five and upwards, who could find half a dozen supporters, and could put down a very small deposit as a guarantee of good faith, was free to stand. I often asked electors what they thought of the candidates who were seeking election, and I found that their entire freedom of choice was inducing a sense of responsibility. 'In the old days', one man in East Pakistan said to me, 'I had to vote as I was told, or take the risk of a beating-up. Now I am able to vote for the man I want, and I am choosing him very carefully.' 'What kind of man do you want?' I asked. He replied: 'I am illiterate myself: I am going to choose an educated man whom I can trust, he will do better for me and for everyone else than someone who is uneducated.' 'Have you any of the right type standing here?' I asked: he replied: 'We have five candidates: three are no earthly use to anyone: two are very good, and I am making up my mind between them.' The choice of the voters did really seem to be based on merit: in some places I found that there was impressive support for an illiterate man because everyone trusted him and everyone admired his drive and energy. I think this point is worth noting, because, when the election results were complete, there was adverse comment from some quarters on the fact that, in all, about 10,000 illiterate people were chosen by the voters of East and West Pakistan out of a total of about 80,000 successful candidates. Most of the illiterate members were elected from West Pakistan constituencies; East Pakistan chose only some 800 of them. To my mind, this is no sign of political immaturity on the part of the electorate: it indicates an intelligent choice, because almost everywhere educated candidates were also available. There is no evidence at all that illiterates voted for illiterates and labourers for labourers—rather the contrary.

Among the highlights of our tour of Pakistan during the weeks preceding the first Basic Democracies elections was the time we spent with the President on his special train in the course of his tour of West Pakistan. He was throwing the whole weight of his personal influence into urging the people of Pakistan to accept and work the Basic Democracies scheme. He had toured extensively in East Pakistan before we arrived from England—it was a tactful move, to take East Pakistan first—and he was now completing his campaign in the Western wing by touring the large and populous areas between Sargodha and Peshawar. The train, named 'Pak Jamhuriat Special', in which the President travelled, was linked by radio and radio telephone to the whole of Pakistan, and to the outside world as well. There was an excellent link with London—a facility of which a number of foreign

newspapermen made great use—and the G.P.O. co-operated by assigning to their own end of the link an officer who spoke excellent Urdu.
The communication-system of the train, which was the responsibility
of the Pakistan Signals Corps, proved impressively efficient: the
President sent a message to us asking if we would like to call up anyone in London. We were able to speak to our daughter at Walton-on-
Thames—to her great surprise—from Gujrat in the Punjab. The
connection took only a few minutes. By means of these radio communications, the President remained in touch with the whole of the
country: he could summon his officers: he could give directions: he
could exercise complete control.

He worked tirelessly, both at governing the country and at carrying
on the campaign itself. In the course of three days we accompanied
him to fourteen meetings and heard him address many hundreds of
thousands of people. The days began very early: by 7 a.m., in the
bright, sharp cold of a Punjab winter morning, we would be out of
the train and inside our cars, driving along gaily decorated roads
lined with cheering people. Boy scouts, cadets, schoolboys, and
schoolgirls were much in evidence, waving flags, cheering, singing,
and shouting 'Pakistan Zindabad' ('Long live Pakistan'.) Soon we
would come to an open marquee, where a company of a hundred or
two of the leading citizens of the place we were visiting were
gathered to receive the President. These smaller meetings were of the
'Question and Answer' type: the President would give a short address,
explaining Basic Democracies: anyone present could question him on
this or any other matter. He sat back, completely relaxed, in his chair,
with no one to prompt him: he answered all the questions 'off the
cuff' with simplicity and frankness. There was always a small block of
seats reserved for women, some wearing the burqa and some un-
veiled. He seemed to make a particular point of inviting questions
from them, and of insisting upon the importance of the part which
they had to play in building up Pakistan. His gift for sensing the
'feel' of his audience was obvious: he knew at once whether a questioner
was airing a private grievance, or was voicing an opinion widely held.
The former class he dealt with wittily and effectively: a twinkle
would come into his eye, and he would deliver a terse comment which
would evoke an appreciative roar of laughter from his hearers. The
latter class of questioner he would treat very seriously: taking great
pains to elicit the real point at issue, and not infrequently ending: 'You
have really got something there: I think we may have made a mistake.'

He would then beckon to a Staff Officer behind him and say: 'We must look into this: let me have a report at once.'

These Question and Answer meetings were timed to last an hour, but if important topics came up, the President would never cut them short. When they were over, we would all go to an adjacent Circuit House or Rest House for a very welcome cup of coffee, while we waited to allow the audience at the Question and Answer meeting, and the people who had lined the streets, to make their way to the main public meeting where townsfolk and villagers from many miles round had gathered to hear the President. A procession of cars was formed, with the President's car in the lead, which drove through the city under triumphal arches and amidst showers of flower-petals and garlands, to give those unable to attend the public meeting a chance to greet him. The drive finished at the place fixed for the main gathering —either the local sports stadium or an arena specially arranged— where an enormous crowd of many thousands of people were assembled sitting packed together on the ground. Here, too, there were special arrangements for seating women, curtained tents were always provided to accommodate those who are not accustomed to appear in public.

After the recitation of verses from the Quran by a *maulvi*, the President would deliver a short, forceful address, explaining the principles of Basic Democracies and asking for the co-operation of every citizen in making the scheme a success. In this gathering, too, questions were invited. There was one question which made its appearance in every place we visited. The president would be asked, 'You have saved our country from ruin—things are looking up. We are quite content for you to lead us because we trust you. Why not leave well alone? What is the reason for this new thing? Why make a change now?' His reply always followed the same line. 'You are citizens of Pakistan—the country belongs to you. It is because you took no interest in public affairs that we encountered all these misfortunes which we are now overcoming. You must learn to run things for yourselves! This scheme is a beginning—take it! Remember that I and my colleagues cannot be with you for ever to run things for you!'

From the main meeting, we would all hurry back to the train, and move on to another place, where the same pattern of Question and Answer and public meetings would be repeated to a different audience. Not infrequently, there would be three such patterns in a single day, along with many unheralded and impromptu 'whistle-stops' at which the President would address great crowds packed on some small station platform, festooned in the trees, and swarming over the permanent way. I recall that in a brief interval between engagements, the President turned to my wife and said: 'You know, I do get *so* tired of speaking!' But he never failed to do it very well indeed, and to carry his immense audiences along with him.

The infectious enthusiasm which his presence aroused no doubt helped to keep him going through these strenuous days. However tired we ourselves felt, it acted like a tonic on us too, even though we were not the objects of it. The scene at Peshawar railway station, for example, was unforgettable. Here the President was among his own people, a Pathan among Pathans. The cheering crowd broke through all the cordons guarding the platform and swarmed towards the train. According to the standing instructions which guided our movements, as soon as the train drew up we left our own carriage to make our way, along the platform, to the President's saloon, where we were to join up with him and his personal staff. At Peshawar, it proved impossible to penetrate the solid mass of cheering, shouting humanity which blocked our path—immense men, almost all of them over six feet high, and broad in proportion, wearing the customary equipment of the local gentry—revolver, sword, and dagger. When the President appeared, they engulfed him bodily: clapping him on the shoulder, taking their turbans from their own heads and setting them on his, and even shedding tears of emotion.

The President, smiling broadly, and seeming to enjoy every minute of a scene which must have given all his Security Officers a thousand shudders, towered above the crowd, shaking hands, welcoming old friends, and shouting greetings above the din of laughter and cheering. My wife and I were swept almost off our feet, like leaves in the wind, by the pressure of apologetic but enormous Pathans, who grinned cordially as they pushed past us, saying: 'Forgive me—Madam and Sir—it is *my* President—I *must* touch him.' Everyone was so happy, so good tempered, that even the most confirmed solitary could hardly have felt alarmed: but it was slightly disconcerting for my wife to find her handbag, with our passports and money, immobilized inextricably behind her at the length of her outstretched arm by the sheer pressure of the crowd. Before long, the Foreign Minister was flung up beside us, smiling imperturbably, and as firmly jammed in the crowd as we were ourselves. But our plight was soon noticed: the broadest and most bulky Pathan Inspector of

Police whom I have ever seen came to our rescue. By sheer weight of bone and muscle, he ploughed a path through the press. The crowd grinned cheerfully and yielded what ground it could: behind him struggled the Foreign Minister. My wife clung firmly to his coat with one hand and to me with the other. At last we were on our way to our cars and to the next meeting. The sight of the President, alone but perfectly at his ease, entirely cut off even from his personal staff by this milling crowd of formidably-armed warriors, helped us to understand something of the position which he holds in the respect and affection of the people of Pakistan. It seemed probable, indeed, that his personal support of the Basic Democracies scheme would suffice, by itself, omitting all the other favourable factors, to give the project a good start.

We left Pakistan for England before the elections were entirely finished; but we were able to keep in touch with the results, and we received by airmail official analyses of the kind of candidates who had been returned, and overall reports on how the elections had been conducted. Altogether, 8,266 Basic Democracies were set up in East and West Pakistan together, of which 7,114 are Union Councils in the countryside: 816 are Union Committees in the cities: and 218 are Town Committees in the smaller urban centres. There are also 75 Cantonment Areas and 43 special areas. The total number of constituencies for the country was 50,561, returning 78,376 seats. Of these seats no fewer than 49,000 were won by agriculturalists: the bulk of the remaining successful candidates had small private businesses and were self-employed. There were 2,586 people who were in business in a fairly big way: there were 391 retired Government Servants—a most valuable element: there were only 288 lawyers! Altogether, it was plain that a good cross-section of the middle- and lower-income groups had been successful, only something under 8 per cent of whom had in the past been affiliated to any political group. The Hindu minority did well, winning nearly 5,000 seats in East Pakistan, and being well represented also in the Sind and Baluchistan areas. About one in every seven of the successful candidates throughout the whole country was illiterate.

An impressive characteristic of the elections was the care taken to provide against any improper pressure or influence. One instance which came under my notice may illustrate this. An Army Colonel went on leave to his own village while the elections were being held. Quite properly, he kept entirely aloof. But a defeated candidate, annoyed at his own failure, accused the Colonel of exerting influence against him. An inquiry was at once held by the Deputy Commissioner: a second inquiry was held by the Provincial Government: a third was instituted by the military authorities: the poor Colonel had to spend most of his leave under close examination. He was completely exonerated, and the false accuser was prosecuted: but the authorities had shown that they would stand no repetition of the scandals which had disgraced too many previous elections in the period before the Revolution.

The elections had been successfully held, and the Basic Democracies had been brought into existence: it remained to be seen how they would work. That the Revolutionary Government intended to make full use of them was shown by the fact that in February 1960 it asked the Basic Democrats to decide, by secret ballot, whether they wanted General Ayub Khan as President. A vote for him was to be taken as a general endorsement of the policies of the Revolutionary Government: but his opponents were left entirely free to record their dissent which, under the rigid precautions taken to preserve the secrecy of the ballot, could involve them in no penalties. Opposition there was, but it was numerically negligible: 96 per cent of the Basic Democrats—roughly 80,000 strong, and all men and women chosen by the electorate on personal merit—supported the President and his policies.

The Basic Democracies scheme interested my wife and me so much that we were very glad to accept from President Ayub Khan, whom we met again in England when he attended the Commonwealth Prime Ministers' Conference in May 1960, an invitation to visit Pakistan at the end of the year to see how the scheme was working out. We were particularly anxious to form our own personal impressions, because, as the year went on, not much appeared in the British Press about what was happening: and, such information as was given seemed to have been derived at second-hand, as it were, from sources which viewed the Basic Democracies with scepticism or even with distaste. Accordingly, we reached Karachi in the middle of December 1960, and were able to make a rapid but intensive tour of West and East Pakistan, in the course of which we personally visited several dozen Basic Democracies, talked to the Basic Democrats, and collected first-hand impressions about how the scheme was going. We went, as before, exactly where we chose to go, sometimes selecting villages and towns which we knew well, sometimes breaking fresh ground by penetrating to remote places which were new to us. My wife often visited purdah ladies, while I was chatting with the menfolk. Between us, I think we did enough field-work to provide us with a pretty accurate assessment of the situation. Our Pakistani friends, particularly the higher officials, had warned us, with characteristic 'canniness' not to expect too much: and we ourselves had also certain broad questions in our own minds to which we were seeking answers. In particular, we wanted to find out whether the general enthusiasm which we had observed a year previously had declined, and whether the new institutions had in fact progressed beyond the 'blue print' stage. The detailed notes which my wife and I made of our visits to individual Basic Democracies, if reproduced here, would unduly expand this book; and I shall have to confine myself to a few samples of a kind which may be taken as representative. But first, in order to set the background of what we saw, I will begin by recording some general impressions.

We soon found that the Government 'drive' to enlist public support for the scheme, so far from slackening off when the elections were finished, had, if anything, been intensified. The inexpediency of leaving the Basic Democrats 'in the air' was fully realized: from the moment of their election, every care was taken to convince them that they had important work to do, and that it was their duty to learn how to do it. The response had been whole-hearted and prompt: the Basic Democrats showed themselves willing to devote both time and energy to their jobs. In maintaining their enthusiasm, the personal influence of President Ayub Khan has proved a decisive factor. Everywhere we went, we learned of the visits he pays to Basic Democracies, of his talks with the Basic Democrats, of his tireless energy in touring the whole of Pakistan to visit them. He has been largely responsible for instituting the new campaign to galvanize Basic Democracies into effective action.

The Government, using the Village AID structure in its newly-expanded National Development Organization form, had set out to help the Basic Democrats by providing a network of nation-wide facilities for instruction. Carefully thought-out training courses, of two weeks' duration, were made available at appropriate centres up and down the country: and by the time we reached Pakistan, some 60,000 out of the 80,000 Basic Democrats had attended them. Before the courses were thrown open, intensive experimental work had been undertaken to decide upon the subjects to be covered and the methods of instruction to be used: the two Village AID Academies—one at Peshawar and one at Comilla—had pioneered this research. Test-courses were first tried out on a small scale: comment and criticism was invited both from Village AID officials who had to do the actual work of instruction, and from selected Basic Democrats who acted as 'guinea-pig' audiences. Eventually, a standard course and method were evolved, with the two-fold aim of instructing Basic Democrats in their responsibilities to their own constituents, and of orientating them in their position relative to other parts of the national administration.

The course familiarized the Basic Democrats with what they would need to know if they were to perform efficiently their duties as laid down in the 1959 Order: it instructed them in the proper conduct of council meetings, in the rules of procedure, in the regulation of discussions: and in the taking of majority decisions. Although each Council is provided by the Government with a clerk to keep the minutes, to conduct correspondence, to prepare the Budget and to keep accounts, the Basic Democrats were taught how to supervise his activities and how to keep him up to the mark as a Council functionary. They were instructed in the sources of revenue at their disposal, and in the social and economic developments to which the Council income should be devoted. They were taught how to prepare schemes of local improvement both for execution themselves and for submission to higher authority. Quite as important as all this for the proper discharge of their duties was the instruction they received in the functioning of the official world—a world hitherto regarded by many of them as remote, arbitrary, and Olympian. They were taught the position and the responsibilities of every official with whom they would come into contact—revenue, police, education, public health, engineering, irrigation, civil supplies, and the like. They learned exactly to whom they should go for whatever particular advice or help was needed. They also learned who his superiors were, in case complaints had to be made!

Both in East and in West Pakistan, these training courses were very popular, and attendance at them had become a matter of prestige. Basic Democrats who happened to be illiterate would bring their schoolboy-sons to take notes, so that nothing that had been learned should be forgotten. I found that the keener Basic Democrats often came back for special refresher courses after their initial experiences of practical work: in these courses, particular problems were discussed, and the solutions adopted in various places were compared. Tape-recordings of proceedings were played back for comment and criticism: successes and failures were discussed and analysed. The good the courses did is not confined to these practical ends. They really are bringing the people and the officials into close touch, as each side learns more about the other, and begins to gain an understanding of the development-work to be shared between them. Further, by a real touch of genius, it is not only the Basic Democrats who are expected to undergo an intensive course of training in the implications of the 1959 Order: parallel, but of course more advanced courses have been instituted for the officials themselves. At subdivisional and *tahsil* level, departmental officers are instructed in their duties towards the Basic Democracies: how authority must be delegated: how consultation must be arranged: how development-schemes must be co-ordinated: how personal contact must be established and maintained between departmental officers and the Chairmen and members of all the Union Councils. At the higher levels, courses are arranged at the Peshawar and Comilla Academies for Heads of Districts and their assistants, and for senior officers of the technical services—agriculture, engineering, health, co-operative, veterinary and the like—at which advanced specialist instruction is given in the practical, social, and psychological problems of village development, in the ways of encouraging local initiative, and in methods of co-ordinating administrative and specialist functions to avoid overlap. Moreover in all these courses for officials, at whatever levels, great stress is laid upon a new aspect of official life: the individual officer must henceforward combine with his duties to the Government his duties to the public: he must be a public servant as well as a Government official. A special pamphlet entitled *The Expanding Role of the Public Servant in a Democratic Pakistan*, prepared by the Chief Administrator of Village AID, has been circulated to all Government officers.

I made a point of inquiring both from officials and from Basic Democrats what they thought of the change which has thus been introduced into the relations between them. Would the transformation of the executive officer into a kind of Chairman of committee, charged with the task of carrying along with him in all he does colleagues who are representatives of the public, prove over-clumsy in operation as compared with the old practice of the officer taking decisions, and doing all the work himself? Many people seemed to think that any delays which the new system might cause would be more than offset by the advantages which close co-operation between the officials and the public would bring.

In the highest ranks of Government service, several of the older and more senior officials frankly confessed to some initial scepticism when Basic Democracies were first introduced. They had not believed that the kind of men who would be elected to Union Councils and committees would be able to make a useful contribution to the advanced level of development work with which the Divisional and Provincial Councils are concerned. But a short experience of the actual working of the scheme had, they said, shown them that they were mistaken. The Basic Democrats with whom they sit on these high-level councils have proved to be extremely well-informed, highly practical, persons with a knowledge of local conditions, and an acquaintance with local opinion which makes them most valuable colleagues—men indeed, from whom even the highest official ranks have been able to learn a great deal. At the District level, both in East and West Pakistan, I found real enthusiasm among the Collectors and Deputy Commissioners over the transformation that had taken place in their work since Basic Democracies had been introduced. Time after time, I heard the Head of some District which I happened to be visiting say proudly: 'I have the best bunch of Union Councils in the whole country! They come to see me, I go to see them: we all work together. And look what they have done!' Then I would be given a long list of achievements—the expansion of Service co-operatives for the supply of seed, implements, and materials for improvement and for tube wells: the relief given to the technical departments now that the Union Councils are taking over the execution of so many local duties: the building of roads and culverts: the extension of the social services. Particular satisfaction was expressed by many District officers at the readiness which Union Councils are showing to tax themselves for the purpose of putting in hand local improvements. One interesting by-product in many areas has been a reduction of formal litigation. 'When a case comes up to me,' more than one District Magistrate told me, 'I now send it for report to the Chairman of the Union Council of the area. Almost always, I never see the case again—it has been settled locally!' So successful has the plan proved that the Government later gave formal sanction to it by authorizing the setting up of a Conciliation Court, with the Union President as Chairman, in each Union; and by encouraging would-be litigants to take their grievances to these courts in the first instance. The change has considerably eased the work of the District and Sub-Divisional officers. Even so, what they seem to value most highly is the new close relationship between the administration and the people, which is substituting direct human contacts for mere paper-work, and is giving the officer himself a new interest and a new joy in his duties.

From the official angle, indeed, one of the most useful results of the institution of Basic Democracies has been to spread among the people an increasing knowledge of how Government works, of what its difficulties are. The old idea that Government can work miracles, and only does not work them because it is selfish and unresponsive to popular needs, is gradually disappearing. This increasing grasp of realities is found in practice to achieve two things: it stimulates self-help and local initiative; and it induces a willingness to believe that if Government cannot always do what people want immediately they want it, there is probably a good reason behind its apparent failure. A case which came under my notice illustrates this new attitude. In one District, a cholera epidemic threatened to break out: local supplies of vaccine were inadequate: angry feelings developed and strong criticism of the authorities was voiced. Immediately, through the Union Councils, the public was told exactly how much vaccine was made in Pakistan: what the demand for it was: what the equitable share of the District in the available supplies amounted to: and what steps the Government was taking to import more. The public were entirely satisfied that Government was doing its best, and showed themselves ready to accept what could be provided immediately and to wait for the rest. In the case of other temporary shortages, for example, white sugar in certain towns, the function of the Basic Democracies in eliciting the facts and publishing them, has proved equally useful.

From the standpoint of the public, the change that has come over the general relations between the people and the officials is highly esteemed: a notable element in it has been the discovery that Government officers are human beings, who can be approached, reasoned with, and persuaded, who have definite functions to perform, and are subject to strict limitations upon their powers. 'I never knew what a difficult job the administrators have to do', one Basic Democrat remarked to me, 'until I had to sit with them and help them to do it.' 'We see so much more of our officers than we used to do,' is a common observation, 'they seem really interested in us.' Several Chairmen of Union Councils told me that their Assistant Commissioners or their Sub-Divisional officers have become their personal friends. 'We know them as man to man: they come to our houses—we go to theirs.' In East Pakistan, the difference between the new Basic Democracies and the old Union Boards was the subject of many conversations in which I took part. 'In the old Union Board,' I was told by a Union Council Chairman, 'the sub-divisional officer ran everything and gave all the orders—the Government and the people were in opposite camps. Now we all sit together. The Sub-Divisional officer discusses and advises, but he has to listen to us—he does not issue orders himself. Moreover, if he should try to throw his weight about too much, we can always get the matter taken up to the District, Divisional, or even Provincial Councils through our fellow-Chairmen who sit on these bodies. So we have no trouble—we all work together!'

It is time to set against the background of these general impressions some specific examples of how the Basic Democracies scheme is working in practice. The great city of Karachi, once the capital of Pakistan, was for long a separate *enclave*, but is now incorporated in the general administrative structure of the country. The whole urban area has taken on a 'new look' since the Revolution: order, cleanliness and fresh signs of progress, of which the P.I.D.C.'s shipyard and foundry: the new fishing harbour: and, of course, Korangi, are examples, have transformed the setting in which the Basic Democracies are now functioning. But Karachi presents particular problems of its own. I encountered there a comment on the local Basic Democrats which I found nowhere else in Pakistan—namely, that the candidates who had been returned by the electors were by no means always the best people available. My informants told me that in Karachi the influence of the old-type Party politicians, now deprived of the scope and opportunities to which they had become accustomed, is still far from negligible (which is among the reasons no doubt why the capital has been moved) and that this influence had been from the beginning hostile to the whole idea of Basic Democracies, condemning them in advance as unworthy of the attention of substantial citizens. The result had been to discourage some very good individuals from standing, even though, by and large, a representative cross-section of the population had been returned.

I was curious to find out how the scheme was being applied to this extensive civic complex, in which some 2 million people live. I found that, in all, there are 125 Basic Democracies working, 94 in the

Municipal area: 17 in the cantonment area: and 14 in the rural area—of which 9 are Union Councils and 5 are Town Committees for places like Korangi. In the Municipal area, the Union Committees function like Ward Committees: and to elect the new Municipal Committee, the Wards were divided into thirty groups, each of which returned one member to the Municipality. In the Municipal area, the Municipal Committee holds the purse-strings, but the Union Committees are entitled to put forward development schemes and to follow them up through their representatives on the Municipal Committees. They can also impose their own cesses—which they are doing very vigorously—for small projects of Ward improvement. Ward-life is active: the special problems of an urban population are being carefully studied to promote civic consciousness, local initiative, and the spirit of self-help, along the lines already established in the countryside. I think that Pakistan is unique in this effort, which I found in other great cities besides Karachi, to apply the principles of community development work to purely urban conditions. The aim is to give the inhabitants of each Ward the sense of 'belonging' to a definite community, such as a villager enjoys in the rural areas. The women's organizations play a prominent part in this work. One of the best ways of keeping the Basic Democracies actively employed and of maintaining their keenness has been discovered to lie in promoting competition between them. The rivalry which emerges between adjoining areas through such institutions as sports gatherings, tournaments, exhibitions, and fairs readily extends to competition in such fields as the establishment of maternity clinics, dispensaries, adult education centres, and welfare work.

The Basic Democracies in the Karachi area, I was told, are concerned with two main kinds of development schemes. The first kind comprises all that they can do with their own resources, both on a self-help basis, and with the aid of the cesses which each Committee imposes to raise its own 'internal' fund. Generally, the Committee decides for itself what kind of taxation it will impose, and Government rarely interferes, believing that the Committee itself is the best judge of whether a tax is practicable or not. I saw a great deal of work being done in this way—cleanliness drives, paving of roads, small drainage schemes, repair of wells, and the like. As a result, Karachi has become a much cleaner place, and it is rare to find refuse lying about. The small shops too, are cleaner, and food is more generally covered as a protection against flies and dust.

The second kind of development scheme is more elaborate, and is based upon 'external' funds. These are of three classes: first, money set aside by Government for specific development actitivities in such spheres as education, health, birth-control and the like: secondly, money allocated by Government for the Basic Democracies to use for approved schemes for the expansion of local services, for the building of bridges and embankments, and for other works not figuring in some larger departmental plan: thirdly, money allocated by District Councils from their own sources of revenue to Basic Democracies in connection with District development plans. An interesting feature of all these development-projects of the second kind, which depends upon 'external funds', is that when its plan is first formulated by a Ministry or Department of Government, priorities must be settled in consultation with the Basic Democracies, which can call the Ministry or Department to account if nothing much happens. The Basic Democrats are so closely in touch with the people as a whole that they are well fitted to voice public complaints authoratitively.

At the end of 1960, when we were inquiring into the application of the Basic Democracies scheme to Karachi, the training-scheme for Basic Democrats had been in operation for the best part of a year. Six classes were held every day throughout the area from 6 to 7 p.m.: every single Basic Democrat had attended them, except for an occasional individual man or woman who had been exempted because of previous long experience of local government institutions. As is the case elsewhere in Pakistan, the actual training was imparted by Village AID officials: it was obviously successful, because the Basic Democrats were showing keenness and competence in the performance of their duties. On the whole, as might be expected in an urbanized area, the typical Basic Democrat in Union and Town Committees is fairly well educated, and possesses considerable sophistication. The result is that a second-grade Government clerk is proving adequate for the general run of Union Committees. But in the nine Union Councils in the rural area, where the members need more guidance, it has been found desirable to appoint clerks of a higher grade.

To pass from great cities like Karachi, Lahore, and Dacca, with their highly-organized Municipal structures, their integration of the Basic Democracies into an urban framework, and their far-reaching plans for civic improvement, into the remote rural areas of West and East Pakistan is to gain a lively impression of the varied circumstances in which Basic Democracies are now working. These variations are reflected in the composition of the Councils and Committees. On the outskirts of the larger towns, it is not unusual to find a Union Council which has elected as its Chairman a retired Government official of high standing, and counts among its members a doctor, a surveyor, a sanitary engineer, a building contractor, and perhaps a barrister. In the really rural areas, the Basic Democrats are almost entirely agriculturalists, with the addition, perhaps, of a retired schoolmaster or a retired member of one of the subordinate services. The former category of Council can often supply from its own membership a great deal of the expert advice which it requires for the improvement schemes which it is putting in hand; its suggestions to higher authority are framed with great cogency and formidable drafting ability. Illiteracy among its members is virtually non-existent: the general level of competence is high, and the record of work accomplished, in hand, and projected, is already impressive.

It is the Union Councils of the second category which really test the usefulness of the whole scheme, and it was among these that my wife and I spent most of our time. We felt that if Basic Democracies worked successfully in typically rural areas, removed both by distance and by difficulties of communication from anything but the most occasional official contacts, the scheme would have proved its worth. We found, in fact, that it is working, and working well. For this, great credit is due not only to the keen interest and astonishing initiative of the Basic Democrats themselves, but also to the skilful and devoted efforts of the original Village AID worker. He, with the bicycle which enabled him to cover astonishing distances, had become a familiar figure in the countryside. He held such a key-position among the Basic Democrats that before long they 'took him over' altogether. To begin with, he was their friend and counsellor, the link between the villages and the Government departments concerned with development. He received, week by week and month by month, a perpetual stream of information dealing with improved agricultural methods, advice about crop pests which threaten, improved varieties of seeds, precautions against epidemics, advice on all types of elementary construction from improved cooking stoves to new culverts, suggestions for reclaiming waste, and for planting trees. He was always at hand to explain the admirably clear and instructive posters which he set up on the village notice-board, to read pamphlets to the illiterate, to outline Government policy in things which interest the rural population. In the areas where Village AID had penetrated, the Basic Democracies scheme found the ground prepared. The habit of co-operative effort had become familiar: a village council had often been set up: there was an awareness of local needs and the will to satisfy them. But if Village AID has helped Basic Democracies, Basic Democracies have more than repaid the debt. Even from the first, the working conditions of these devoted servants of the public were quickly transformed. The Basic Democrats backed the Village AID worker in all that he did; they provided him with facilities which he had never enjoyed before; they put pressure on conservatively-minded farmers to adopt his methods; they put their hands into their pockets ungrudgingly to help his work forward. Finally, they took him over altogether, and embodied him in their own organization, to the enormous benefit of all concerned.

Wherever practicable, we arranged to attend one of the regular meetings of a Union Council, so that we could see for ourselves what kind of work is done. In cases where no meeting coincided with our visit, we called on the Chairman, and he was usually able to collect most of his colleagues so that we could talk to them. In a very high proportion of cases, we found that the Union Council had built a special house for itself, with an office for the Chairman, an office-cum-record room for the clerk, and a meeting room for the Council itself, which is often stocked with books and periodicals and used as a village library. Sometimes the house was a free gift: one of the Union Councils in the Montgomery District meets in a house given by a villager, who has moved into a second house he happens to own. In this case, a free dispensary, stocked and maintained by the Union Council, occupies part of the same premises. In other cases, the elected Chairman, if his house chances to be big enough, sets aside two or three rooms for the exclusive use of his Union Council. But in whatever kind of accommodation a Union Council is housed, one thing is common to almost all of them. In the meeting room, the walls are covered with charts, diagrams, and tables embodying complete information about the resources of the area for which the Union Council is responsible: how many men, women, and children: how many ploughs, oxen, bulls, cows, sheep and goats: how many tube-wells: how many tractors: how much land under what crops: how much waste land, and of what kind. The figures are constantly revised and kept up to date, so that the Basic Democrats have always in front of them the hard facts with which they must reckon.

The way in which Basic Democracies are working may be illustrated from my notes of a meeting of the Kahna Union Council, which I attended in a village some miles from Lahore in December 1960. This Council had held nineteen meetings, built itself an excellent council house, formed a youth club at its headquarters, settled ten local disputes without resort to the courts of law, raised its post office to branch level, secured electricity connections, cleaned streets, improved drainage, and dug a channel a mile long to relieve water-logging. It received, in common with other Union Councils, a Government grant of Rs. 2,500. to start it off: since that time it had quadrupled its financial resources with voluntary subscriptions. The meeting was a full one with all fifteen members present: there were no absentees. The Chairman sat at a table in a large roofed veranda, on his left was the clerk, a retired schoolmaster who wrote a most beautiful hand and had all his papers in apple-pie order—I later inspected his record-room. The Council members sat on chairs in a semicircle facing the Chairman. Small boys and interested villagers sat on the walls surrounding the neat little garden in which the house stands. Whether this interest was focused upon the meeting itself, or upon the unusual spectacle of two European visitors, I should not like to say! Anyhow, perfect order prevailed and there were no attempts at intervention in the Council's activities.

The first item on the agenda was the provision of a Girls' Primary School and the enlargement of the existing Boys' School. The level of debate was high: each Basic Democrat spoke his mind, often quite tersely: eloquent oratory was viewed with disfavour: any wandering from the point at issue was promptly checked by members rising and appealing to the Chairman to stop irrelevant talking. It was decided to use the present Boys' School for the new Girls' School, and to move the boys to a new school in a neighbouring village where a suitable site existed, and where a school was needed. Until this was done, boys and girls would use the same building at different hours. The next item was the starting of adult education classes. Where should they be housed? There was a suitable building, publicly owned, at present occupied by a refugee. Would it be fair to turn him out? Or there was an abandoned Sikh *gurdwara* (temple): was it worth repairing? It was quickly decided that the refugee ought not to be turned out: that the *gurdwara* was too dilapidated to be patched up. But why not use the present school building after nightfall—electric light was available? This was agreed. Next, how could classes be started? In the discussion which followed, it became for the first time possible for me to realize

222

that some of these Basic Democrats were illiterate, because one or two of them stated quite frankly that they could not help other people to learn to read and write, but they would gladly attend classes themselves. The literate members of the Council quickly offered to hold classes in reading and writing, saying that, as adults themselves, they would be able to cope better with the difficulties which adults would encounter than professional teachers accustomed only to instruct the young. Accordingly, a sub-committee was appointed to select the most suitable teachers, to persuade people to attend the classes, and to report back to the Union Council at the next meeting.

Two items then came up for discussion which were dealt with in a way which seemed to me to illustrate the general atmosphere of the Council pretty clearly. There was need of a new well: one of the proper sanitary type would cost Rs. 600. The suggestion from the chair was that the Council might find half the money: and that the Development Directorate might be asked for the other half. This did not meet with favour. Speaker after speaker rose and pointed out that the Council was quite able to find the whole sum itself: that the work ought to be put in hand at once to save delay. It was so agreed. Next came a complaint from one Basic Democrat that some of the farmers who were his constituents were grumbling about the bad quality of certain seed supplied to them by the distributors employed by the Department of Agriculture. Could not the Council, he asked, take over the work and deal directly with the Department? But, if this were done, was there any way of testing the seed locally to ensure good quality and save the farmers from wasting money? The Chairman turned to the Village AID worker, who was sitting in the background, and asked him for his opinion. The worker answered that testing was a simple matter: he had been himself trained to do it, and he would gladly do the seed-testing for the Council if the suggested plan were were adopted. Again, the Council registered its assent. The Chairman said that he understood from the Department of Agriculture that they would be only too happy to be relieved of the responsibility for arranging seed distribution: and the clerk was instructed to write, formally proposing the new arrangement.

Under the last head, of which the English equivalent would be, 'Any other business', there were some serious complaints about the water shortages due to the cutting down of supplies from the Indian side. What was the Government doing? The Chairman said he had already taken this matter up: the position was that the Government, knowing that India had reduced the flow from the expected 56 to 26 cusecs, had made strong representations: but India had replied that two bad monsoons had drastically reduced the amount of canal water available to both countries: and that she was doing her best to share the diminished supplies equitably between the Indian and the Pakistani cultivators. There was some general grumbling about the position; but it was agreed that the Pakistan Government was not to blame at all, and that there was nothing to be done except to see if tube-wells would help. The Council decided to get into touch with the Department of Agriculture and seek its assistance.

At this point, after two and a half hours most useful and practical work, the Council adjourned: the members, along with my wife and myself, were hospitably entertained to tea by the Chairman. After this we were shown over the admirably-kept office by the secretary.

I have described this meeting in some detail, because it is broadly typical of what we found going on everywhere we went in West Pakistan. Local problems were being tackled with enthusiasm: there was a keen and business-like determination to show results. Some of these were remarkable. Take, for example, Union Council No. 20 in Montgomery District—an area which contains 202 Union Councils. No. 20 is centred on Kadirabad, half a mile from any metalled road. A considerable proportion of the members, including the Chairman himself, can neither read nor write: but since the Council started work, they have done these things—built half a mile of link road, raised against flooding, and with plenty of culverts: raised the street level in the village to allow proper drainage on each side: planted 10,000 saplings on reclaimed waste ground—widows and other indigent persons are paid a regular stipend for watering and caring for them: introduced cotton-sowing by drill and secured its acceptance for 75 per cent of the crop with very beneficial results: maintained a free dispensary which treats 200 patients a month and is served by a qualified dispenser whom the Union Council pays to give two hours' attendance daily. When we visited this Union Council, it had just decided that the Village AID worker, who had been with it for some time and had helped it greatly, could now move his headquarters to another village in the Council's area, which had not been advancing so quickly. The Council had collected a good deal of money, both by cesses and by voluntary subscription to supplement the Government's 'starting-off' grant of Rs. 2,500s. and the Chairman had contributed

Rs. 500. which he had saved up for a wireless set. 'My wireless can wait', he said, 'until we have got the village on a bit.'

To take another example—Deona Union Council in Gujrat district. This serves a population of more than 7,000, living in ten villages. All the Basic Democrats are literate. The Council started work in July 1960, and had held fifteen meetings by December. It had dug two tube-wells costing R. 12,000. on a self-help basis: it had built a High School and found Rs. 5,000. towards the cost: it had set up two soil conservation centres: it had brought 200 acres of land under new irrigation: it had made link roads 'jeepable' by building culverts: it had paved village streets, removed rubbish heaps, and dug refuse pits: it had set up two Development Societies with a capital of Rs. 14,000. to give loans for productive schemes, and it was planning a third.

We also attended meetings of Town Committees, in which we found the level of competence and of education impressively high, and improvement schemes of considerable local importance well in hand. As a rule, these Town Committees have more money to spend than Union Councils because their resources are greater: we found that they were generally spending it intelligently and liberally.

The work of the Tahsil Councils is mainly of a co-ordinating nature. Haripur is a good example. It meets monthly, and deals with schemes which come up to it from the thirty Union Councils for which it is responsible. Haripur is prosperous, and many of the Union Council Chairmen in the area have returned to Government the initial grant of Rs. 500s. which each of them receives as an honorarium. Free gifts of land worth Rs. 10,000. or Rs. 15,000. on which the Union Council offices have been built are not unusual. The Tahsil Council finds that the main questions sent up to it by the Union Councils refer to such matters as taxation-powers: fund-raising: extension of irrigation: construction of new roads: girls' education: and adult literacy campaigns. At a higher level, again, the District Council is concerned mainly with schemes which come up from the Tahsil Councils, although, as already noticed, there is a strong element of Union Council Chairmen who sit side by side with the Deputy Commissioner, officials of the Development Directorate, and representatives of technical departments. We were not able to attend meetings of the Divisional and of the Provincial Councils, since we were concentrating mainly on the lower tiers: we felt that if the Union, Tahsil and District Councils are working well, the success of the superior Councils is assured. We were interested to learn that small but high-powered 'flying squads' have been set up to visit each division to ensure that development work is pushed on quickly: while each Divisional Commissioner now has a 'flying squad' of his own to keep the Deputy Commissioners in his area in line with the general advance.

The working of the Basic Democracies in East Pakistan, for particular reasons, some of which have already been explained, present fewer problems. In comparison with West Pakistan, the population is more sophisticated, the level of literacy is higher. Further, the Union Boards of East Pakistan, in spite of their obvious deficiencies in certain directions, had trained the people in the rudiments of local government and given them an advantage in this respect over the people of West Pakistan. In East Pakistan, rural areas had become accustomed to the operations of the Debt Settlement Board and of its local representatives: co-operative effort in many directions had become a well-established feature of village life. The new Union Councils have inherited from the old Union Boards, along with other valuable assets, a working financial system based upon twenty-three well-established items of taxation. Broadly speaking, therefore, the Basic Democrats of East Pakistan have not found it necessary to supplement their resources by voluntary financial contributions in the same way as their colleagues in West Pakistan, where taxation-powers are entirely novel, and, in the earlier stages, have depended far more on local initiative. East Pakistan pins its faith to voluntary labour, rather than to voluntary subscriptions, for initiating and carrying on local development schemes. In the Eastern, as in the Western, wing, the Village AID movement has proved invaluable in setting the stage for Basic Democracies: the Village AID Academy at Comilla, with its frequent conferences for Civil Servants, Circle Officers, school teachers, Development Officers, Ansar (cadet) leaders, and others, builds upon the foundations already laid by its scientifically-framed training courses devised for Basic Democrats and administrative officials. Its influence spreads far and wide. Thanks to an unique arrangement, the Comilla Academy is now the development authority for the Thana in which it is situated. A Thana Council, held in the Academy, provided us with the opportunity of meeting the members. Their interest in local development schemes put up by the Union Councils was both helpful and constructive: the standard of work was impressively high. We visited some very progressive villages in its area whose economy has been wholly transformed for the better by water-storage schemes and by the installation of co-operatively-owned electric pumps, which make possible winter crops and provide employment during what has hitherto been the slack season. The plan has remarkable potentialities for many other parts of East Pakistan.

The institution of Basic Democracies has supplied a fillip to East Pakistan at least equivalent to that which it has administered to West Pakistan. We visited a number of Union Councils, and were favourably impressed by the progress which is being made. The Basic Democrats to whom we talked spoke warmly about the change that has come over the official attitude—they feel that the officers and the people are now on the same side, instead of being in opposite camps. One change that we noticed is the greater prominence of village women in development activities: they are now getting together, starting their own co-operatives, attending classes at centres like the Comilla Academy for instruction in poultry-raising and sericulture, and interesting themselves actively in adult education. Few of them are Basic Democrats, except in the larger towns, but more than half the female electorate registered their votes in the elections, and they keep closely in touch with all that the Union Councils, Union Committees and Town Committees are doing.

As in West Pakistan, there is a noticeable difference between the highly-educated, highly-powered Basic Democrats in the vicinity of the larger towns, and the members of the Union Councils in remote areas such as the Chittagong Hill Tracts—where the smooth working of Basic Democracies has been temporarily complicated by large movements of population under resettlement schemes resulting from the Kaptai project. But the general level of keen interest, hard work, and hopefulness was noticeably high. Everywhere Government and the people are closer together than they have ever been before: we felt that East Pakistanis no longer think of themselves as living in a neglected backwater. Whereas the budgets of the former Union Boards had averaged only about Rs. 3,000., of which 75 per cent had to be spent on pure watch and ward, the average budget of the new Basic Democracies now stands at Rs. 13,000. The people pay the taxes—levied on land, buildings, hearths and the like—quite cheerfully because almost all the receipts are expended on *visible* improvements, such as roads, bridges, embankments, tube-wells, agricultural demonstration farms, nurseries, poultry farms, and training in new methods. Of the 40,000 Basic Democrats in East Pakistan, only some 800 are illiterate; while of the Chairmen, 67 per cent have had secondary education and nearly 20 per cent have been to college.

Under this new impetus, rural development is going ahead fast. There is a Circle Development Officer to every two or three Union Councils; while every Council now has an Agricultural Assistant, a Veterinary Assistant, and a Health Assistant. Altogether there are 411 Thana Councils in East Pakistan, of which the Chairmen of Union Councils and Town Committees are members. Each Thana Council sits with the Agricultural Officer, the Fisheries Officer, the Inspector of Revenue, the Co-operative Officer, the Inspector of Schools, the Veterinary Officer, and the Sanitary Inspector; the main work is to co-ordinate and to supervise the execution of the schemes put up by the Union Councils. As in West Pakistan, the enlargement of the powers and responsibilities of the Basic Democrats has made them an important factor in national life; and when we visited a number of them in 1962 we found them well out of the experimental stage, and an accepted element in the structure of society throughout Pakistan. It seemed to us that they were wholly deserving of the key-position which the new constitution—as will be seen later—has entrusted to them.

The good impression made upon the people as a whole by the institution of Basic Democracies and by the resulting change in the official attitude has been greatly strengthened by the dynamic personality of Lt.-General Azam Khan, the creator of Korangi, whom President Ayub Khan afterwards sent to East Pakistan as Governor. With the full support of the President behind him, he soon became something of a legend in the Province: every village knew his name. He visited spots which had never, since British times, seen any official of higher rank than a Thana officer: his tours of cyclone-stricken areas, his warm human sympathy with the sufferers, and his prompt and effective relief measures, gave the public a wholly new conception of what good government can mean. His plans for improving the living conditions, and developing the resources of the Province proved far-reaching: they ranged from the extension of the inland water-transport services, and the construction of cyclone-proof houses and protective walls, to the development of the delightful seaside resort of Cox's Bazaar into an attractive centre of the tourist industry with modern rest-houses and motels. His institution of East Pakistan Week—an annual gathering which combines athletic contests, folk-dancing, exhibitions of traditional arts and crafts with a kind of social 'get-together' of representative deputations from every part of East and West Pakistan—served the double purpose

228

of fortifying pride in local culture and of making East Pakistanis feel that their claim to 'count' as an intrinsically important part of Pakistan is firmly established. Long before he left in 1962 they had come to believe, along with him, that if East Pakistanis pull together, the Eastern Wing can become the most prosperous part of Pakistan.

Our successive tours in East and West Pakistan in 1961 and 1962 have convinced us that the scheme of Basic Democracies is no longer an experiment; it has become an integral part of the national life of the country. Perhaps its greatest achievement, to date, is the narrowing of the gap between rulers and ruled which had opened so dangerously in pre-Revolutionary times. Thus one of the main aims which inspired President Ayub Khan to set Basic Democracies on foot is in a fair way to be achieved. On the twin foundations of self-help by the people, and team-work between the people and the Government, the stable edifice of the Pakistan of the future can safely be erected.

The President realizes clearly, as he has several times told me, that in the day-to-day affairs of his country, it is institutions which count, not less than the men who work them. He believes that in Basic Democracies he has found a machinery which the people as a whole can, and will, successfully operate within the limits, already familiar to them, which it has been designed to cover. These limits are by no means narrow. Mention has already been made of the extension of the Basic Democracies' duties to arbitration and conciliation work. These duties now also include the responsibility for ensuring that the women of Pakistan are protected in the legal rights secured to them under Quranic law. Intention to divorce must be reported to Union Council Chairmen, who will refuse sanction unless an Arbitration Council, specially appointed, makes a favourable recommendation. Heavy penalties are imposed for polygamous marriages contracted without permission: and the marriage-age of girls has been raised from fourteen to sixteen. The tendency, indeed, has been to entrust the Basic Democrats with more and more responsibility. Mention has already been made of their taking over the 'village worker' organization of the former Village AID structure as part of their job of fostering rural development of the countryside. They have also been entrusted with such important duties as recommending loans to farmers, preparing schemes of local improvement, and watching the execution of larger projects sanctioned and paid for by the District Councils out of public funds. It seems clear that there is still considerable scope for the extension of their duties; and the manner in which they are coping with the responsibilities already assigned to them gives bright hope that the part which they will play in the nation-wide process of reconstruction envisaged in the Second Five Year Plan will prove invaluable.

Chapter 12

AN END AND A BEGINNING

One problem which the President had been considering for some time was how to link the new and promising machinery of Basic Democracy with the higher levels of Governmental responsibility. The institutions of Parliamentary democracy inherited from the British had proved unsuitable because the essential prerequisites for their successful functioning did not exist in Pakistan. The conduct of public affairs degenerated into a spoils-system which set political life at the mercy of vested interests and removed it entirely from the comprehension, as well as from the sympathy, of the masses of the population. Possibly Parliamentary democracy could have been made to work if Quaid-i-Azam had lived: he would have altered and adapted it in accordance with Pakistan's needs. But since it would be highly imprudent to entrust the destinies of the nation to the chance that leaders enjoying the prestige and personal ascendency of a Jinnah or an Ayub Khan will always be forthcoming, institutions must be devised which will, so far as human foresight allows, combine an assurance of political stability with provision for an undeviating pursuit of the public interest.

From the time when I first met him as President, Field-Marshal (as he now is) Ayub Khan has impressed upon me his conviction that democracy is essential to Pakistan because, without it, there can be no political stability. But he is equally emphatic in his belief that this democracy must be the kind that Pakistanis can understand and work: a kind which will kill the relics of feudalism, promote equality, and encourage the spirit of service. 'I tell the people I meet,' he once said to me, 'that there is nothing like serving others and doing one's bit for the country. I say to them that I have got a kick out of this all my life—do try the same thing! You will get as much of a kick out of it as I do.' This attitude of mind no doubt underlies his insistence that Government officials must learn that it is not enough to give orders: that it is now their duty to work along with the public in the service of the country. Only in this way, he thinks, can the old gap between the Government official and the ordinary man be bridged finally: and it is here that Basic Democracies come in. 'The Basic Democrats know what they are doing,' he once told me. 'When the West Pakistan Government tried, to begin with, to stop the Basic Democracies from levying their own taxes, I said: "Please leave them alone!—they know their own business." So they went ahead, and you've seen for yourself what is happening.'

The President's own approach to the main question at issue has been governed by his conviction that no scheme will work which removes political life from the understanding of the masses and sets those who engage in it apart from the ordinary man. It is for this reason that he likes the idea of a strong Executive, with a Head of State elected by some sort of plebiscite, and thus standing in direct contact with the people as a whole, as the American President does. Field-Marshal Ayub Khan is particularly suspicious of any system which would give the Legislature unrestricted power to remove, or to fetter unduly, the Executive, because he fears that this might open the way to a reversion to the former disastrous régime of party politics, intrigue, and corruption, which so nearly involved the country in ruin. He also believes that it should be the function of the judiciary to guard and to enforce, not to make, laws. In short, he is a convinced adherent of the 'separation of powers'.

It was with these general ideas in his mind that he set on foot an expert inquiry in February 1960. He appointed a Constitution Commission under the chairmanship of Mr. Justice Shahabuddin to advise the Cabinet on the form of a new constitution for Pakistan. The members of the Commission were drawn from eminent men in several walks of life; their mandate was to frame suggestions for securing a democracy suitable to Pakistani conditions: adaptable to changing circumstances: based upon the Islamic principles of justice, equality and toleration: calculated to consolidate national unity, and to produce a firm and stable system of government. The Commission sent out a questionnaire which brought more than six thousand replies; it personally interviewed between five hundred and six hundred people in both wings of the country.

While the Commission was at work, I had the opportunity of talking to some of its members informally, and I found that they were impressed with the difficulties of the task assigned to them. Two problems, in particular, loomed large before them. The first was the need to ensure that East and West Pakistan worked harmoniously together:

this meant, in view of the strong feelings of East Pakistan on the subject, that there would have to be a considerable measure of local autonomy. Could this be reconciled with the admitted need for a strong government at the centre? The second problem was that of reconciling the theory of the Islamic State with the needs of a modern polity. Underlying both was the necessity of learning from the disastrous experiences of the past, and thus of avoiding a plan which might look well on paper, but would lay itself open to the old abuses. A further complication lay in the fact that so many people whose opinions on constitutional matters would normally be entitled to great respect have been brought up in the former British Parliamentary tradition, and cannot think outside the lines of the Westminster model. That this limitation is a serious one was quickly shown. Although the proceedings of the Commission were confidential, some of those who gave evidence before it did not hesitate to publish their views. A controversy, as premature as it was undesirable, arose in the Press, and this raged so violently that it reminded me of the old, sterile quarrels which had bedevilled the former Constituent Assemblies. I myself, and I am sure a great number of other people also, experienced considerable relief when the Government stepped in, and officially forbade such polemics until such time as the Cabinet had made up its own mind.

The Commission submitted its report—which was later published in full—in May 1961. It proved to be an excellent working draft, but the Cabinet took no chances with it. Several Cabinet committees were appointed to examine it from every point of view—practicability, satisfaction of the country's needs, respect for the feelings of both wings of the country, effect upon the development programmes and the Second Five Year Plan, and the like. These detailed examinations lasted all the summer, and during October 1961, the Cabinet as a whole began the ultimate definitive scrutiny, which included ascertaining the views of a number of senior administrative officers on the practical problems which the working of the scheme would involve. When all this was at last completed, and the Government had made up its mind on all the details, one final task remained, which was in some respects the most difficult of all. The President insisted that the new constitution should be drafted in terms which could be made intelligible not merely to constitutional experts and trained lawyers, but to the ordinary citizen. He argued that the people of Pakistan could not be expected to work it and to defend it unless they understood it; he wanted a draft which could be turned into simple and straightforward Bengali and Urdu as well as being readily intelligible in its English form. The President had his way, but the task presented difficulties which few but constitutional lawyers can appreciate. It says much for the skill and judgement of the draftsmen, chief among whom were Mr. Manzur Qadir and the Australian expert, Mr. Quayle, who assisted him, that the new constitution in its final form can be read and understood by anyone, whether lawyer or layman, who cares to study it, while at the same time it is so clearly expressed that there are few, if any, loopholes for ambiguity or conflicting interpretations.

All this took time; and when I was in Western India in January and February 1962, I encountered a good deal of scepticism among my Indian friends about whether the new constitution would ever see the light of day. Even in Pakistan, where my wife and I found ourselves late in February, there was a certain disappointment over the delay. East Pakistanis, with their keen political sophistication, were becoming impatient, and the leaders of the Calcutta-inspired Communist campaign, to which reference has been made on an earlier page, exploited this impatience with their customary skill. Certain malcontents of the former political parties, disgruntled by their exclusion from place and power under the Revolutionary Government, started an agitation; some Hindu money seems to have been involved. The Government thought it wise to place Mr. H. S. Suhrawardy under house arrest; but the general confidence which the country as a whole placed in the honesty of intention of its rules was shown when the student-demonstrations in Dacca and Rajshahi fell flat because of the refusal of ordinary citizens to join in. In the event, the delay was entirely worth while, as was conclusively shown when the final result of all this devoted labour was hailed with real enthusiasm throughout Pakistan.

The President had set the 1st of March 1962 as the final deadline. He refused to extend it, even at the earnest plea of the draftsmen, who were working up to the fifty-ninth minute of the eleventh hour, clarifying, simplifying, and polishing the language. The actual text which he signed, after formally promulgating the new constitution in a broadcast to the nation on March 1st, still contained some final changes in pen and ink. Yet every line of this text quickly became public property, as it was eagerly studied and freely discussed.

Perhaps the characteristic of the new constitution which struck the people of Pakistan most forcibly immediately after its promulgation is

the fact that it is designed for *them*, not for anybody else. Outside observers may approve or disapprove; but it is tailored for Pakistan's
own needs, and only Pakistanis really know what those needs are.
They think that the Presidential system is what they want, at least at
the moment; for they have come to realize that they do not possess at
present the various sophistications—such as high levels of education,
prosperity, public spirit and integrity—which the Parliamentary
system on the Westminster model requires for successful working. In
particular, they know that there is no effective public opinion to prevent members of a House in which the Executive needs the support of
a majority from changing sides if their own profit is at stake. They
agree with the President when he told them: 'Don't let us kid ourselves and cling to clichés and assume that we are ready to work such
a refined system, knowing the failure of earlier attempts. It will be
foolhardy to try it again until our circumstances change radically.'

The main outlines of the constitution are simple and straightforward. There is a President, a Central Legislature, and a Legislature in
each Province. The normal term of all is five years; but the first elections operate for three years only, in order to give experience of the
working of the scheme and allow for any modifications which experience may suggest. Judicial power is vested in the Supreme Court at
the Centre, and the High Courts in the two Provinces. There is only
one list of subjects for the Centre—subjects of a national character;
but the Centre can legislate in the Provincial field in such matters as
security and co-ordination of economic development, although execution will rest with the Provinces. The underlying theme is that all
that can be done in a Province ought to be done there. As an earnest
of the Government's intentions in this direction, East Pakistan has
been given control of its railway system; it has its own wing of the
Pakistan Industrial Development Corporation: its own Water and
Power Development Authority; while Dacca has been declared the
Second Capital and the permanent seat of the National Assembly. It
has further been provided that the Supreme Court shall sit there at
least twice a year. The constitution lays down certain principles of
lawmaking and of policy which embody fundamental rights, the safeguarding of minorities, parity between the Provinces; and, in accordance with the idea of the 'separation of powers', the responsibility
for observing these principles has been vested in each organ of the
State. Provision is made for the establishment of an 'Advisory Council
of Islamic Ideology' supported by the existing Islamic Research

Centre, and consisting of men of eminence in theology, economics, administration, and the like, whose advice will be available to the President and the Legislatures to ensure that laws conform to the requirements of Islam and observe the constitutional principles of lawmaking.

It is in the detailed provisions which fill in this broad outline, and in the built-in safeguards to resolve possible conflict between the various organs of the State that the President's own ideas find their clearest expression. These ideas are based upon his practical experience of the needs of the country; and I personally think that his intimate and instinctive understanding of the feelings of ordinary people has rarely done Pakistan better service. He told me that it took him a lot of hard work and a great deal of argument before he could bring some of his colleagues round to his own way of thinking, which entailed including some original and indeed unorthodox conceptions.

'When I was working out what was wanted, and what we were trying to do, in order to make sure that the people of Pakistan are the final arbiters of who shall govern them, with the right to hire and fire their rulers,' he said, 'I found that I had to begin with myself, as President, and shed off a lot of power.' While bills passed by the National Assembly will require the President's assent, his veto can be overridden by a two-thirds majority of the members. He can be impeached by the Assembly for misconduct, or removed for physical or mental incapacity, but this requires a three-quarter majority, and if the supporters of the motion fail to get the support of at least half their colleagues, they lose their own seats! In certain circumstances, the President can go to the electorate over the head of the Assembly; but if he dissolves the Assembly, he must at the same time seek re-election himself. He appoints his own Ministers, but they need not be members of the Assembly, although they have the right to speak there if they are not members. Each Minister has a Parliamentary Secretary for his department, who is an Assembly member, and sits and votes in the House. No President can be elected for more than two terms without the permission of a joint meeting of the National and Provincial Assemblies.

A very ingenious provision to reduce the chances of conflict between the President, as Head of the Executive, and the National Assembly, as custodian of taxation-powers, takes the form of a distinction between taxation already sanctioned, and new taxation. When the Assembly has once passed a budget, this carries on, and cannot be altered without the President's consent; but all fresh taxation requires the sanction of the Assembly. This device prevents the Legislature from paralysing the Executive, but gives full powers to those who represent the taxpayers. In accordance with the same belief in the division of functions which runs through President Ayub Khan's thinking, the Legislature has been made responsible for observing the principles of lawmaking which the constitution lays down. The Courts have the duty of taking notice of, and rectifying, any breaches of laws so passed; but are unable to challenge the validity of the law itself—a position which resembles that prevailing in England and obviates the chance of rich litigants holding up beneficial schemes on the pretext that the Legislature has exceeded its powers in making a law to enforce them. In the Provinces, the Central picture is, roughly speaking, reproduced to regulate the relations between the Governor, the Legislature, and the Judiciary.

The President's conviction that political party activity was largely responsible for the plight into which Pakistan fell during the 'wasted years' posed this problem: How were candidates for the Presidency, and for seats in the National and Provincial Assemblies, to canvass the voters without the aid of a Party machine? This difficulty was got over, at least for the moment, by giving the State itself the duty of enabling all candidates to enjoy equal opportunities to press their claims upon the electorate. A very senior and experienced official, Mr. Akhtar Hussain, was made responsible, as Election Commissioner, not only for demarcating the constituencies which return members to the National and to the Provincial Assemblies but also for ensuring that in each constituency, every candidate could address gatherings of the electorate on his own behalf, as used to be the case in the old 'hustings' system in Britain. Later on, if the National Assembly so decides, Party organizations may possibly be revived, but care will be taken that the parties are limited in number and possess 'respectable and healthy' national programmes.

One feature of the Constitution upon which President Ayub Khan consistently laid the utmost stress in all the preliminary discussions is the employment of the Basic Democrats as the Electoral College. This has been criticized in India, Britain, and—to a lesser extent—in the United States as 'undemocratic'. In my view, such criticism is based upon a misunderstanding both of the circumstances of Pakistan and of the actual way in which universal adult suffrage operates in an Asian country. When I was informally discussing with certain members of the Constitution Commission—before their report was drafted—the possible function of the Basic Democracies in any future set-up, I was asked whether I thought that the Basic Democrats would provide a better electorate than the system of direct adult suffrage. I replied in the affirmative, and, when asked my reasons— as, no doubt many others before me had been asked—I said that the Basic Democrats had been elected by adult suffrage in small consti- tuencies on the simple basis of personal merit confirmed by the inti- mate knowledge of those who voted for them; and that persons of this kind—whose sterling work for their community I had myself observed and admired ever since the beginnings of the system—did in fact provide a responsible, instructed, and intelligent electorate of a kind which would provide an invaluable foundation for any higher consti- tutional structure. By contrast, ordinary direct elections, based upon adult suffrage but conducted on Party lines, are often illusory as re- flections of the real feelings of the voters, who are influenced by al- most every possible consideration other than the personal merits of the candidates. I doubt whether anyone who saw the Congress Party political machine at work during the 1962 Indian elections would dis- sent from this view, even though the Indian voter is by now relatively experienced as compared with the Pakistani voter.

My own opinion, for what it is worth—and it is founded not only upon personal experience of the kind of people Pakistan's Basic Democrats are, and of the work that they are doing, but also upon nearly half a century's study of the people of the sub-continent—is that President Ayub Khan and his advisers have been quite justified in making use of the Basic Democrats as an Electoral College. Apart altogether from the fact that this plan enabled the first elections to be held in April and May 1962—within a few weeks of the promulgation of the Constitution—it does in fact hold almost illimitable possibilities of getting closer and closer to the real feeling of the people. At the time when the elections were held, there were 80,000 members of the Electoral College, half in East Pakistan and half in West Pakistan, every one of whom had been directly elected by adult suffrage on the basis of his or her personal reputation as a trusted and trustworthy individual, ready to work for the community. Very shortly, the dis- appearance of the nominated members will make the small 'neigh- bourhood' constituencies even smaller and more intimate, as the number of elected members in each Union Council, Town Commit- tee, and Union Committee rises from ten to fifteen, and the Electoral

238

College expands from 80,000 to 120,000. There is nothing to prevent it from rising still higher.

The membership of the Assemblies, National and Provincial, is adequate without being unwieldy. Each Wing of the country has returned 75 members to the National Assembly—150 in all—together with 6 women members, 3 from each Wing—who were chosen by the Provincial Assemblies. There was nothing to stop women standing for general seats; several did this, although some very able ladies who are the wives of men in Government service were forbidden to stand in accordance with the pledge that the Government itself, though it had undertaken to give full facilities for every candidate, stood wholly aloof and supported no individuals. The constituencies which returned 150 members to each Provincial Assembly were, of course, smaller than those which elected the members of the National Assembly; each Assembly, when it met, elected 5 women members.

In light of the country's previous experience, as well as of close observation of what went on elsewhere during election time, rigid rules were laid down to ensure, so far as possible, both the secrecy and honesty of the ballot. The voter, after marking his paper in privacy, was obliged to put it into the proper box before he could leave the polling booth—thereby circumventing the practice, not unknown in other countries, under which the voter carried out an unmarked paper with him, and disposed of it for a good price to a waiting agent, who thereupon marked it with the name of his own candidate, entered the polling booth, and disposed of it in the appropriate box. The penalties for tampering with nomination and ballot papers were severe. As President Ayub Khan himself remarked, it would be unrealistic to expect a 100 per cent result in honesty and impartiality in a society which is still in process of maturing; but all the information available suggests that the Electoral College did its work well, and that the first members of the National and the Provincial Assemblies are not only broadly representative of Pakistan, but, when they settle down, are likely to operate the new Constitution in the spirit hoped for by its framers.

With the meeting of the National and Provincial Assemblies in June, the last traces of martial law disappeared, and Pakistan embarked upon a Constitutional régime. I know of no other instance in history where a Head of State enjoying the unrestricted powers wielded by President Ayub Khan has thus deliberately and of set purpose devolved those powers so extensively upon a people who would gladly have endorsed his personal authority for a much more extended term. His unselfish, disinterested policy merits real admiration. That it is not more widely recognized at its true value only underlines the general unfamiliarity with conditions in Pakistan which prevails so widely in Britain and America.

My wife and I left Pakistan before the elections were held, but we stayed long enough in the country to gather two firm impressions about the prospects of the new Constitution.

The first was that no pains have been spared to familiarize the people with all its features, to explain it to them, and to enlist their enthusiasm in working it. As soon as it was promulgated, President Ayub Khan, his Ministers, and the senior officers of all the administrative and nation-building departments of Government threw their energies into an educational campaign which covered the whole country. As was the case when the system of Basic Democracies was being introduced, the machinery of Government was employed to expound the possibilities which the new Constitution opened to the nation as a whole. Particular care was taken to impress upon the Basic Democrats the great responsibilities which had been assigned to them, and to urge them to use their powers with patriotism and integrity. The President himself toured extensively, expounding, exhorting, explaining, answering questions, removing doubts and resolving misapprehension. His Ministers followed his example, and the entire country soon realized that a new era was beginning. It was not only the masses, and their representatives, the Basic Democrats, who were the objectives of this educational campaign; particular attention was also paid to lawyers, schoolmasters, college teachers, college students, and professional men. Some of the doubts raised by the unusual features of the constitution were sincerely held; but most of them were allayed by the frank discussions which were a part of the campaign, and by the obvious honesty with which the President justified the details of the plan.

The second impression which we took away with us related to the character and sources of the criticism which the new Constitution aroused in certain quarters. It was easy to generalize, as certain Western commentators did, about the hostility of the educated classes. In my observation, this was incorrect. While it is true that most of the early enthusiasm, which was real and deeply felt, came from the masses and from the lower income-groups among the middle classes, many lawyers and other leaders of educated opinion, including

members of the old land-holding aristocracy who had lost their former
economic prominence, quickly lent their support to the 'new deal'.
Religious leaders from the first backed it whole-heartedly, and they,
thanks to the wider range of studies which they are officially encouraged to pursue, can no longer be regarded as an obscurantist
element in the nation. In East Pakistan, as no doubt the Government
had expected, the general reception of the Constitution was predominantly favourable—it gave the East Pakistanis exactly that
measure of equality with the Western Wing, and just those opportunities for developing along their own lines, for which they had been
long fervently hoping.

It seemed to me that such criticism as defied conciliation—and its
bulk was small—was derived from four main sources. The first came
from disgruntled politicians, some of them still men of local influence, who can see no good at all in anything which is done by the
régime which displaced them from power and office. The very
clemency of their treatment at the hands of the Revolutionary Government had been an injury to their pride; but they could console themselves by the reflection that they were the true custodians of consti-
tutionalism and the martyrs of martial law. Now this consolation no
longer lay open to them as they saw the martial law régime vanishing
into a form of constitutional Government in which they stood little
chance of success against political leaders of better reputation in the
eyes of the public. Their hostility was inevitable, even though it was
likely to be impotent. Resembling them in their implacability, but perhaps even fewer, were the hard core of Hindus, mainly resident in East
Pakistan, who have never really reconciled themselves to being Pakistani citizens, and continue to hanker after an undivided Bengal, independent of Pakistan, and possibly linked with India. Their opposition to anything which is calculated to draw the two wings of Pakistan
into closer partnership and better understanding was to be expected.

Two other sections of opinion, more to be respected than the above,
also stood out as critics of the new Constitution. The first were those
—and there are men of reputation and learning among them—who
hold that the Westminster model is the only example for Pakistan to
follow. They consider that the country could, in fact, work Parliamentary institutions if it were given the chance to do so; and that the
earlier failure to make good was due to conditions which the Revolutionary Government had radically changed for the better. Most of
Pakistan, I think, considers them mistaken; and believes that the risks

Q   241

involved in adopting Parliamentary Government are too great to be faced for the present. But they will have their chance: the new Constitution can be amended. Indeed, President Ayub Khan has already done this under a section which gives him authority to remove initial difficulties, and ministers can now be members of the National Assembly. The second section of opinion is more pathetic than formidable. It consists of those who ignored President Ayub Khan's appeal for support of the Basic Democracies, because they considered themselves too important to associate themselves with a movement which started from such humble, and 'grass-root' beginnings. They now find themselves excluded from the Electoral College, but not, of course, from standing as candidates. 'If only we had known', several of them have lamented to me, 'what the President intended to do with the Basic Democrats! Now, we feel that we have "missed the bus".' But their troubles are temporary only; and the next election for the Basic Democracies will no doubt see them represented in full force.

To foresee the future of the new Constitution, one would need to be a prophet rather than a historian. But it has sensible built-in provisions for the kind of changes and modifications which the country may need now and in the future. It is neither too rigid nor too elastic; it promises stability as well as progress. But, above everything else, it is based upon practical experience as well as upon a far-reaching trust in the common sense of the citizens of Pakistan. I feel sure that Quaid-i-Azam would have approved of it, just as he would surely have approved of the work of those men, headed by President Ayub Khan, who saved the country which he founded from destruction and regained touch with the ideals which had originally inspired its creation.

SUGGESTIONS FOR READING

In the course of the fifteen years of Pakistan's independent existence, a considerable literature has grown up; and the books listed below are only those which I myself happen to have found useful, or interesting, or both.

BOOKS BY PAKISTANIS

OFFICIAL

ANNUALS

The series *Pakistan 1954–55, 1955–56, 1956–57, 1957–58* and following years surveys in outline the main governmental activities and contains very useful statistics. There is also a chronology entitled *Pakistan 1947–1957* which surveys the first decade.

OCCASIONAL

The Pakistan Government publishes from time to time well-written monographs dealing with particular problems; e.g. *Minorities in Pakistan*; *Buddhism in Pakistan*, issued by Pakistan Publications, Karachi. The same organization issues useful cultural miscellanies containing essays by specialists (*Pakistan Miscellany Volume I and Volume II*) and the like. Since the revolution of 1958, and, in particular, since the inauguration of the Ministry of National Reconstruction, the progress of Pakistan in the social, economic and cultural fields can be followed in detail in the excellent monthly publication *Progress of the Month*. The new Constitution has been well outlined by President Ayub Khan in his broadcast address to the nation on the 1st of March 1962, published in a pamphlet entitled: *The Constitution*. There is also a fair amount of controversial literature setting out Pakistan's point of view on current international issues, particularly Kashmir. Broadly speaking, as soon as the inquirer makes up his mind on what particular aspect of Pakistan his interest is focused, his best course is to consult the Press Attaché of the Pakistan High Commission, who will readily advise him about the available literature. The Government Tourist Bureau (Headquarters Rawalpindi) publishes excellent brochures on tourist attractions.

UNOFFICIAL

As general introductions to the Pakistani outlook the following are to be commended: Qureshi: *The Pakistani Way of Life* (Heinemann); *Crescent and Green* (Cassell); Ikram and Spears: *The Cultural Heritage of Pakistan* (Oxford University Press); S. A. Vahid: *Iqbal* (Murray).

For constitutional and political development there are many good books such as G. W. Choudhurry: *Constitutional Development in Pakistan* (Longmans). One of the best and latest is Khalid bin Sayeed: *Pakistan, the Formative Phase* (Pakistan Publishing House, Karachi). There is a good deal of rather techincal stuff on the economic side, regarding which I am not really qualified to advise; but *The Economist* published a most admirable Pakistan Supplement at the end of 1961, which I found very informative. There is a considerable literature on the Kashmir dispute by Pakistani authors. Aziz Beg: *Captive Kashmir* (Allied Business Corporation, Lahore) is particularly telling.

BOOKS BY FOREIGNERS

For the general background, written from the Indian point of view, of the emergence of Pakistan, V. P. Menon: *The Transfer of Power in India* (Longmans) is valuable. The late Lord Birdwood's two books: *A Continent Decides* and *Two Nations and Kashmir* are full of clearly-presented facts (Robert Hale). Symonds: *The Making of Pakistan* (Faber) is a useful little book. Mr. Hector Bolitho has written a very readable *Life of Mohammad Ali Jinnah* which Pakistanis do not regard as really definitive because certain valuable sources of information were not at his disposal, but Western readers can learn much from it. Percival Spear: *India, Pakistan and the West* (Oxford University Press) gives a good overall picture; while geographical influences are set out in *India, Pakistan, Ceylon and Burma* by Dr. Dudley Stamp (Methuen). There are some excellent travel sketches, like Peter Mayne: *The Narrow Smile* (Murray), Elizabeth Balneaves: *The Waterless Moon* (Lutterworth Press) and Ian Stephens: *Horned Moon* (Chatto & Windus)—the last particularly good on the frontier areas. Penderel Moon: *Divide and Quit* (Chatto & Windus) is a vivid account of the author's personal experiences during the stormy days of partition.

But everyone who starts to study Pakistan will before long build up his own list of books to be remembered: those mentioned are only my personal selection. If I had not happened to have spent so much time in the country, the choice would, no doubt, have been quite different.

INDEX

Abbottabad, 78
Abdul Ghaffar Khan, 36, 66, 67
Abdul Qayum, 67, 69
Abdullah, Sheikh, 56, 80, 81, 86
Abdurrahman, Amir, 62, 63
Adam Khel, 70
Adamji (family), 33
Afghanistan, 19, 62, 63, 65, 69, 72, 74, 75, 123
Afridis, 69, 72, 164
Afro-Asian *bloc*, 118
Agricultural Development Corporation, 163, 171, 175
Ahmadiyas, 147, 149
Ahmed, Sir Sayyid, 17
Akbar Khan, Brigadier, 60
Aksai Chin, 121
Al Azhar, 128
Aldershot, 96
Algeria, 91, 115, 116
Ali, Mohammad, 18
Ali, Mr. Mohammad, of Bogra (*see* Bogra)
Ali, Chaudhuri Mohammad, C.S.P.
  Cabinet Secretary, 150
  Prime Minister, 150–2
Ali, Shaukat, 18
Aligarh, 17, 25, 56
Alishah Khan, Raja (of Baltistan), 59
All Souls College, 13
Allahabad, 13, 17, 21
  Muslim League Conference at, 21
  University, 13, 17
Amritsar, 49
Apartheid, 115
APWA (All Pakistan Women's

Association), 159, 181, 191, 202. *See also* Basic Democracies, Refugees, Women
Arab World, Pakistan and, 116
Askandria Fort (Skardu), 53, 57
'Ataturk', 19
Auchinleck, Field-Marshal Sir Claude, 33, 81
Australia, 107, 108, 117, 157, 161
Azad Government of the State of Jammu and Kashmir, *see* Azad Kashmir
Azad Kashmir, 60, 76, 77, 78, 82, 83, 84, 85, 87, 88, 89, 90, 91–5, 105, 163
  Azad Kashmir Radio, 92, 93
  basic democracies in, 92
  bitter feeling in, 89, 90, 91
  conditions in, 88
  progress in, 88, 89, 163
  relations with Pakistan, 91, 92
  seeks international recognition, 91
  Village AID in, 88, 174
Azam Khan, Lt.-General, 147, 185, 191–2, 228
Ayub Khan, Field-Marshal Mohammad, President of Pakistan, 13, 44, 68, 106, 114, 116, 121, 122, 123, 124, 125, 128, 145, 149, 182, 184, 185, 186, 193, 194, 197, 198, 199, 206–10, 212, 229, 233–8, 239, 240, 241, 242
  Defence Minister, 149
  Commander-in-Chief, 149
  intervenes with President Iskander Mirza, 182–3